DRAMA IN EDUCATION

The Annual Survey

DRAMA IN EDUCATION 1

The Annual Survey

Edited by

John Hodgson and Martin Banham

Pitman Publishing

First published 1972

SIR ISAAC PITMAN AND SONS LTD.
Pitman House, Parker Street, Kingsway, London WC2B 5PB
P.O. Box 46038, Portal Street, Nairobi, Kenya

SIR ISAAC PITMAN (AUST.) PTY. LTD.
Pitman House, 158 Bouverie Street, Carlton, Victoria 3053, Australia

PITMAN PUBLISHING COMPANY S.A. LTD.
P.O. Box 11231, Johannesburg, South Africa

PITMAN PUBLISHING CORPORATION
6 East 43rd Street, New York, N.Y. 10017, U.S.A.

SIR ISAAC PITMAN (CANADA) LTD.
495 Wellington Street West, Toronto 135, Canada

THE COPP CLARK PUBLISHING COMPANY
517 Wellington Street West, Toronto 135, Canada

Printed by photo-lithography and made in Great Britain at
the Pitman Press, Bath
G2—(G.3515:13)

Editorial

DRAMA IN EDUCATION is, as our subtitle promises, the Annual Survey.
It is our intention that a book shall be published every year, and we
already have the first five numbers planned! Clearly, therefore, our
purpose is not merely to collect a few splendid articles, statements of
faith, exhortations, cris de coeur, and to offer them as our contribution
to the rapidly developing interest in the general application of drama and
theatre in the areas of education in its widest sense. DRAMA IN
EDUCATION is aimed to serve as a central forum for the growing,
vigorous, and continuing study of everything and anything that needs to
be stated, argued, exercised or debated wherever anyone in this field
is working. This first number has tried to collect together the facts
and information that state the position of drama in education as we see
it today – and to lace that information with some ideas from the fringes
that may act as stimulus or detonator.

One of the editors' first problems was the matter of title. What
should we call the book, in order to be both explicit and interesting – and
for that matter accurate. "Education" often seems a dull word – which
is a strange observation about such a lively topic. "Drama" is a staid
relation to "Theatre" but the word "Theatre" also has limitations that
"Drama" avoids. What did we want our book to include within its scope?
Our answer was almost anything that concerned the relationship between
creative work in drama, theatre, film, television, dance, movement,
speech, and the learning process, whether formal or informal, for old
or young. Therefore, street theatre is as much our concern as the
drama lesson; the creation of syllabuses as important as psychodrama;
the training of the actor as vital as the child at play. Various titles
might have taken us somewhere near our target. Perhaps something like
'The Joyful Game,' as Brian Wilks has called his contribution to this
first number. It would be nice to have something snappy and romantic,
but in the end we saw that we had to accept the full and rich meaning of

our two central words, "Drama" and "Education" and thus DRAMA IN EDUCATION we are, but our stage is all the world.

When this publication was well into its final planning stage the editors read an interesting article in 'Speech and Drama', in which a drama teacher, John Norman, expressed his loneliness, and the vulnerability that he felt as a drama teacher in a secondary school. His article asked for some kind of support, some strong and authoritative voice to counter the cynicism, the lack of imagination, the prejudice that faced the drama teacher in so many schools. We all know that John Norman's predicament is a common one, and that it spreads far outside the formal teaching situation. What difficulties do street theatre groups face in applying to local authorities for support, what obstacles do theatre in education teams find themselves facing from doubtful schools, what inhibitions do children develop when told to sit still and keep quiet when "the play" is on? And yet, as everyone should know, Newsom has stressed the essential and central function of the creative arts in education. In other words, the drama teacher is not the poor relation with the fringe subject but the man at the centre of an educational revolution. Given the inherent conservatism of the educational establishment, however, it is necessary for this fact to be shouted loudly and coherently and with logic and example. We intend that DRAMA IN EDUCATION shall serve in this respect and become not only a vehicle for discussion, reference, and assessment but also a meeting place for everyone concerned with all aspects of drama in education, and a statement of their aims, ambitions, and achievements.

In order to fulfil this editorial policy, future numbers of DRAMA IN EDUCATION will each concentrate upon different major and immediately relevant themes. Each will also have sections devoted to Ideas and Projects in which we shall record activities of interest, discuss current trends, report on conferences, books, and events, and draw attention to recent imaginative and exciting work. We hope that anyone will feel free to write and report upon important developments, whereever they occur. Our Ideas and Projects section could become a focal point for the exchange of information and stimulation. Major themes that will be the concern of future numbers include speech, movement, improvisation, dance drama, drama in the secondary schools, in the primary schools, in Colleges of Education and Universities, theatre in education teams, actor training, educational television, youth and community theatres, theatre centres and arts laboratories.

Our contribution as editors will aim to be diverse and exploratory. It may even at times appear to be contradictory.

In DRAMA IN EDUCATION 2 our main themes will be: **Why do we teach drama at all?** – this will include a range of approaches, opinions and viewpoints – and **What is the school play?** We will examine a number of different practices and attitudes and attempt to evaluate specific projects from varying points of view.

This annual survey, then, has two principal functions: on the one hand we want it to be a permanent point of reference for what is happening, and being thought about; and on the other we want it to be a lively point of interchange and provocation which will serve anyone practising in drama and education.

October 1971   John Hodgson
                                                Martin Banham

Looking Ahead

'The Reverend King' at Primrose Hill Secondary School, Leeds

Primrose Hill School is situated close to the centre of Leeds, serving
a new council housing estate on one side and an older part of the city
on the other. As in many other large industrial cities this means that
the school accommodates a large immigrant community as well as the
local white children. In the case of Primrose Hill School the immigrant community is largely West Indian, though there are children of
many other black and white immigrant groups. 'The Reverend King',
presented as "the school play" in July 1971, was conceived by the
teacher in charge as an improvised exploration of the history of the
black man and his relationship with whites, with the purpose of honestly
facing the conflicts in any black/white community and bringing understanding of the other's attitudes to each group. The result, to many
observers, was startling in its honesty, impact, emotion, and was
clearly a most positive and purposeful exercise for the children.

The play was based greatly upon improvisation and movement, and
was built by the group over a long period of experimentation, contribution and discussion of ideas, argument and stimulus. The confrontation
between black and white is established early in the presentation, with
an emphasis upon the manner in which misunderstanding and ignorance
have contributed to racial conflict and prejudice. An instance of this
is a scene where a black child holds out a small wooden cross towards
some white ladies, and his gesture is misinterpreted as an attempt to
molest them. The development of this situation leads to the lynching
of the black child who is realistically hanged at the top of the simple
rostrum unit that is the only feature of the acting space. Fights, in-
sults, aggression — all these aspects are clearly stated by the play,
which has as its commentator a Martin Luther King character, using
many of that great man's own words to pray for tolerance and understanding.

QUESTION RAISING

It is difficult in a brief summary to indicate the full range of this presentation. It was a totally committed as well as a skilled one, and the dedication of the children was very apparent. It raised interesting questions. Should a school in a racially conscious area stress racial conflicts and tensions? To what extent is an attempt to bring understanding and tolerance more likely to reinforce hatreds and prejudices? If gangs of white youths attack gangs of black youths "on stage" doesn't that underline what happens (or may happen) in the outside world? Isn't racial conflict too delicate a subject to bring openly on to a school stage and present to young children who may be gradually being weaned away from the intolerances of their parents? How far should the school play aim to cope with such real, sometimes explosive, community issues, and to what extent is it running the risk of disruption, or self-indulgence, or simply misdirection if it does so?

In the case of Primrose Hill School the children who took part in the presentation were in little doubt of its value. They spoke afterwards of the change in their own attitudes as they came, through the play, to a greater understanding of others. They talked openly of their parents' fears about the play when they first heard about it, the ostrich-like attitude, the prejudices on both sides — but the children were sophisticated to a degree far beyond their parents in coping with racial issues, and probably greatly as a result of this play. But how much is there a risk of completing "solutions" via the play in the school situation that will fall apart when the child goes out of the protected environment? How much will stick?

DRAMA IN EDUCATION 2 will concentrate upon The School Play, and in that issue we shall develop this particular example in much greater detail and also discuss the purpose of the school play, and instance many different approaches to it. We invite information and contributions on this theme, and the editors brazenly solicit invitations to see school plays that their creators believe have something to offer.

Contents

(*Note: Apart from 'Views and Opinions,' all items not attributed in this list of contents are by the editors*)

xi

ACKNOWLEDGMENTS

The drawings accompanying 'Views and Opinions' are by Susan Bradbury. That on page 168, illustrating the proposed Drama Centre, University of Leeds, is by A. P. Waterhouse. The editors' thanks go to both.

The editors would also like to thank all those who have contributed photographs, including:

Ric Jerome, cover, pages 12-13;
Rob Inglis, pages 75, 111, 154;
David W. Johnston, pages 43, 150;
J. Crawford, page 100;
John Cura, page 131.

The theatre plans on pages 52-63 are reproduced by kind permission of the Editor of TABS magazine.

Finally, grateful thanks are due to Dorothy Clark, for secretarial assistance.

Views
and
Opinions

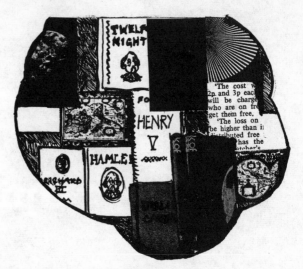

A lot of teachers ....

        have to take a lot of blame ....

                for putting a lot of people ....

Off Shakespeare

Judi Dench
Actress
Royal Shakespeare Company
Stratford upon Avon

Improvisation is the curse
visited upon education.

Gareth Lloyd Evans
writer, critic and lecturer

The study of theatre involves aspects of literature, history, economics, art, architecture, fashion, sociology, technology, ideology and sex. What more does one need for a well-rounded education?

Bamber Gascoigne
Critic and writer

Theatre education companies are like a randy old uncle back from
Tangiers telling a bedtime story that is more shocking than Mum's.

Colin George
Crucible Theatre
Sheffield

For me, what matters about drama is that it can be art, and what essentially matters about art is the intrinsic value to which it gives access. Any work of art can be used instrumentally; but such use has nothing to do with its most important quality. My hope is for a constant awareness among educators that, whatever else it may be able to do, drama can at best give rise to works of art which, as such, have no use, but have unique value. A Lautrec may teach you (and teach you very effectively) something about social history; but this is not why it is a work of art. Drama may teach many things, but its greatest excellence is to cause us to have self-sufficient experiences we could not have had otherwise.

George Hauger
Lecturer and playwright

Old values die hard. Who would have thought that as late as 1964 no survey had been made of the teaching of drama in our schools? This, of course, was a hang-over from the days when the three Rs were all that was thought necessary for the children of working-class parents.

Between 1964 and 1970 I had the good fortune of being given responsibility for the Arts, and a great deal of publicity was given to the fact that a Labour Government had given them a higher priority than ever before, expressed in practical terms by the trebling of financial support. But sometimes it is the less publicised activities that have produced more long-term results. One such was promoting a survey of the teaching of what at one time was considered élitist subjects, suitable only for the children of the well-to-do. I was fortunate in being able to have surveys made of the teaching of drama, the visual arts, music, and the proper use of museums and galleries, in our schools. I was doubly fortunate in having some of the most able Inspectors in the Department of Education and Science for this work. Outstanding among them was Mr. John Allen, who knew of the pioneer efforts of some class teachers, heads of schools and local authorities, and who also knew how under-financed and inadequate this whole field was.

When Mr. John Allen's survey was brought to my desk I was particularly delighted to find that one of my own firmly-held views was reflected in this official survey. I have always felt that drama, not only as a subject in itself, but as a method of teaching, was an ideal way of giving children of diverse abilities the opportunity of working together and of appreciating their dependence on one another. One child may have a gift for making electrical gadgets work, or making furniture, for enjoying research when this can help with costumes and the rest needed for a particular project. Another child may have no craftsman's interest at all, but be a natural poet responsive to fine literature, or even a child with exhibitionist tendencies who feels he must simply go to the front of the stage.

There is a great deal of criticism of the comprehensive system in education, although it was never challenged when applied to the great public schools where the children came from the same social background. I do not underestimate the difficulties that parents face where a comprehensive school is in a sub-standard area, but there is no doubt at all that if we want to give reality to our claim that we are concerned to give equal educational opportunity to all, the comprehensive is the way of the future. I know no subject that can make a greater contribution to an understanding of what enlightened educationists are seeking to achieve than the encouragement of children to act for themselves, externalise their dreams, and of course have opportunities to visit first-class theatre groups.

The Rt. Hon. Baroness Lee, P.C.

In a recent television documentary entitled 'Three Looms Waiting', Dorothy Heathcote talked of her work, particularly that centred upon handicapped children, with engaging freshness and honesty. There were no vast generalisations, no hiding behind jargon, or behind the vague nature of Speech and Drama itself. Her frankness, her determination to evaluate, and if necessary reject, hours, days, weeks of hard work which did not measure up to highly uncompromising standards, seemed for me to highlight and contrast with a disturbing weakness within the Speech and Drama profession – 'ostrichism' – however cryptic and quaint, this word does so accurately describe a state of mind in which the sand exercises a strange fascination, whenever problems appear.

From the student unsure of his motives, to the teacher suffering an imperceptible erosion of standards, the deception, unconscious or perpetrated, continues. What of the various training institutions who send new entrants into the profession armed with actual or implied promises of a land flowing with spots and rostrums, guarded and encircled by the loving arms of LEA'S and local drama advisors? What of the professional societies who do not know, or indeed wish to know, that the whole field is "in a state of chassis"? Without question, imagination is a quality much needed by the teacher of Speech and Drama, but when practical pressures and an uncertain status induce a creeping self delusion, and the balance of personal realism and the ability to recognize and state the truth is missing, it may become a destructive agent blurring objectives and standards.

In the teaching situation the means of survival may well be not to ask that perpetually ruthless question – why? Why did I allow work of poor standard to drift by? Why was that lesson not a success? Why did that glazed expression haunt the faces of my pupils? – and to those who fondly imagine Speech and Drama to be an established and accepted part of English Education, why is it not? Why is it disorganized and sectionally counter productive? – Why do we not know the precise statistical situation as to schools and specialists, and ultimately why does it appear that we do not wish to know?

Answers to these questions may well regenerate enthusiasm for some, indicate failure for others, but they cannot be more damaging than those blissfully birdlike attitudes which inhibit the proper development of our work.

John L Norman
Teacher
Huddersfield

Pin-striped Drama

Sam Beckett – the story goes – was being pursued down a Paris street. The American interviewer was trying to find out if Mr B knew why he wrote in French.

Sam continued down the street for a while, then replied unambiguously: "No." He walked on a few paces more still reflecting, then added thoughtfully, "Nor, for that matter, why I write at all."

Drama in education is a bit like that. Why do we do it, why are we doing it increasingly, when young actors already have drama schools and young directors can go into theatres instead of coming to us?

But our industry, as they say, is expanding so rapidly that we have plenty of time in front of us to offer our various explications; and generations of climbers to tackle that particular Everest.

We are visibly on the crest of a wave, but the real question is the one posed by Gogo: what do we do, now that we are happy?

Leaving Didi's unhappy reply aside, all we can do at this stage is conclude with a point of departure, so to speak. The future of this discipline lies in a play of words: not educational drama – which relegates the dramatic element of the phenomenon to the mental institution, or to a slot in the school week roughly comparable to cricket on wet Wednesdays – but drama in education. Consciously or unconsciously, the editors of this book have pointed the way to a subtle but crucial realignment of emphasis.

By the very fact of putting Gogo's question, we move from pragmatism to projection, but even already we are obliged to claim that drama in education has finally become respectable, and the pin-stripes of recognition are beginning to clothe us all.

So what do we do now that we are recognized? Welcome advances from municipal councillors, interest from school boards, money from educational authorities – and set about making ourselves unrespectable, no doubt. The rest will then be, simply, history.

Kevin O'Malley
Fellow in Drama
University of Essex

Film is probably the most intense experience any kid has. The size of the screen, the use of colour and the dramatic qualities of all films speak directly to the child. With an intelligent selection of material I would have thought film could make the most, the best, impact in getting across complex ideas. Complex emotional ideas about the way people behave, complex emotional ideas about the way they relate to each other, as well as enabling them to have a very realistic feeling about what a play is all about.

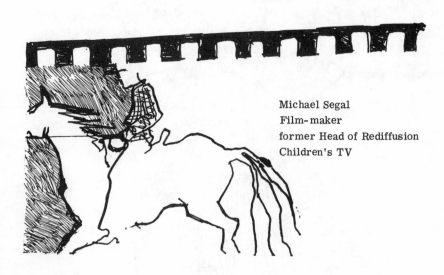

Michael Segal
Film-maker
former Head of Rediffusion
Children's TV

Work in children's theatre is part of the extension of the child's horizon. Adults working in this field have a responsibility here and they should not be afraid to exercise it. The child is especially vulnerable – his attitudes and opinions are being formed so we have to watch carefully what we do. Of course the child has to learn about all sides of life but the process has to be selective and gradual. The very young child at first remains within the security of the home and then he is encouraged to play within the confines of his garden. But there are clear restrictions; "Don't go outside the gate because of the motor cars!" Later you take him across the road and gradually help him to a point at which he can cross safely on his own. Then you can leave him. So this kind of extending horizon is a principle we can apply through all aspects of life – first house, garden, field, street until the child is ready to undertake a long journey. It's only much later that he can set off on his own for Japan. So, it is my belief that the plays we present to children should have constructive value – not everyone need have a moral, but if there are morals, they should be "good" ones.

Gerald Tyler
Drama Advisor
West Riding C C
Yorkshire

1. From the Past to the Present

The Joyful Game

*A comment upon selected reports and recommendations concerning
the teaching of drama in schools from 1919*

To trace the growth of the teaching of drama in schools through the
examination of official reports over the past fifty years is to follow an
unfolding pattern – one which begins simply and concludes both complex and diverse. From the role of drama as a minor contribution to
the teaching of English there is a process of refinement and enlarge-
ment which leads towards the present day explorations of drama as a
central and fundamental educational exercise. The growth is continuous and at times rapid. Much of the early investigation has a relevance
beyond the specific recommendations of its day which sharply indicates
the gap that has existed between the exciting theories about teaching
and the slow pace of adaptation in practice.

A sensitive and alert reading of the documents concerning teaching
half a century ago proves rewarding at many levels. It also offers the
opportunity for an appraisal of the aims, methods and purpose of teaching drama in schools. Such a study sets a high standard of scrutiny
and enquiry while also placing the subject in its right historical perspective. For the dramatic method of teaching has an ancient lineage.
In our own culture it was long established as a method of teaching before
that usurping subject English adopted it as one of its minions.

Here a selection of reports is examined briefly in order to indicate
the gradual emergence of the variety of activities that we now meet
under the heading of "the teaching of drama in schools". The main
points made in the various reports are stated and the overall development of the subject plotted.

Now, as ever, there is the need to see the teaching of drama in
perspective; to see its place in the overall education of children by
reference to its strengths as shown in its contribution to learning in
the recent past.

This outline covers the period in which the teaching of English became a respected and accepted part of the curriculum of the schools of

14

the nation. The first report consulted, (Board of Education 1919, 'The Teaching of English in England'), is a spirited defence of the teaching of English as a subject in its own right. Much that was sown in the 1919 report was to grow sturdily into the full blossoming of English as an exploration of experience and communication that we enjoy today. The radical nature of this early report and the vision of its committee provide an excellent starting point for the consideration of developments in teaching English and drama. In all aspects of its work the 1919 committee established a poise and clarity which should serve as a model for investigation and definition.

1. 1919 THE TEACHING OF ENGLISH IN ENGLAND H.M.S.O.

In this report, for the Board of Education, a distinguished committee, including such eminent figures as Sir Henry Newbolt, Sir Arthur Quiller Couch, Caroline Spurgeon and John Dover Wilson, found it necessary to argue a case for the inclusion of English as a subject to be taught in all kinds of schools. Interpreting their brief as widely as possible they launched a swingeing attack upon the state of national education and instead of seeing English as of "inferior importance" declared that it was the sole true basis of all education:

> ".... the one indispensible preliminary
> and foundation for all the rest" (1)

With the zeal which we find in the current apologists for creative drama, the 1919 committee argued a convincing case for English that was to become the keel for the whole structure of lively, relevant and experience-centred English teaching which we now have. With Wordsworth's 'Prelude' as their inspiration they recommended that education to be "real" should transmit "the influence of personality and the experience of human life", and, they concluded, English literature was essential for any liberal education, being, "the most direct and lasting communication of experience by man and man". As English then, so with drama now. The 1919 report placed the teaching of English in the centre of any discussion of curriculum. There are those who would argue that drama in schools should also command such a position.

While claiming priority for English studies this report summarised with great clarity the various branches of those studies. The section concerning "The Drama in Education" is of interest for its brief historical outline and the tenor of its advice to teachers. Reminding readers that drama was a "favourite Renaissance method" in the classical languages and later in English, it crisply defined the value of drama in schools under three headings:

    i) as something to be written

   ii) as something to be read

  iii) as something to be acted

The order here seems significant. As exercise in writing, the use of dramatic forms was considered more valuable than the use of the essay and it was suggested that, at times, it was possible for the class to create a play with the teacher acting as a scribe. The advice in this first sub-division was positive and near in feeling to the documentary method which is proving so popular today:

> "The collective composition of a play may be attempted by quite young pupils. As soon as boys are old enough to enjoy a ballad or story in verse they should try to dramatise it....
>
> .....Consider the training involved in the composition of a drama on the subject, say, of Sir Walter Raleigh."   (2)

The discipline of writing for acting was considered to be an excellent training in "practical English composition," such as "periodical attempts at essays will never give".

Inevitably, much of the advice concerning the reading of drama was to do with the reading of Shakespeare. His plays were seen as difficult, for they were for the most part "written in a language that not every Englishman understands". But his work was considered worth study. The emphasis of the recommendations was upon the lively presentation of the plays, including wherever possible the use of models, reference to the period in which Shakespeare lived and seeing the plays performed. There is a refreshing concern for the true dramatic reading of the text rather than the arid intellectual study of the words and images that examinations often seem to encourage:

> "A discussion of Shakespeare's language and style can be valuable and a delightful lesson for senior pupils: but it is a lesson that has nothing to do with the drama, and certainly nothing to do with a dramatic reading."   (3)

With confidence the report warns that there are dull passages in the great plays which the teacher had "better omit", just as there are minor plays which are quite unsuitable for pupils to study. There is a stern warning for the teacher with the temerity to value the minor plays above the major:

> "Enthusiasm for Shakespeare .... is very delightful: but a teacher to whom 'Twelfth Night' and 'The Taming of the Shrew' are both equally Shakespeare is not a person who can be safely trusted with Shakespeare at all."   (4)

In the final section, "The drama considered as acting", there is a further sub-division of this "ancient and honoured form of literature" into three headings:

(a) the performance of scenes or pieces in class
(b) the public performance of plays by pupils
(c) visits by pupils to professional performances of suitable plays (5)

Confident that experience of "good" drama will give children standards for discrimination, playgoing is considered a necessary part of education as "preparation for life". Moreover, actual performing in plays is found to be wholly beneficial:

"The pupils who take part in performances of plays must learn to speak well and to move well, and to appreciate character and to express emotion becomingly, to be expansive yet restrained, to subordinate the individual to the whole and to play the game, to be resourceful and self-possessed and to overcome or mitigate personal disabilities. It will hardly be suggested that these are negligible accomplishments."
(6)

We may withhold full support from every detail of this statement, but, nevertheless, it contains much that would still be considered important. The development of control, flexibility and overall poise remains a chief aim of drama in schools. A further virtue noted was the particular value of performance for the less able:

"Incidentally it has been found that boys or girls usually regarded as stupid, and incapable of learning, have exhibited unsuspected ability in acting and have gained a new interest in themselves and their possibilities." (7)

To enable the child "regarded as stupid" to discover such a "new interest" in himself remains a priority in education and a valid aim for the drama teacher.

The performance of classroom plays, seen as "joyous and instructive adventures," is recommended. "They may range from happy improvisations to a formal show on a special occasion".

The recommendations of the 1919 report clearly contain the early formulations of the later growth and development of the teaching of drama in schools, both as a contribution to English and as a subject in its own right.

Fifty years ago it was English itself that needed to be recognised as an important foundation subject in schools: today much the same arguments are put forward to support the teaching of drama. In their defence of English as a basic subject for a liberal education the 1919 committee defined the importance of studies in English Literature and

Language in all its branches. Their report created the first impulse
of what was to be steady dynamic growth. With an emphasis upon experience and expression, maturation, communication and the sharing
of experience between man and man: with a concern for even the
"stupid" and those "incapable of learning": it looked forward to much
that still occupies our thought and attention in the development of the
teaching of English. We can only regret that so few of its recommendations seem to have been acted upon. We cannot fail, however, to
see the influence of the report on the thinking related to the teaching
of English and drama and to acknowledge that many of its recommendations are worthy of further thought. The formal recommendations
for "The Drama" provide a good basis for discussion of the place of
drama in education:

THE DRAMA

96 That as soon as children are old enough they should attempt to
    dramatise familiar ballads, stories or fairy tales, or famous
    historical incidents: and that schools in districts where a genuine
    dialect survives should make use of any traditional fragments of
    old folk plays.
97 That the reading and acting of plays should be encouraged in
    schools of all types and in Training Colleges.
98 That Universities should seriously consider the possibility of
    granting a Diploma in Dramatic Art....
99 That lectureships on the Art of the Theatre .... and also Chairs
    in Dramatic Literature, might well be established. [8]

2. EDUCATION FOR A CHANGING WORLD

**1931 Report of Board of Education Committee on Primary Schools,
H.M.S.O.
1938 Report of Board of Education Committee on Secondary Schools,
H.M.S.O.
1937 Board of Education Handbook for Teachers, H.M.S.O.**

The Board of Education reports of 1931 and 1938 look back over a
decade of development in teaching with the realisation that life and
education alike were fast changing. The focus of the scrutiny of teaching methods and aims seems, in these investigations, to have narrowed
and to be directed to detail in curriculum matters and towards the individual nature of each pupil's needs. Some very sure and positive
advances have been made in the teaching of drama and there is evidence
of a growing awareness of the variety of work possible and the diversity
of its contribution to learning and the refinement of skills.

Among the more usual claims for drama's validity we find the first mention of the benefit of work in "movement":

"Drama both of the less and more formal kinds, for which children, owing to their happy lack of self-consciousness, display such remarkable gifts, offers further good opportunities of developing that power of expression in movement which, if the psychologists are right, is so closely correlated with the development of perception and feeling." (9)

Linked with comments upon the teaching of "physical welfare" we find an early reference to the use of games in education and the possibility of learning through "activity at once joyous and disciplined." Reference is also made to the possibility of integrating work in drama with literature, music, dancing and handicraft. Once again we find dramatic work recommended for the "dull child." It is interesting to note the gentle epithet after the plain "stupid" of a decade before!

"The dull child is as a rule singularly slow in talking in front of the class and the teacher. He has little to say, and does not know how to say it. In the past what he has ventured has seemed stupid to others and he has grown shy and monosyllabic. Simple homely talks, storytelling, dramatic work and the like, might be freely used in the lower classes to draw the dull child out of his shell." (10)

Linked with such enlightened encouragement for the adventurous teacher we find equally sound advice on the nature of the space needed for work in drama.

Plays were clearly seen to need acting:

"....drama is a most effective method for improving the clarity and fluency of children's speech. It should be realised, however, that drama is also a good deal more than this. In the school it may perhaps be appropriately defined as a training, a study and an art ..... The mere reading of parts round the class has nothing to recommend it. However simple the play may be, it should always be prepared – an attempt should be made to understand the characters, the movements, the situations; it may be produced in the hall or an empty classroom or even in a clear space in front of the class." (11)

Later there is reference to the need for children to explore space and to have large spaces in which to work:

"Young children are naturally inclined to put their conceptions of other modes of life into dramatic play and so it is important that children in the junior school shall have ample space, as, for example, in a commodious school hall, in which they can give free rein to their dramatic propensities. Through a free expression of these, children find their way to mature forms of speech, feeling and behaviour, and when their conceptions of life are thus openly expressed in dramatic action faulty

ideas are exposed and can more easily be set right."
(12)

Throughout the evidence of this book there is a strand of sympathy for children and their need to discover forms of expressing their view of experience. Together with the early report on primary schools, that of 1931 quoted above, the handbook of suggestions shows that there had been considerable progress towards defining the benefits that drama offered beyond those of performing in formal plays. There is evidence of a growing awareness of the need for training in sensitivity, indeed in the 1931 report a whole section is devoted to the need for systematic development and training in the "Sensory Capacities". Albeit these were not seen as the particular province of drama teaching, the suggestion that sight, hearing, fine muscle-control, touch and movement should be explored and refined in school was a pointer towards much that was to follow. There is an interesting comment on "seeing" that looks forward to today's emphasis upon concentration:

> "The fact that children see an object a hundred times a day
> without acquiring consciousness of it suggests that the teacher
> needs to converse with the children about the most obvious
> aspects of their day to day life." (13)

Already some of the more specialised aspects of the teaching of drama are beginning to appear in the thinking and advice presented in official papers, in particular the suggestion that work in sensitivity, work in the developing of awareness of the senses, control and perception, is now considered a high priority in work in schools and colleges.

But it is not merely in the details of exercises and methods recommended that these early reports are of interest. The preface to the handbook for teachers warns that while teachers may consult it for information about their own particular subject, they should try to see their subject in relationship to other disciplines and school subjects. Seeing a subject in the overall perspective of educational aims is still a matter of importance. One of the great difficulties confronting teachers of drama is that of linking their work with the rest of the activities of their school. The future for drama in schools is bound up with the kind of contribution that it can make to the curriculum of the school and the overall life of the local community.

The handbook of suggestions reminds teachers of the nature of the modern world, of its rate of change and the need for re-thinking of roles and relationships:

> "It must be recognised that world distances have shrunk and
> that the peoples of today are nearer to each other and their
> lives more closely linked than ever before." (14)

In summary it is possible to discern in the reports of the thirties an overall concern for the development of each child's skills and abilities, the provision of opportunity for learning through experience and the development of skills and scope within society. All the subjects of the curriculum

"should be thought of in terms of activity and experience rather than of knowledge to be acquired and facts to be stored."
(15)

This emphasis upon learning by doing, upon "experience" and activity, suggests that the thinking of those persons who wrote the reports and handbooks was moving towards the same ideas that now inform the work in much of the drama taught in schools. The priority upon "doing" clearly points the way towards the total activity offered by sustained and disciplined work in drama and its associated activities as we now see them practised.

Before leaving the reports of the thirties it is worth noting at some length the support for drama as an aid to the development of "Confidence and Freedom in Self-expression":

".... But the most vital thing of all is that the young child should move in an environment of easy, pleasant and continuous speech....
.... Particularly in dramatic activity the child will find a joyful game in which he is almost unconsciously trained in all the virtues of effective expression. Perhaps the best starting point for drama in the infant school is the use of simple occupational mimes. This can be followed by the acting of familiar stories in which one or two of the characters speak. By the time he leaves this stage of his school career the child should have acted frequently in suitable classroom plays. There is no need for these plays to be childish and sentimental affairs. Many teachers may prefer to dramatise the well-known children's stories .... But the language should be straightforward and expressive. The children should know **why** they behave and speak as they do. There should be much preliminary discussion and reading before the play is actually rendered.... In all modes of expression the children must be encouraged to gain and retain self-confidence."
(16)

By 1940 many of the preoccupations in educational thinking centred upon the personal development of the individual child and the need to provide opportunity for each child to develop to the full his mental and physical resources. At that time drama contributed little to the overall development of the child; it was still seen as most useful for work in speech, bringing poise and confidence in its wake. It is tempting to conjecture that had official reports and recommendations been given more attentive reading there would have been equally more exciting

21

and dynamic drama teaching to read about. However, the groundplan
was drawn and the foundations securely laid.

3. THE SHARED EMOTIONAL EXPERIENCE AND
THE CREATIVE OUTLET

1947 The New Secondary Education. Ministry of Education H.M.S.O.

As may be expected after the 1944 Education Act there is an accelera-
tion in the development of what we now may call "modern" methods.
In 1947 there is clear indication of the realisation that schools should
provide more than the syllabus of curriculum subjects.

> "It is now fairly generally acknowledged that impulses with
> their accompanying emotions ought to be expressed and not
> repressed. This does not mean that it does not matter how
> they are expressed. It is important that they should be ex-
> pressed in a way that is at any rate harmless to society, and,
> if possible, actually beneficial. It is obviously preferable
> that the aggressive impulses should be expressed in the form
> of dogged perseverance rather than in the form of assault and
> battery. Much will, of course, depend on the early stages of
> this process in the home: but the school also has its part to
> play in providing legitimate outlets for impulses and emotions
> and so getting them into some sort of order." (17)

The arts are seen as valid in this document in so much as they provide
the opportunity for children to share real emotional experiences. So
highly was Literature considered as an opportunity for children to
share insights into others' experience of life that as far back as 1938
the Spens Report on Secondary Education had recommended that "....
books should no longer be prescribed in the school certificate examination" for this practice prevented the possibility of the child encounter-
ing the writer's experience in any other than a dull and depressed
manner. It was in the next decade that real progress was made throughout the British Isles in the provision for drama in schools. And it was
at this time that the first substantial report devoted entirely to the teaching of drama (in Wales) was produced.

4. FOUR DOCUMENTS REPRESENTING ENGLAND,
SCOTLAND, N. IRELAND AND WALES

**1951 The Curriculum of the Primary School - City of Aberdeen
Education Committee**
1954 Drama in the Schools of Wales - Ministry of Education H.M.S.O.
**1956 Association of Assistant Mistresses in Secondary Schools -
Memorandum on the Teaching of English, London University Press**
**1956 Programme for Primary Schools - Government of Ireland,
Ministry of Education, Belfast H.M.S.O.**

These four texts amply illustrate the rapid development over the next
decade of teaching. To read each in turn gives a good introduction to

the problems facing the teacher of drama and an insight into some of
the worthwhile and less obviously useful aims that were current when
they were published. As may be expected, the memorandum from the
A.A.M.S.S., while seeking to be progressive, added little to the aims
set out in 1919. Most work would be, it suggests, rightly on Shakespeare, 'Midsummer Night's Dream' being the obvious play with which
to start. There are many now who would see this play as quite unsuitable for younger children: but we must allow for neat evasions of the
play's real concern which still left the scenes with the fairies. But to
be fair to this memorandum there is healthy emphasis upon practical
work and the exploration of ideas for ways of playing scenes etc. The
tone of "correctness" and forced enjoyment prevails, however, and it
is all too easy to imagine the kind of well-drilled "nice" performances
that its recommendations too often brought about.

In Aberdeen things were much brighter. This handbook draws together much of the previous thinking and adds more that was fresh at
the time:

> "**Aim.** Dramatic work is of the utmost value in developing
> the children's grasp of reality. Children act things out in
> order to understand them. Even when the infant stage is
> left behind, dramatisation is one of the ways in which experi-
> ence of persons and situations in real life and in books can
> be clarified and illumined." (18)

We find improvisation explained and advised and a first consideration of the special role of the teacher of drama as an encourager and a
provider of ideas and stimulus rather than as pedant or authority. The
teacher is advised to let the children experiment and to support them
in their games and imaginative activities:

> "If the children are not accustomed to activity in the classroom
> and are afraid to be wrong, they will never do playmaking at
> all, nor indeed anything else creative." (19)

Also in the Aberdeen notes is a brief outline of the need for technical training before children act. Slowly the requirements of drama
are being appreciated. Whereas at one time it seemed enough to state
blandly that the children "will act," it seemed at this point necessary
to suggest that there was a need for some training and previous activity
before the children were thrown into an "acting" situation:

> "A word or two must be added about the techniques that lie
> behind this acting. They are speech and mime. From what
> has been said above, it will be clear that speech training
> not only contributes to dramatic work but derives incentive
> from it. The purpose of mime is to train the observation
> and the imagination and to develop an expressive and well-
> poised body." (20)

The process of refining and particularising the various elements of drama that need to be investigated and taught in schools was a slow but steady one. We have already come some way from the crisp statements of 1919 and are moving towards the fuller and richer pattern that had emerged by the end of the next decade.

It is in the suggested programme for primary schools published in Northern Ireland that even more exciting ideas are expressed. Accepting that the need for dramatic work is established as a recognised part of English studies, the writers go further, suggesting that there are those who see "dramatic activity as a development of the creative play of childhood", and who "consider it essential to the harmonious growth of a child's personality". Drama is now seen as a popular subject, both with young and older children, as a mode of expression and an emotionally satisfying and necessary activity. Far above this in importance is the writers' claim that dramatic activity in school calls for a special relationship between the teacher and the taught. In what must still be a very important exposition of the value and scope of drama in teaching we find a warmth and depth of insight that is appropriate to its context:

> "Dramatic activities transcend the traditional but largely artificial boundaries of school subjects, fusing them into a unified and significant whole. The broader sympathy and the wider knowledge of one's fellows which dramatic activity inculcates enrich understanding." (21)

The good teacher of drama will be one who knows his or her pupils well, who, basing judgement upon experience and knowledge, will be able to establish a conducive atmosphere and rich environment in which drama can be taught. Emphasis is given, rightly, and for the first time in this kind of report, to the special nature of the discipline needed for good work in drama:

> "The relationship between teachers and class is perhaps the most important feature in the success of the dramatic activity lesson. The freest possible type of discipline is necessary if the children's powers of self-expression are to be encouraged .... Directions from the teacher should therefore be as few as possible; suggestions and criticisms should come rather from the class. To encourage the children to see, think and feel imaginatively will be the teacher's most vital contribution. Her aim should be to give stimulus and encouragement and to present her material so that for the children it always provides a creative experience, an opportunity for the free use of the imagination and the exercise of self expression."
>
> (22)

There is much here to ponder, not least the importance of the personal reaction between the teacher and the children. The section on drama in this publication is brief but fecund. It lifts the established view of drama into a new plane.

24

The fullest report, at this time, was that of the Central Advisory Council for Education (Wales), devoted entirely to the provision for the teaching of drama in Wales. In some ways this is a disappointing document, even if predictably limited by the nature of the experience it was exploring.

The Welsh report takes the traditional divisions of dramatic activity in schools, describes them as they are found in the schools of Wales and goes, disappointingly, little further. In some ways it seems to deny those areas of growth which would seem to be happening elsewhere. There are local and historical reasons for this, but it seems a pity that the report, so promising in its scope and brief, should limp so pitifully behind. To take a single example, the school play is seen as "a welcome relief from the essential discipline of learning," a view that should surely have been out of fashion with the 1919 report. Almost at one blow we are plunged back into seeing drama in schools as something less exacting and less important than curriculum subjects. Even the report's more positive conclusions lack edge and the value of insight:

> "First and foremost it is the devoted, enthusiastic and informed teacher who can make it (dramatic activity) a lively handmaiden to instruction, a fruitful means of self-expression to all pupils and a source of joy in the life of the school." (23)

However, the report does define the various areas of activity that we now accept and expect schools to be involved in: the dramatic method of instruction, visits to the theatre, children's theatre, the school stage and drama in the sixth form. While defining these activities it does little to explore the real philosophy and opportunity that dramatic work in schools should raise in the minds of teachers and administrators. Fortunately in a later report, the Gittings report on the Primary Schools of Wales 1967, there is an excellent account of creative drama which more than compensates for the earlier piece of work.

5. EMANCIPATION, ISOLATION AND COMMUNICATION

So far, then, perhaps some early views were more enlightened than we had thought and the emphasis of various recommendations has been less predictable than we had imagined. On the whole, however, the pattern of the growth of drama teaching, from a small contributing section of English teaching towards a valid place as a curriculum subject in its own right, is a pattern of gradual development. Now with the vigorous activity of the sixties, and the major reports of enquiry into all aspects of teaching, the growth becomes more rapid, radical and far-reaching.

To take stock of the position is to see a subject that can contribute as an extra-curricular activity in most cases and as an accepted discipline in others. A subject, moreover, that demands sympathetic and sensitive teachers who are able to establish the best relationships with their pupils. We see a subject that is considered valuable for the way in which it encourages children to develop ways of behaving and ways of meeting and responding to other people. We read of a subject which enables children to experience, in play, emotions and ideas that otherwise are not safely available to them.

Drama can help the dull child; it can provide a means of expression for those whom one report describes as "those who as it were think with their hands". It can provide the opportunity for subjects to be integrated and to be taught as a coherent whole. Exploration in drama can put children in touch with the best ideas of the past in ways that they can readily perceive and understand. Drama can train children in modes of discrimination as well as giving them insights into ways of employing their leisure time. Work in practical drama can help them refine and develop their physical and mental skills. Theatre visits and experience of Children's Theatre can enrich the life of a class, school or community, while school plays provide a focus and a social undertaking for the school as a community in its own right. There are the well defined contributions that work in drama makes towards the development of speech, self-confidence and poise as well as the obvious benefits of the completing of tasks undertaken, and challenges accepted.

So far so good. The next decade that we consider, however, the sixties, defined a new challenge for education and posed new problems for teachers. Major enquiries were undertaken in all aspects of education and all came to agree that the rate of change in our way of living, together with the tremendous pace of technological development, called for a radical reorientation of resources and a fundamental reappraisal of educational thinking. Those reports which we know as Newsom, 'Half our Future', and Plowden [24] provided a challenge that lies before all teachers but which has a special appeal to teachers of drama.

The implications of these reports can be quite briefly stated. The exploration of solutions and their implications would take considerable time.

The Plowden and Newsom reports provide a polarity in their statements concerning the use of dramatic activity in schools. The Plowden report continues the pattern that we have met so far. We have a level-headed if brief description of what drama can achieve, with a plea for unscripted informal work. The work is obviously accepted as valuable.

The Newsom report, on the other hand, is pessimistic in its honesty. There is much evidence that in the teaching of the less able children of the country we are failing, and failing not in particular situations, but right across the board.

Evidence submitted to the committee is typical of the situation:

"We feel bound to record our impression that very many of these less gifted young people are socially maladroit, ill at ease in personal relationships, unduly self-regarding and insensitive: their contact even with their peers is often ineffectual; they understandably resent being organised by adults but show little gift for organising themselves." (25)

And here is the real opportunity for the teacher of drama. Not, that is, the producer of the school play, but that teacher who can establish sympathetic working relationships with young people and help them towards formulating and possibly solving their particular and "special" problems. The elements lacking in the children described are just those that the sound teaching of drama is able to provide and help the pupils towards.

Moreover, the report continues:

"This matter of communication affects all aspects of social and intellectual growth. There is a gulf between those who have, and the many who have not, sufficient command of words to be able to listen and discuss rationally; to express ideas and feelings clearly; and even to have any ideas at all. We simply do not know how many people are frustrated in their lives by inability ever to express themselves adequately; or how many never develop intellectually because they lack the words with which to think and reason. This is a matter as important to economic life as it is to personal living: industrial relations as well as marriages come to grief on failures in communications." (26)

We need go no further to seek the concerns of the trained teacher of drama. The whole structure of drama teaching must be so arranged that it tackles all the problems given above with competence, patience and understanding. Once we can discover and clarify those aspects of creative dramatic activity in the classroom, school hall, youth club or whatever, that have a bearing on the above desperate need, then we shall clearly see the true nature of drama's contribution to modern education. For drama is the engagement between man and man, from isolation to contact, where that which normally evades expression and even contemplation becomes understandable or at least apprehensible. In play the boy who lacks words can find means of expression, in improvisation complex ideas become manageable and less diffuse; for dramatic play is the process of interchange in listening, talking and communicating in a host of ways.

The Newsom report is explicit concerning the value of the teaching of drama for less able children. With this report we now find the teaching of drama occupying the precise place of the teaching of English at the turn of the century. Instead of being a small contribution to the subject of English, itself then a new study in schools, the teaching of drama is seen as a crucially important lifeline for children who are in desperate need of help:

> "Though drama comes, by school tradition, into the English field, it is a creative art embracing much more than English. Perhaps its central element is, or should be, improvisation. It involves movement as well as words – that is one reason why an outsize classroom or small hall is really essential for English teaching .... drama can offer something more significant than the day-dream. It helps boys and girls to identify themselves with well-known men and women of whom they have heard and read. By playing out psychologically significant situations, they can work out their own personal problems. Here is one way in which they can be helped to reconcile the reality of the world outside their own private worlds. Once this begins, education has something on which to build. In short, drama, along with poetry and the other arts, is not a "frill" which the less able can safely omit or relegate to some minor position on some Friday afternoons. Art is not an expensive substitute for reality. It is through creative arts .... that young people can be helped to come to terms with themselves more surely than by any other route." (27)

So strongly did the members of the committee feel about the need for drama that they suggested:

> "It is a matter of some concern that the educative experience of drama in all its forms is too often, despite notable exceptions, restricted or denied to pupils." (28)

6. THE PRESENT POSITION

1967 Primary Education in Wales (Gittings)
Department of Education and Science H.M.S.O.
1967 Education Survey 2: Drama
Department of Education and Science H.M.S.O.

Together, the 'Gittings' report and the Education Survey 'Drama', provide an excellent picture of the state of drama teaching today. They admirably scan the whole landscape of the various activities that are presently being explored, investigated and created as the current contribution of drama to education.

The Gittings Report is valuable in an apparently eccentric way. No entry will be found under "drama" in this report, instead the relevant information is to be found in a section entitled 'Physical Education, Expressive Movement and Dramatic Movement'; thus far have we come from examining drama as part of English. The contribution of

this report is of particular value for its emphasis upon the teaching of
expressive movement and its overall commonsense and expert advice
on all aspects of movement work.

Of the 'Education Survey No 2: Drama' there is so much to say that
this work merits a full study to itself. The most comprehensive exploration of drama teaching in the country ever undertaken, it is a
central text, as much a handbook of examples of current habits as anything else, for any discussion of the aims, methods and philosophy of
the teaching of drama. It is fitting that some fifty years after the first
sustained attempt to make English the cornerstone of a liberal education, we have a wide-ranging survey of the whole scope of what is now
being undertaken in drama.

From 1919 there has been a continuous development in the teaching
of drama in schools as an aid to expression, self-knowledge, group
sensitivity and understanding. Slowly the belief that drama was extra-
neous to the real concerns of education has given way to a more sensitive and enlightened view of drama as valuable at all levels in our educational system. By nature of drama's necessary concern with people,
their ideas and their involvement one with another, whether this be in
documentary or imagined form, dramatic activity provides means
whereby pupils may experience and explore a variety of modes of expression. Exploration in drama is exploration of ways of living, feeling
and communicating: as drama is the art of the enactment of imagined
history so it involves young people in activities and thought relevant to
their own feelings and experiences.

Any survey of the state of drama teaching in schools and colleges
undertaken in the past fifty years will show the increasing amount of
time given to experimenting with dramatic activity as a means of engaging children in activities which, while appearing to be play and
simple enjoyment, are carefully planned developing programmes of
work. The nature of the work undertaken has often been the refining
and developing of skills and talents while the ultimate aim has been the
articulate and confident child; a child resourceful, nimble in mind and
body and sensitive to the needs of others.

It is encouraging to find that this concern for activity that produces
competence and poise is no new fad thrust upon us by gadfly enthusiasts.
The teaching of drama, having a thoroughly respectable place in classical education, has in our own recent history been given high value as
an intrinsic part of growth in powers of understanding and communication. What is now needed is mature and objective study of the part that
dramatic experience plays in the child's development. While it is

accepted that drama can aid and assist growth in understanding and sensitivity, much remains to be shown about the precise nature of the help offered.

While the children play the joyful game and learn through experience in dramatic activities, their teachers should be aware of the overall shape of the work undertaken and be constantly re-examining its underlying philosophy.

Brian Wilks

NOTES

1 Board of Education, Report on the teaching of English in England. HMSO 1919. Page 10
2 Ibid Page 311
3 Ibid Page 314
4 Ibid Page 315
5 Ibid Page 315
6 Ibid Page 316
7 Ibid Page 316
8 Ibid Page 319
9 Board of Education Report on Primary Schools. HMSO 1931. Page 76
10 Ibid Page 164
11 Board of Education, Handbook of suggestions for teachers. HMSO 1937. Page 375
12 Ibid Page 108
13 1931 Report. Page 33
14 Ibid Page 6 (1944 edition)
15 Board of Education Report on Secondary Education. HMSO 1938
16 Handbook for teachers 1937. Page 361
17 Ministry of Education, The new Secondary Education. HMSO 1947. Page 17
18 City of Aberdeen Education Committee, The Curriculum of the Primary School 1951. Page 12
19 Ibid Pages 13-14
20 Ibid Page 13
21 Government of Northern Ireland Ministry of Education. Provision for Primary Schools Belfast HMSO 1956. Page 34
22 Ibid Page 34
23 Ministry of Education, Drama in the Schools of Wales. HMSO 1954. Page 27
24 Ministry of Education, Report Half our Future (Newsom). HMSO 1963:
    Ministry of Education, Children and their Primary Schools (Plowden). HMSO 1966 (two volumes)
25 Newsom Report. Page 15
26 Ibid Page 15
27 Ibid Page 157
28 Ibid Page 157

The Thoughtful Playground

A survey of some pioneers in educational drama

The value of play activities in education has long been recognised,
though we have not always appreciated the relationship between the
many meanings and facets of the word itself: "to play," "a play" and
all the subtleties which context and a variety of epithets can give.
Play as a means of education had been recommended by both Plato
and Aristotle and their cry renewed by some Renaissance teachers.
In the eighteenth and early nineteenth centuries, education pioneers
like Rousseau, Pestalozzi and Froebel all emphasised that education
was activity rather than solely a matter of book learning. Yet, while
they recognised the value of **play** in educational discovery, none of
them considered specifically the importance of **dramatic** play or play
in which impersonation or symbol featured largely.

VALUES IN ACTOR TRAINING

Goethe was primarily a man of the theatre, yet, in his concern to raise
the status of actors, he began to consider their training and it seems
that as director of the theatre in the Duchy of Weimar he had to cope
with a very poor specimen of actor. Perhaps because of this, Goethe's
Overseer explains in 'Wilhelm Meisters Wanderjahre' that there is no
theatre in the Pedagogic Province. Nevertheless, Goethe had many
useful and important things to say about acting and the value of acting,
and when he talks of excluding drama it seems he is more concerned
to exclude the professional theatre. Goethe saw that in acting there
was an opportunity for training both the memory and the person, and
it was through drama that dexterity in speech and gesture could be
acquired. Goethe especially knew the value of improvised drama, ie
drama in which there is a plan, action and division of scenes, pre-
determined and discussed, and in which the actor extemporises, filling
up all that lies between. He saw this as "the best mode of drawing
men out of themselves and leading them by a circuitous path back into

themselves again". In other words, he saw how improvisation, by
drawing upon the personal resources of the individual, helped to release him, to release his inhibitions and establish confidence. It is
interesting, too, to note that music plays its part in improvisation and
that it could stimulate and guide the movements of the body – "dance
affording them animation and the skill to measure it". Goethe saw
that, although there were dangers and problems in the misuse of drama,
yet, used well, it was an instrument of the highest value:

> "If one could communicate to thronging multitudes a fellow
> feeling in all that belongs to man by the portraying of happi-
> ness and misery, of wisdom and folly, nay of absurdity and
> silliness; could kindle and thrill their inmost souls and set
> their stagnant nature into movement free, vehement and
> pure!"

Drama could not only fire men's enthusiasm, provoke their thoughts
and imaginations, but also, by the very communal act of its presentation, unite a group in a shared experience. Goethe is setting out his
ideas in a novel: his characters are the characters of fiction, but the
ideas have begun and something of a theoretical approach to drama in
education is under way. He saw also, however, some of the bad
effects which could result from mishandling of the drama and it may
well be that this aspect of drama in education has frightened some
away from investigating its place sooner.

One of the points about acting and the theatre which worried Goethe
was its apparent emphasis on the artificial and it does not seem to be
until the advent of Stanislavsky that we find the professional theatre
once more able to be identified with reality. The actor was then required:

> "To reflect all that is best and most profound in his creative
> spirit .... to store up within himself this great inner content
> and identify it with the spiritual life of the part he is playing."

To judge from Goethe's "Rules for Actors" his system had been most
external and artificial and in banishing theatre Goethe was condemning
not the art itself but his own presentation of it. Stanislavsky, as Lee
Strasberg puts it, made:

> "A sharp break with traditional teaching and (established) a
> return to actual theatre experience.... The works created
> are never copies or imitations of one another, but are
> original creative achievements. That is the purpose of the
> Stanislavsky idea. It teaches not how to play this or that
> part, but how to create organically."

Stanislavsky's work came after thinkers had begun to investigate the purpose of play earlier in the nineteenth century. Froebel had maintained that play:

> "Is the highest expression of human development in childhood
> .... to one who has insight into human nature the trend of the
> future life of the child is revealed in his freely chosen play."

STUDIES OF PLAY

Other thinkers had begun to classify and discuss the nature of children's play. Herbert Spencer, for instance, put forward a theory that the play of children is a discharge of excess energy, and in 1896 Carl Groos published his study of 'Play of Animals', and then a few years after came his work 'The Play of Man'. He saw play as the expression of instinct, grouping this into seven main sections with sixty sub-divisions. Stanley Hall, at the turn of the century, considered that in children's play there was a recapitulation of the development of the human race: "true play never practises what is phyletically new:..... I regard play as the motor habits and spirit of the past, of the race persisting in the present, as rudimentary organs".

So, on the one hand there was thinking about the dangers and opportunities of the art of acting, and on the other investigation and consideration of the value of play as education. Then, into this climate of opinion came a young teacher from Oxford, Henry Caldwell Cook, who united the feeling for "play" as an activity method in education with a feeling for "the play", as a means of enabling young people to express and develop their own resources.

THE PLAY-WAY IN EDUCATION

It was at Oxford that Henry Caldwell Cook began to develop his interests in education and the theatre. After his finals, he stayed on to take a Diploma in Education and, even at this stage, we find him very concerned about the passive nature of education. He worked for a time at Bromsgrove School and then offered his services to Dr. W.H.D. Rouse at the famous Perse School at Cambridge. His degree was in English and so he came to teach that subject, but his outlook was wide. Dr. Rouse says, "He threw himself into his work with a whole heart, not only the intellectual part, but to acting, singing, dancing, swimming, and, most wonderful of all, he made his boys poets and dramatists."

At the basis of his work, Caldwell Cook said that there were three propositions:

1. Proficiency and learning come not from reading and learning,

but from action; from doing and from experience.

2. Good work is more often the result of spontaneous effort and from interest rather than of compulsion and forced application.

3. The natural means of study in youth is play.

Right from the start, he aimed to break away from the domination of the book approach to education, and it is from his experiments and adventures that we come to think of the Play-Way approach to English, but he was quite emphatic about the value of books – it was the use of them which for him was important:

> "We yield to none in our love of and feelings to literature – our complaint is against that pedantic misuse of books which repre-sents the greatest part of what is called education at the present time."

He was eager to see the breakdown of formal relationships between teacher and taught, and realised that, if a lively interest in education was to be established and maintained, the physical conditions under which young people worked must be such as to establish the right atti-tude of mind. He soon began to request a theatre in which his work could be carried out, not for the putting on of annual productions and school plays, but as a place in which the day-to-day work of drama in education could take place. Originally, he thought of a reproduction of an Elizabethan theatre on the lines of 'The Swan', but lack of funds made him replan and the result was the first room for drama, 'The Mummery', at the Perse School. This was a room to be used for act-ing and dramatic activity and contained a raised area at one end, joined by a step to the lower end. The raised section had an inner "stage" which could be cut off by curtains and, in the Elizabethan manner, a wide forestage.

In shape and actor-audience relationship this atmosphere seems not unlike that of the Mermaid Theatre created by Bernard Miles. It minimises any break between those who act and those who share in the acting. Caldwell Cook established The Mummery in 1914 – Bernard Miles didn't bring about the Mermaid until 1956.

In this atmosphere of the Play-Way, all kinds of work could take place and, although at first most of the work was based on texts, he brought the texts quickly to life by the use of costumes and simple props. Then, by giving out the parts a week in advance, he ensured that the actors had time to come to some understanding of the play be-fore the acting began. The acting was nearly always carried out so that the boys themselves could discover and enjoy the texts.

One day, at the suggestion of one of the members of a class, to "let us write a play, sir," Caldwell Cook established the practice of the children writing their own texts. As a basis, following a precedent set by many established playwrights, they used mythology or history, or a story told by one of the boys. From this they set about improvising the dialogue, very much it seems in the manner which Goethe had described in his novel. Rough notes were made about the development of character and the shape of the plot and finally a small committee was appointed to add the final touches and establish the complete drama. The value of such enterprises was that the youngsters made discoveries about the art of the dramatist and began to explore drama creatively. In his own words:

> "It is not acting we teach boys but the value of action. If it is said that boys are born play actors, we do not agree, but, to use the words in a wider and more natural sense, every one knows that boys love to play and live to be active."

People went to Perse School to watch Caldwell Cook at work and one might feel that here there was not only good theory on drama in education but a practical example which could easily be followed. Yet Cook seems to have remained a pioneer and rather isolated. Under a later Headmaster he does not appear to have received the same encouragement and although many speak today of the Play-Way, few follow his excellent practice.

BETWEEN THE WARS — OFFICIAL VIEWS

Still, however, after the First World War drama was a matter for public discussion and enquiry. In 1921 the President of the Board of Education constituted an Adult Education Committee to promote the development of liberal education for adults, who prepared a report on the Drama in Adult Education which was published in 1926. This gives a wide survey of dramatic activities in adult education and indicates something further of the realisation of the value of drama. The committee obtained from a number of witnesses a variety of views on the nature of drama as a form of art. Sir Barry Jackson, for instance, declared that

> "It teaches humanity quite directly to what it should aspire and what it should cast aside as base and worthless."

The Board, the Ministry, or the Department of Education and Science, has always recognised the value of drama in education. Each report or official publication includes references to drama, but not until the publication in 1967 of 'Drama', the survey of John Allen and his colleagues, has anything like full official consideration been given to its nature and purpose and, above all, its scope in the pattern of educational progress. The 'Handbook for Teachers in Elementary Schools' (1929 edition) accepted the need for education of the feelings and saw that through the arts this could best be achieved. There was very cautious reference to drama in schools:

> "The dramatic sense is very strong in most children and the reading and acting of plays should not be omitted."

This is the kind of benevolent approval which has been reiterated up to and including Newsom's Report 'Half our Future'. By 1937, and again in 1942, the Handbook was prepared to be a little more emphatic:

> "In recent years there has been a notable growth of interest in dramatic activity in the school and it is certain that drama is the most effective method for improving the clarity and influence of children's speech."

But it is now prepared to see beyond this and recognise its value as an art form:

> "In the school it may be appropriately defined as a training, a study, and an art; it is an excellent discipline in speech and self confidence; it affords remarkable opportunities for literary study and it is a natural and effective mood of artistic expression for the child."

Official thinking to this point stresses the oral and speech side of drama. The use of dramatic and dance movement was also beginning to be appreciated, but it was not until Rudolf Laban's arrival in this country that movement became respectable and more officially advocated.

A MOVEMENT CENTRE

The rise of Hitler and the Nazi movement on the Continent led to many artists moving their sphere of activities to Britain and America. Amongst the pioneers who left the Continent prior to the Second World War was Rudolf Laban, who had been Director of Choreography and Ballet at the State Opera in Berlin. When Hitler came to power it is said that Goebbels expelled Laban with the remark:

> "In Germany there is room for only one movement – the National Socialist Movement."

Laban was more than a Choreographer, for he began to examine at once movement in relation to the whole of man's movement activity:

> "Man moves in order to satisfy a need "

and Laban studied, analysed and classified the movements and efforts
and applied these explorations to all walks of life. With F.C. Lawrence,
he undertook researches into the movements of various workers, in
order to find the techniques which would suit them best, and such was
his approach that he was able to cooperate with dock management,
medical authorities, and even the R.A.F. for whom he investigated
the techniques of parachute jumping. After some work at Dartington
Hall in Devon, Laban eventually established a movement studio in
Manchester, working with Liza Ullman and a number of other pioneers.
It very soon became clear that his work had strong educational implications and he began to develop his ideas on movement with special reference to his work in schools.

With the work of Dalcroze and others, rhythmic movement had
become accepted in many areas as valuable in aiding the child's sense
of coordination and expression. Laban's work set all this activity in
an even wider frame of reference and paved the way for much of the
work which was to follow. In 1940, A.L. Stone became Headmaster of
Steward Street Primary School in Birmingham and in the H.M.S.O.
publication 'Story of a School' he tells how in these most unpromising
surroundings (bounded by factories and builders' yards, with no sign
of grass for at least half a mile), expressive work in movement, drama
and art, developed:

> "I wanted the child to be as free to develop himself in the
> material given him in school as in the material provided
> by nature: for a child to be free, the first essential is for
> him to move easily."

He tells how, in the hopes of achieving this, he began work in paper
and clay and then led on to:

> "Block mimes and massed movements (the channels of
> dramatic feelings) and to music in a happy, informal
> and contented setting."

Although at first apparently unaware of Laban's work, Stone seemed
to be travelling along paths very close to the spirit of Laban:

> "Before coming to Steward Street we began to feel that
> this type of dancing (ie country dancing) was not giving
> us what we wanted for dramatic movement, so, instead,
> we told tales in rhythmic movement and mime."

This work he developed, using the hall in the school for mimed history
lessons, scenes from Hiawatha and other incidents from literature.
The breakthrough seems to have occurred when two of his staff returned
from a course in "modern dance." This surely must have been con-

ducted by Laban or Liza Ullmann, and Stone tells how they then became associated more clearly with his work and how it formed the basis, leading into dance on the one hand or drama on the other. All the expressive work which seems to have dominated the whole attitude of the school arose from movement and:

> "After they had been through this dance or movement experi-
> ence they used their bodies to the full extension .... the body
> easily responded to the emotional stimulus aroused by the
> part the children were playing."

Stone's work was later carried on by Kenneth Scott and the school became a pattern which others could follow. All this was taking place with children aged between seven and eleven, and this kind of free movement and drama developed most readily in junior schools.

In spite of the fact that the Ministry gave its official blessing to such an enterprise, by issuing the 'Story of a School' as one of its pamphlets, very few Heads of Junior Schools seem to have followed this lead. Here and there throughout the country good and lively experiment was going on, but very much, it appears, in isolation.

AN ART IN ITS OWN RIGHT

Then in 1943 a group of teachers and others formed the Educational Drama Association, aiming to foster an interest in drama in schools. That same year Peter Slade became the Drama Adviser to the County of Stafford and established the Pear Tree Players, a professional company devoted entirely to drama in education. Professor Cizek had pointed out that there existed in painting the form Child Art, which had to be seen and appreciated on its own level and not measured against or by adult standards. Peter Slade pointed out that, in the same way, there was a Child Drama, also an art form in its own right and with its own forms and developments.

Mr Slade became, in 1947, Drama Adviser for the City of Birmingham and at Rea Street devised the Experimental Drama Centre, which is an all-purpose adult/children's theatre. Then, in 1954, his book 'Child Drama' was published and in this he set forth his ideas and observations based on twenty years of study and understanding, research and experimentation, in connection with drama in education. He is careful to point out that child drama is more closely associated with play than the theatre. He wisely underlined the fact that performance by children to an audience, especially in the early stages, is likely to do more harm than good, by building tension and placing the emphasis away from the thing being done to the people for whom it is presented.

39

Like Caldwell Cook, he recognised the need for an atmosphere of friendship in the activity and that out of the child's way of "thinking, proving, relaxing, working, remembering, daring, testing, creating and absorbing", which is his life, his play, there are moments when "clear characterisation and emotional situations arise." This can be recognised as a special kind of play, namely dramatic play. Peter Slade recognises two main forms of play:

Personal Play

This, in Peter Slade's terminology, is characterised by movement and impersonation, and it is linked at times with dance and the delight in physical exertion and the making of noise, eg the child, with a wooden sword at his side, will become a warrior and fight against demons and savage animals. He is totally absorbed in this role and uses his whole personality in presenting the character.

Projected Play

For Slade this is a more mental and imaginative play. The child is less physically involved in himself, but uses toys and symbols which may take on a personality of their own. The child, as it were, projects his dramatic instinct into these objects, eg the child may take toy animals, or a dolls house and, simply by moving the pieces around within this imaginative framework, can animate the scene from within his mind with the minimum of physical effort.

All this was an important development in educational thinking about drama, and we may say that Peter Slade's most valuable contribution was to work in junior schools, where his appreciation that drama had great therapeutic value gradually began to establish itself. He also did pioneer work in secondary schools. Kenneth Scott, too, after working for some time at Steward Street, became Headmaster of a Secondary Modern School and explored the possibilities of a similar approach at the secondary level. An organisation gave the work a focal point. A magazine 'Creative Drama' was established and this ensured the regular circulation of ideas. Drama in schools could begin to spread.

VALUES OF PERFORMANCE AND INVOLVEMENT

Working for some time with Peter Slade in the Midlands was Brian Way. After a while Brian Way moved to London where he established and directed the Theatre Centre. He continued to develop and extend the ideas he had worked on in Birmingham and from his London Centre sent out a number of companies to present drama in the schools, using the performance for children as a stimulus to the children's expressive work. It is interesting to find him in his book 'Development Through Drama' insisting that the two activities of theatre and drama should not be confused. Theatre, he maintains, is largely concerned with communication between an actor and an audience: drama, he says, is largely concerned with the participants, being irrespective of any function of communication to an audience. In this he is at one with Mr. Slade, though it always seems a pity that both should feel that "communication to an audience is beyond the capacity of children and young people". Much, it seems, will depend upon the size and relationship of the audience, as well as the material being communicated. While it is right to be cautious about where and when the audience becomes involved, there is surely some educational value in children learning this kind of communication and, above all, in discovering the pleasure and benefit from sharing endeavours with others.

Brian Way sees that drama in education has a two-fold function, namely that of being "a method as well as an art", and stresses that drama is a useful tool for teaching other subjects only after it exists within its own right:

"We cannot use number to solve interesting problems until we have experienced, and to some extent mastered, number itself; no more can we use drama to understand and experience history or bible stories, or literature, until we have experienced and mastered certain aspects of drama itself."

Even in his own work from the Theatre Centre, he has come more and more to involving the younger audiences into developing drama themselves, and less and less into using the dramatic experience as the stimulus.

It is only in recent years, too, that teachers of drama have been recognised to the point of their being included as a separate category on Department of Education and Science returns. Drama in education may not yet be of age but it is growing. The survey which John Allen undertook for the then Minister for the Arts, Jenny Lee, indicates that the subject if still in fact very young and that much of what goes under the name of drama is of doubtful value and of uncertain aim. Far more basic thinking has still to be done. With a subject which is so active and demonstrative it naturally arouses much attention and, because many judgments are made on a superficial viewing, drama sometimes remains misunderstood. Nevertheless, alongside many of the other areas of our school curriculum, there is considerable room for fundamental thinking to be carried out.

Amongst those who have undertaken some of this pioneer consideration is Dorothy Heathcote, of the Institute of Education at the University
of Newcastle. Though working along her own lines, her approach is
not dissimilar to that of Peter Slade and Brian Way. She quotes Kenneth
Tynan's definition of drama as a useful starting point: in a book called
'Declaration' he said:

> "Good drama for me is made of the thoughts, the words and
> the gestures that are wrung from human beings on their way
> to or emerging from a state of desperation."

Dorothy Heathcote draws our attention to the idea of some element of
desperation and goes on to explain:

> "Very simply, it means putting yourself into other people's
> shoes and by using personal experience to help you to under-
> stand their point of view you may discover more than you
> knew when you started .... Drama uses the six elements of
> stillness, movement, silence, sound, darkness, light, in
> every possible combination and gradation."

These are the means which drama uses and it is through these
that we communicate in the drama to each other and to an audience if
there is one. Drama is basically a living-through situation or, as
she put in another context:

> "Play is a problem and the actors set about the task of
> exploring this in action."

In many ways, the common ground between those who have undertaken pioneer work in education in the twentieth century is greater
than their differences. The main points of controversy and uncertainty
seem to have arisen from lack of clarity in understanding the basic
elements. But it is pertinent at this point to realise and acknowledge
the debt contemporary thinking about the creative uses of play owes to
these pioneers. Perhaps greater knowledge of what has gone before
might steer us more purposefully into even sounder activities in the
future.

The Players in Conference

A report of the Clifton Conference on 'Drama and Theatre in Education,' Clifton, March–April, 1969

The account of the sporadic but extremely varied nature of the work being done in schools and other institutions under the name of drama which was given in 'Education Survey 2: Drama' (Department of Education and Science 1967) revealed very vividly the confusion existing in the minds of many teachers about the claims made for drama as an integral part of the education of all children. The first response to the challenges proffered by the survey a few weeks after its publication was a one-day conference held at Goldsmith's College, London, which was attended by several hundred people, amongst them three from Bristol who represented respectively the Local Education Authority, the Bristol Old Vic Theatre Company and Clifton College. They returned from London convinced that a conference on a much larger scale was called for, particularly to answer the challenge in the quotation from the survey which later appeared on the programme and on many other documents relating to the Clifton Conference:

> "What needs to be done is not to define the frontiers of a
> subject where no frontiers exist, but to establish clearly
> the contribution of dramatic activity to the growth and
> education of children."

A small committee representing the three sponsoring organisations agreed that the conference should open with a survey of current practice and thinking, and that the second day should be devoted to the presentation of a variety of approaches through demonstration and description. The main aim was to involve all members of the conference as much as possible and the object of these presentations was to heighten the discussions which would occupy the third and fourth days, when small groups of members would be asked first to consider the place of drama and theatre in education generally, but with particular reference to the educational needs of children, and in the later sessions to explore one aspect of the subject more fully. Exhibitions of books, photographs and other materials illustrating the work being done in various parts of the country were also to be arranged and presentations of work for

---

*A full account of this Conference has been published under the title
'Drama & Theatre in Education', edited by Nigel Dodd and Winifred
Hickson, Heinemann Educational Books, 1971.

children by at least one professional company and by children and young
people themselves were to be included.

Once the programme was arranged, a number of interested teachers,
educationists and people from the professional theatre in the South West
were invited to a series of meetings to prepare discussion papers on
some of the core subjects as well as on a wide variety of specialised
topics which were sent to all members before the Conference.

Applications flooded in, a few even from overseas, so that many
people were disappointed, although the committee almost doubled the
number of members originally planned to a new maximum of 330, including teachers representing all the age ranges as well as from all
types of schools, together with members of staff from Universities and
Colleges of Education, a fair number of drama advisers and representatives from at least seven Theatre in Education groups.

Gavin Bolton, Lecturer in Drama at the Institute of Education,
University of Durham, opened the conference by tracing very amusingly
the changes of attitude to drama during the period of his own career as
a teacher. He also acted as chairman at most of the sessions during
the second day, when five speakers presented their individual approaches
in varied ways.

John Hodgson, Head of Drama Studies, Bretton Hall College of
Education, talked on 'Improvisation and Literature', illustrating his
points by allowing the conference to see and hear his students working.
Probably the point made most strongly by this session was that while
improvisation makes literature appear more immediate and compelling,
since it takes place **now** as opposed to the more indeterminate time suggested by the printed word, it will modify the particular work of literature for the student through the varied contributions of those taking part.

Dorothy Heathcote, Lecturer in Drama, Institute of Education,
University of Newcastle-on-Tyne, gave consideration to drama as a
system rather than a subject and so analysed the particular needs of
the teacher who would use drama to "create learning situations for
others". She spoke of both teachers and students as being at once
senders and receivers and pleaded particularly for teachers to know
their own security boundaries and to work within them.

Movement as preparation for drama was demonstrated by Veronica
Sherborne, External Examiner for London University Institute of Education, with a heterogenous group of students, all of whom had, however,
worked with her previously in their varied contexts. She successfully,
and very quickly, demonstrated how to use different relationships in

movement terms to help people to work sensitively and creatively together, but she proved also that a considerable movement vocabulary was essential to both teacher and student if this aim was to be achieved. Yet her film 'In Touch', which was shown several times during the conference, was equally impressive in proving how movement, in her terms at least, can help to develop awareness in even severely subnormal children.

The theatre building in which all the full conference sessions were held was itself evidence of the theatre activities of Clifton College. It was therefore appropriate that the Master-in-Charge, John Hersee, should speak of the school play as a contributory factor in the education of young people, justifying its co-existence with those other activities more often identified with the term drama in education.

Mark Woolgar, Staff Producer with special responsibility for schools at the Bristol Old Vic, confined his attention to the work being done by professional theatre, both in and for schools, though he acknowledged the contribution made over many years by the travelling children's theatre companies. His talk was deliberately provocative, questioning the value of the various types of programmes offered by particular companies so that lively, if somewhat indignant, discussion was aroused. Later in the conference, the Belgrade Theatre in Education team from Coventry showed the nature of their work in schools by parallel activities at adult level involving members of the conference.

It was perhaps fortunate that the main organisers of the conference, Nigel Dodd (Clifton College), Mark Woolgar (Bristol Old Vic) and Winifred Hickson (Bristol LEA) had never imagined that any clear cut conclusions could emerge even from such penetrating discussions as might be expected from the highly experienced members of the conference, for no such conclusions were reached.

John Allen's amazingly concise summing up pointed to the needs of the future and it is possible that he might admit that the enthusiasm and energy generated by the juxtaposition of so many strongly committed people as were present at Clifton seem to have greatly stimulated the interest in drama and theatre in education in many areas of the country. Certainly the many references that have been made to the Clifton Conference in all kinds of contexts during the two years that have elapsed since it took place have made some teachers say it has become almost a badge of honour to have been there!

Winifred Hickson

PLATO ASCHAM ROUSSEAU PESTALOZZI FROEBEL MONTESSORI GOETHE STANISLAVSKI HERBERT SPENCER FREUD STANLEY HALL FRAZER ARISTOTLE

Development of Drama in Education in the 20th century

Recognition of Play

London Street Games (Norman Douglas 1916)
Play in Childhood (Margaret Lowenfeld 1935)
Imitation, Play and Dreams (Piaget 1951)
Lore and Language of School Children (Opie 1959)
Children's Games in Street and Playground (Opie 1969)

Drama Pioneers

Caldwell Cook (Playway 1917)
Moreno (Therapeutic Theatre in Vienna 1922)
Brecht (Theory 1923 to 1956)
Irene Mawer (Art of Mime 1934)
Rudolf Laban (Modern Educational Dance 1936)
Educational Drama Association 1943
Mary Kelly (Group Playmaking 1948)
Peter Slade (Child Drama 1954)
Brian Way (Theatre Centre 1956)
John English (Midlands Art Centre 1964)
Ed Berman (Inter-Action and Dogg's Troupe)

Official Response

Drama in Adult Education (Board of Education 1926)
Handbook for Teachers (HMSO 1929, 1937, 1942)
Story of a School (Ministry of Education Pamphlet 1949)
Drama in the Schools of Wales (HMSO 1954)
Newsom Report (1963)
English Working Paper No. 3 (1965)
Plowden Report (1967)
Provision of Theatre for Young People
(Arts Council 1966)

Integration and Training

Main Drama in Colleges (first in 1945)
Drama Advisers (first 1934)
Univ. Drama Dept. (first at Bristol in 1948)
Theatre in Education Teams (first at Coventry 1964)
Specialist Drama Teachers (first DES 1967)
British Children's Theatre Association
Theatre Centres

2. Drama in Further Education

Drama and Theatre Arts in the British Universities

Fellows, Theatres, Schemes and Gestures

The British universities are rapidly catching up with themselves. The drama, once so central to the education of the gentleman and scholar, through rhetoric, composition and performance, is regaining its place in the undergraduate curriculum and has established a fair bridgehead into the prestigious graduate schools. Later in this section we shall hear from the big five – Birmingham, Bristol, Glasgow, Hull and Manchester — and hear the history and philosophy of those full Drama Departments, but it is useful to remind ourselves that outside these universities drama studies, in one form or another, are by no means neglected. There is a healthy diversity of approach, and a range of interest that extends from the purely academic to the sponsorship of professional theatre, as this brief (and perhaps incomplete) summary will show:

> **University College, Bangor:** drama courses are taught here at undergraduate level, and a new theatre is planned to accommodate not only university activities but to house professional theatre to serve North Wales.
>
> **University of Bradford:** a Fellow in Theatre is in charge of encouraging and organising dramatic activity, mainly as an extra-curricular contribution to the cultural life of a predominantly technological university. In addition the Fellow has created professional activity to serve Bradford and the towns near to the city.
>
> **University of Cambridge:** the A.D.C. Theatre is a fully-equipped theatre run by undergraduates and used fully in term-time by student companies. The Arts Theatre houses both professional and student productions. There is no curricular drama but a flourishing number of University and college societies.

50

University College, Cardiff: here a big new 'double' theatre is almost finished, the Sherman Theatre. No drama courses are offered, but the Sherman will accommodate student and community productions and professional performances, aimed to enrich the university and the region.

University of Essex: a Fellow in Drama has a new theatre to work in, with an academic contribution to undergraduate work and an M.A. course in drama.

University of Exeter: quietly, but steadily, drama has grown within the context of the Department of English, and now forms a substantial contribution to a degree scheme. A small staff appears likely to be enlarged to accommodate a developing drama programme, and, of course, on the campus the Northcott Theatre serves everybody.

University of Lancaster: a fine drama studio is under the direction of a full time member of staff, plus other academic and technical staff. The studio serves the university through its theatrical and cultural activities, and is also extensively used in the academic programme of the university, particularly in modern languages, and for much of the teaching of an M.A. degree in drama. A professional company, directed by the studio's director, is also operated to serve the region.

University of Leeds: a Fellow in Drama with supporting staff runs an academic programme at undergraduate level (contributing to the English degree) plus an M.A. in Drama and Theatre Arts that is now firmly established. A make-shift studio may soon be replaced by a purpose-built drama centre, where the academic and para-curricular programme of the present workshop may be extended.

University of Newcastle: a new theatre serves as a home for a professional company and accommodates student activity.

University of Oxford: the Playhouse, the University Theatre, houses a resident professional company and undergraduate societies.

University of Southampton: a large theatre, professionally directed, accommodates both professional and university productions.

University of Strathclyde: a new theatre is being built, and

plans are for staff and a professional group to operate from
the theatre.

University of Sussex: a sophisticated arts centre, with professional staff, serves both the university and the community,
with professional and general activity in the arts.

Without doubt much of the activity outlined above has arisen from
a vocal demand by students for the opportunity to work creatively in
the arts, and a growing awareness of the universities of the academic
argument for laboratory work in the arts and the general cultural benefits of dramatic activity. As the recommendations of official reports
on primary and secondary school programmes in drama become implemented it is inevitable that the universities, along with other sections
of higher education, will have to respond in parallel to provide courses
and facilities to accommodate a growing demand.

At Birmingham

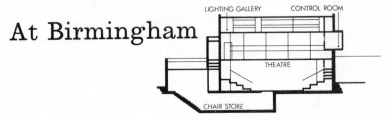

The Cockpit, London, a prototype studio theatre

The Department of Drama and Theatre Arts at Birmingham University
is a development of informal teaching that I undertook for the Students'
Guild Theatre Group and a series of productions for them. In 1963 this
work became formalised as a Supplementary Course within the English
Department, leading to one paper and a practical assessment in the
final examinations. The next step was the formation of a Faculty Committee to make an appointment in drama within the English Department,
and to advise on a syllabus for teaching drama as one of two subjects
for a combined honours degree.

This formative committee was under the chairmanship of the
Barber Professor of Music, Anthony Lewis, and he brought to his work
the talents of scholar, teacher, composer and conductor. From the

first the Birmingham Department was to study both "Drama" and
"Theatre Arts," and practical work was to be basic to its teaching and
take a significant part in the final assessments. Mr. David Munrow,
Head of the Physical Education Department, had already been considering an appointment in dance; as a member of the Drama Committee he
also influenced policy and, through the subsequent appointment of Miss
Jane Winearls, ensured that from the first the study of the actor as
instrument and artist was founded on the tradition stemming from Joos,
Laban and Leder. Professor Terence Spencer of the English Department completed the trio of active founders of the study of drama at
Birmingham, by allowing the English Department to act as parent to
the new development and by his influential support in Faculty, Senate
and elsewhere.

In April of 1964, Faculty and Senate recommended a separate
Department of Drama and Theatre Arts and I was appointed as its Head.
Already the combined honours syllabus had been found too crowded for
a full range of theatre studies, and so a single honours degree was at
this time projected and took its first entrants in 1966. Plans for a new
Studio were also begun at this time and new appointments were made,
Geoffrey Reeves, Jocelyn Powell, Marion Jones and Clive Barker joining in these years of first development. Mr. Reeves and Miss Jones
subsequently left for other work, and Graham Woodruff joined in 1968.
Through all except Mr. Barker, the Birmingham department had important past connections with that at Bristol. Mr. Barker, who had
worked with Joan Littlewood and Centre 42 and had undertaken productions and drama-school teaching in London and elsewhere, brought
practical theatre experience of almost every kind to his work in the
department. Mr. Woodruff had studied in the United States, taught at
the Manchester Department and had been Associate Director at the
Liverpool Playhouse before coming to Birmingham. With this varied
help the Department has grown until its present size.

Now in 1971, twelve single honours and eight combined honours
students are accepted annually, together with varying numbers of
graduate students to study for the M.A. or Ph.D. degrees.   The
department is housed in specially designed quarters, that include two
theatre studios, a design room, sound studio, seminar room, wardrobe, workshop and the usual range of teaching rooms. The main
studio is named after Allardyce Nicoll, who, as Professor of English
and founder-director of the Shakespeare Institute at Stratford-upon-Avon,
had brought his wide knowledge and sympathies to the study of Shakespeare, theatre history and drama at Birmingham in the years immediately

after the Second World War. The equipment of this studio includes a twenty-foot, moveable revolve, stereo sound and a punch-card lighting control which allows three productions to play undisturbed in repertory and encourages experimental use of lights and projections.

Academically, the Department is now much as it was conceived, with practical study central to all its work. So, a course in theatre-history includes model-making and plan-drawing, and a course in play construction includes work with cameras, scissors-and-paste, dramatic adaptations and scenarios. Play-texts are examined through voice, movement and acting, as well as verbal analysis or textual criticism. Practical examinations and assessments are part of Finals. Productions arise, not from the need to provide plays in performance, but from the students' study in any part of the syllabus: the production project may be long or short in time, involve two or three students or the whole department. The most recent was a documentary drama on the Spanish Civil War, researched, scripted and staged under the leadership of Clive Barker.

Because of the origins of the department at Birmingham, relations with other Arts Faculty Departments have always been productive. With the Greek Department there have been studies and productions of works by Aeschylus, Euripides and Aristophanes. Dance programmes, plays in production newly translated from Spanish and Russian, seminars on Beckett and Genet, Jocelyn Powell's productions of opera for the Barber Institute, classes in phonetics, joint drama and sociology research papers, are only some of the evidence of a truly university context for work.

John Russell Brown

At Bristol

Drama, as a subject for study in an academic environment, was admitted to the Faculty of Arts in the University of Bristol as an autonomous Department alongside earlier established disciplines like Classics, Philosophy or the modern languages in October, 1947. This development followed in the wake of the establishment by the Arts Council of an Old Vic Company in Britain's oldest playhouse, the Theatre Royal, Bristol, in 1945, and the creation of the Bristol Old Vic Theatre School under the auspices of the Company in 1946.

It did not gain an ultimate freedom by escaping from former tutelage within a parent department such as English, as had frequently occurred previously in America, or History, as had occasionally been the case in Germany and Scandinavia: nor, for that matter, did it graduate, via Diploma status, from within a conservatoire as was happening at that time in some East European countries. It was simply given the right to exist, as it were "on probation"; either to justify the expenditure of public funds on its development within fifteen years or, failing that, to close down.

Led by a lecturer-in-charge and assisted by a Consultative Committee of Professors in allied disciplines and representatives of the Old Vic Theatre Company and School, it forged its own destiny by trial and error in the form of academic, theatrical and cinematic experiment until, two years before the time-limit originally set by the University Grants Committee was due to expire, the Senate and Council of the University decided to set the seal on its survival by establishing a Chair in the subject in 1960.

The next decade saw the subject accepted into six other Universities in varying forms and with equally varied objectives. Although these new departments and sub-departments could scarcely avoid recruiting a high proportion of staff who had received their training at

Bristol it remained deliberate policy in Bristol itself not to try to exercise any direct influence upon the independent development of these
newer institutions. Each has therefore gone its own way with results
that are different and which are gradually becoming distinct.

In Bristol academic staff appointments have been governed by a
consciousness that a Department of Drama, notwithstanding the practical nature of the subject considered as an art, and its close relationship with professional bodies outside the University, is in the last
analysis the child of an academic parent. Thus, while all candidates
for appointment have been expected to produce some evidence of interest
and ability in practical aspects of the subject they are going to be called
upon to teach, the ultimate yardstick of selection has been scholarly
distinction. No less important is the principle that has come to be
established that while students must necessarily read a majority of
continental European plays, ancient and modern, in translation, the
staff who teach them should do so from a background of close familiarity with the language, literature and culture of the country in question.
Danish, Dutch, French, German, Greek, Italian, Latin, Norwegian,
Russian, Spanish and Swedish drama is now covered in this way from
within the Department itself. These policies have been vindicated by
the respect won for the subject in the Faculty to which the Department
belongs; and from this has stemmed the second Chair, established this
year, to which an election is about to be made.

In adopting these policies the department has applied them uni-
formly to teaching both in theatre and in the modern forms of purveying
dramatic experience to mass audiences: films, radio, and television
have thus figured in the undergraduate curriculum for nearly twenty
years. Great care has also been taken to channel the energies and
talents of those students who wish to apply their knowledge of the subject to vocational ends into appropriate post-graduate courses, thus
giving the undergraduates much more elbow-room to explore the possibilities of the subject, and its relationships both with other subjects
and the development of their individual personalities, than would be
the case if the B.A. curriculum was to be strictly geared to the attain-
ment of specialist qualifications.

The fight to preserve this measure of freedom for undergraduates
has not been permitted to serve as an excuse for ignoring students'
growing concern with careers and vocational training. Two recent
developments are here likely to prove important for the future. The
first is the introduction of a post-graduate Certificate in Radio, Film
and Television presently conducted as a one-year Course, but which it

is hoped to translate shortly into a two-year Course. The second is the establishment at the Old Vic School of a two-year course for Directors and Designers geared to the £700,000 redevelopment of the Theatre Royal with its new Studio Theatre due to open in March, 1972. This major building scheme will give the Bristol Old Vic three theatres, with sections of the resident Company playing concurrently in each, and with the Theatre School and the Drama Department invited to present experimental work in the new Studio from time to time. To meet this new situation the Artistic Director and the General Mananager have invited members of staff in the Drama Department to join them in forming a dramaturgical committee to supervise the planning of the extensive repertoire of plays that will become available to general public and student specialists alike.

In one area at least Bristol has failed over the past two decades to take any active steps to participate in new developments — teacher training. This is largely explained by the curious fact that drama is still not recognised as a principal subject in any of the Colleges of Education associated with Bristol University. In such circumstances, and over a period when the Drama Department has had its own limited resources fully stretched in coping with its undergraduate and building programmes, it has seemed inadvisable to try to take any initiative without either qualified staff in residence, or support from the Department of Education in the University. It can only be hoped that this situation will change in the course of this decade.

Again looking into the future, the time is approaching for all the Drama Departments that are now established on an autonomous basis in British Universities to start to compare notes on their respective aims and objectives. The advantages accruing from regular meetings now substantially outweigh any remaining risks of stultifying or curtailing variety of development; for not only would channels of communication between colleagues who are still thinly spread and geographically far apart be greatly improved, but a more coherent framework for a shared philosophy of aims and methods in teaching should begin to emerge. If the need for action of this sort does not yet appear to be very urgent within the confines of any single Drama Department, it can already be seen to be so in the much wider nexus of common rooms in Polytechnics, Dramatic Academies, Colleges of Education and schools of all descriptions where pupils have to be advised on how best to apply limited funds and time in the pursuit of higher education in drama.

In this quest Bristol has no wish to impose its own policies on others; but it is more than ready to take any initiative which other Departments think to be timely and appropriate.

Glynne Wickham

At Glasgow

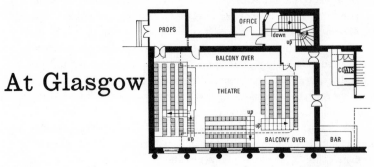

The Close Theatre

On 2nd May, 1470 the University of Glasgow drew up regulations for the celebration of the Feast of St. Nicholas. The day was to begin with the masters and students of the University riding through the streets bearing flowers and branches, and to end with the performance of an entertaining play. After the Reformation, as the Scottish reformers came increasingly under the influence of English Puritanism, such performances would come to an end. In 1745 an attempt by students to get up a production of Addison's 'Cato' was stopped in rehearsal. In 1754 students were forbidden to patronise the first regular theatrical performances in Glasgow. (They were also forbidden to wear lace during term.) Within a decade, however, more tolerant views came to prevail. In the nineteenth century, Glasgow was one of the universities to confer an honorary degree on Henry Irving. A great tradition of Shakespearean scholarship arose.

It was not till 1950, however, that the first step was taken towards the recognition of theatre arts as part of the curriculum, with the establishment of the Certificate in Dramatic Studies. In that year the University participated in the foundation by the Royal Scottish Academy of Music of a college of Dramatic Art, admitting academically qualified students of the new college to matriculation and providing for them a three-year course in theatre history and dramatic criticism, staffed by the English Department, with the assistance of other departments of language and literature.

58

Prompting this development was a faith in the value, for both theatre and university, of bringing together the practical and the academic study of the drama. After fifteen years of cautious advance, the final step was taken in 1966 with the inclusion in the M.A. curriculum of drama in its theatrical aspects, including radio, television and film. This became the responsibility of an independent Department of Drama, responsible also for the course in dramatic studies.

Four courses are provided for M.A. students: a four-year course leading to M.A. (Honours) in drama combined with one of a large choice of subjects; and one or two-year courses forming part of the M.A. (Ordinary) curriculum. There are some hundred students in the first year, thirty in the second, and twenty in the honours class. The course in dramatic studies numbers eighty. The staff consists of a senior lecturer and four lecturers, assisted by part-time teachers.

The main emphasis in all M.A. courses is on the study of the history of the theatre, including architecture, acting, directing, design, dramatic literature, and audience. There is a considerable amount of practical criticism in that first and second years are required to see plays in the Citizens', Close, Athenaeum, University or other Glasgow theatres at least once a fortnight, and to attend discussions on the pre-scribed productions. One of the questions in the honours papers is a detailed review of a performance seen recently.

Although the courses are mainly academic, there is a practical element at all levels, especially in the first and second years. The first year concentrates on the study of the actor. One hour a week is given to movement and to voice production, and once a fortnight a practical seminar is held on the subjects of the lecture courses. All students proposing to study the subject for more than one year are required to take a three-week practical course, normally held in June, where they have an opportunity to act, direct, stage-manage, and make short films. In the second year, when the concentration is on the director, the students are given lectures on stage-management, lighting and design, and required to assist in the running of Depart-mental productions (which occasionally employ professional actors) or those of Arts Theatre Group, a semi-professional company which has the Department as its base of operations. One of the four papers of the honours examination is devoted to directing, when candidates are expected to outline the director's idea, draw a scale ground plan, write notes for the actors, and indicate moves for a production of a scene from a prescribed play. It should be pointed out that all honours students in drama have to complete a one-year university class in a language other than English. The present headquarters of the Department are a Victorian dwelling house. The Department also uses the University Theatre. The facilities of the University Television Service are also made available from time to time. The University library has an excellent section devoted to drama and theatre arts.

The Department is also responsible for post-graduate courses in drama leading to the M. Litt. and Ph.D. degrees. 'Theatre Research/ Recherches Théâtrales,' the journal of the International Federation for Theatre Research, is edited jointly by the Departments of Drama of Glasgow and Manchester.

J. F. Arnott

At Hull

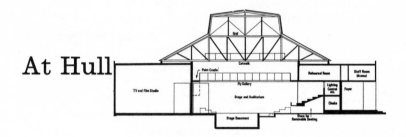

We began, unequivocally, at the beginning — with the human body and little else. Nineteen human bodies, to be precise, belonging to nineteen assorted theologians, American-studiers and Anglicists who had gamely elected to take three terms of drama in the first year of the Department's existence and must have been wondering what to expect. By way of an answer there was one member of staff — no less apprehensive than they — and no material resources of any kind. That was in October, 1963: days of begged lighting, borrowed costumes and stolen rostra, of rehearsals in vacant lecture-rooms amid desks stacked perilously to the wall. Nonetheless, practical classes somehow got under way and, against an improvised setting of builders' scaffolding and placards, a first production was staged. In a determined effort to pluck virtue out of necessity it called itself 'Three Plays Without Décor' and a benevolent 'Guardian' critic was moved to see in it a promising augury for the years to come.

At the same time I was visiting theatres throughout the country

and drawing up specifications for a drama studio of the future. These
were subsequently incorporated with the University's plans for an
audio-visual aids service and in 1964 the architect Peter Moro was
commissioned to design a complex which would be capable of housing
both. Thanks to the energetic efforts of our Vice-Chancellor, the
Gulbenkian Foundation became interested in the scheme and allocated
a grant of £50,000, without which it would have been impossible to go
ahead. Ultimately, after long months of negotiation with the University
Grants Committee over money for equipment, the project became a
reality when the first unlikely-looking hole in the ground was dug in
July, 1967.

Meanwhile the department had grown both in numbers and resources.
We had been fortunate enough to acquire the University's former gym-
nasium, which was converted into an adaptable space for practical
classes, rehearsals and public performances and in which a small
audience of one hundred could be seated. Armed with this Theatre
Laboratory — a title that raised the occasional scientific eyebrow elsewhere on the campus, but more than justified itself by the experimental
nature of the work done there — we were able to think in terms of
teaching drama up to full degree level. The joint honours course was
introduced in October, 1966 and since then we have managed to find
room for thirty candidates each year — a small proportion only of the
seven hundred or so who apply. (Such is the fearsome annual exercise
in selection which confronts all university drama departments.) To
match this expansion further appointments have of course been made,
so that by the beginning of the current session the teaching staff numbered five full-time and one part-time member, while the student body
had swollen to 106 undergraduates, over 90 of whom are reading the
joint course, and three postgraduates. Our next step will be to launch
the special (ie single honours) degree course which comes into being
in October of this year, offering only five places per session to begin
with, but gradually developing to meet the already pronounced demand.

In all our courses we are concerned with four main areas of interest, which complement and to some extent overlap each other: dramatic literature (from Aeschylus to yesterday, virtually), theatre history
(over the same period), art of theatre (an attempt to explore and define
the identity of drama as a performing and communicative art) and
practical work, either in the form of practical classes or of public
studio productions. It seems to me that a university department must
address itself to all four — and endeavour to preserve a roughly equal
balance between them — if "the play in performance" is to remain, as

it should at all times, the focus of attention and the ultimate criterion
of judgement. Only in this way can we view drama as a field of human
activity worthy of study in its own right, without succumbing to the
Scylla of an over-literary or over-theoretical "Theaterwissenschaft"
approach on the one hand or indeed the Charybdis of an implacably
vocational acting-school syndrome on the other. By the same token,
the staff of a university department must operate in all four areas of
interest and engage in creative production work as well as lectures
and seminars; otherwise, a disjunction will inevitably grow up between
the critical and the practical and the two will cease to cross-fertilize
each other. With this in mind, we have in the past eight years mounted
between seventy and eighty production exercises, directed either by
staff or by students of the Department and ranging, with an almost in-
decent eclecticism of style or staging, from Greek tragedy to eighteenth-
century farce, from melodrama to Lehrstück, from son-et-lumière to
three-ring circus and from Everyman via Lefty to Godot.

With its new accommodation in the Gulbenkian Drama Studio and
Audio-Visual Centre, completed in 1969, the department acquired a
sophisticated instrument for this task. Throughout the planning stages
the architect remained in close consultation with us and the design of
the building as it finally emerged was carefully adjusted to the teaching
rôle and production policy of the Department. In addition to a theatre,
the Drama Studio contains dressing rooms, control and ciné-projection
rooms, a stage workshop and scene dock, a property store, a wardrobe
and laundry, a rehearsal room, a seminar room and staff rooms. The
studio theatre itself, as befits our concern with the evolution and presentation of drama in all its guises, is designed to offer a maximum of
flexibility so that our students may gain active experience of as many
known forms of staging as possible — proscenium arch, forestage,
apron, transverse, peninsular, open, in-the-round — and have an
opportunity to experiment with others. For the same reason emphasis
was given in its layout to the provision of functional working space for
staff and students rather than audience accommodation, since we feel
that audiences should not be solicited as paying customers, but invited,
as guests, to make their distinctive contribution to what are essentially
theatrical exercises conducted by students as an extension of the academic course. Moreover, the building also houses the University's
Audio-Visual Centre, in which drama students are given instruction
in the techniques of radio and television by the Director and his staff.

Thus, with the exception of formal lectures, all the Department's
teaching and practical work can now be carried out under one roof,

which makes the Gulbenkian Centre a unique purpose-built complex. It also allows us to contemplate with a fair degree of equanimity, laced with excitement, the arrival of the special degree course in October and the long-term target of an extension in postgraduate work, particularly in the form of advanced theatre studies with a practical bias. So far, our work has borne some fairly gratifying fruit: of the 53 graduates we have produced more than a dozen are actively (and gainfully) employed in the theatrical profession, while about twice that number are either already teaching drama in schools and colleges or are preparing to do so. If we can maintain this record, in roughly the same proportions, during the changing and challenging days which lie ahead both for the theatre and for drama in education, we may eventually help to silence those sceptical voices which can still be heard occasionally asking of drama — as they never do of music, thanks presumably to its academic antiquity — "Why go to the university to study it?"

Donald Roy

At
Manchester

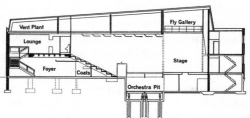

In 1960 Granada Television, at the instigation of its Chairman, Sydney Bernstein, approached the Vice-Chancellor with an offer to provide funds for the foundation of a Department of Drama. The proposal, which included the institution of a Chair of Drama, was welcomed by Senate, and a grant of £150,000 was made available, payable over ten years.

In the spring of 1961, I was appointed to the Chair with effect from September of that year. The department commenced its operations in October, at first offering drama as a subsidiary subject both to the general degree courses and to the honours courses within the faculty.

From the beginning it was, however, agreed that drama, in addition to being a subsidiary subject, should be offered as an honours subject in its own right. A Faculty committee was appointed to consider and recommend the nature of the courses to be offered. It was considered that, in addition to a single honours course of three years' duration leading to a B.A. with Honours in Drama, there should be two subject Joint Honours courses with English, French and German. For these dual honours subjects it was felt that each subject should be studied as closely as possible to the requirements of a full honours course. Four years would therefore be the minimum attendance requirement, and it was proposed that full time must be devoted in the final year of each subject to that subject alone. The method adopted was as follows: both subjects were to be studied jointly during the first two years. During the third year drama was to be studied alone and a final examination taken at the end of that year. During the fourth year the joint subject was to be studied and similarly to be examined at the conclusion of this year. This method made it possible for separate subject classifications to be made, and at a later period separate degree classifications were published; a double-first being a much prized — if rarely obtained — objective.

The committee's recommendations were accepted by Faculty, and the Honours courses instituted in October, 1962. The staff of the department was increased* and new premises provided in a church that stands on the University campus between the Arts Faculty and the Arts Library. This building had conveniently been provided with an upper story which ran its full length, with a good height of some twenty feet to the apex of the roof. It was not therefore a major task to convert this into a fair sized studio. The design of the studio was undertaken by Stephen Joseph who joined us in 1963 as a Fellow in Drama whilst still maintaining his connections with the Scarborough and Stoke-on-Trent Theatres. Stephen later became a full-time member of our staff, and his experience and enthusiasm proved an invaluable stimulant to staff and students alike.

Besides his skill in designing our studio, another task awaited Stephen's ingenuity. The university had decided to build a theatre. This arose from the fact that a somewhat inadequate building, known as the Arthur Worthington Hall, which had previously been used both

---

*The present staff allocation is 1 Professor, 1 Senior Lecturer, 7 Lecturers, 1 Fellow in Drama, 1 Secretary, 1 Studio Technician, 1 Wardrobe Technician. In addition, the department has regular assistance from special lecturers in movement, speech, cinema and broadcasting.

by university dramatic and operatic societies as well as by the Drama
Department, had to be demolished to make room for other purposes.
The U.G.C. accordingly agreed to provide funds for its replacement
on a new site. This gave us the opportunity of providing a purpose-
built theatre to supply both our own teaching needs as well as the needs
of the university societies. Architects were appointed, and the services
of Richard Southern were obtained as theatre consultant.

It was through the ingenuity of Southern and Stephen Joseph that
the University Theatre was built as one of the most attractive and
practical theatres in the country, provided with a fully adaptable stage
containing lifts for fore-stage and orchestra use, as well as theatre-
in-the-round. A small workshop was incorporated as well as dressing
rooms with showers, a profitable bar and coffee and snacks counter.
In consequence, the theatre has been able to attract two fine resident
companies: the present resident company being The Sixty-Nine Theatre
Company under the direction of Michael Elliott.

It must, however, be understood that, whilst this theatre is under
the direction of the Professor of Drama, it remains a theatre for the
whole University, and is not purely a workshop for the Drama Department. In fact, the department's practical work is almost exclusively
confined to the drama studio, the theatre being used by the department
for some three major productions each year, together with a three to
four week Summer Season.

Practical work is one of the major problems that confront the
teaching of theatre art as a university subject. We have at present
some seventy-five students reading drama as an honours subject and
some forty-five who take it as a subsidiary. These numbers make it
impossible to devote adequate attention to a comprehensive training in
speech, movement and basic acting techniques, and yet it has to be
recognised that, unless a modicum of skill is developed, practical
work in the study of theatre is largely valueless.

Drama is not an ordinary "arts" subject. It is in fact a hybrid,
partly theoretical and partly practical. Theory and practice must go
hand in hand, and practice demands not only a degree of practical
ability from the student, but professional qualifications from those who
are to teach him. The department is fortunate in having attracted to
its staff lecturers with experience, not only in acting and directing,
but also in design. Practical classes are offered on a voluntary basis,
although all honours students during their first year are required to
attend at least one practical course.

The basis of our courses is, however, the study of drama within its historical and social context, and in this it does not differ greatly from similar courses at Bristol and elsewhere. A study of television and radio drama as well as cinema is included, but practical work in these fields is not undertaken at undergraduate level.

Perhaps one of the most interesting developments of the department has been the institution of a Diploma in Drama for post-graduate students. This one-year course is purely practically orientated, and is intended for those who wish to enter the theatre or its allied arts as professionals. The special subjects offered are acting, design, directing, playwriting and administration. Practical work in acting and directing is conducted by the Manchester-Polytechnic School of Acting. The latter is a fully qualified Acting School which has recently been formed, again with help from Granada Television who provide a number of bursaries for students from acting schools to take a final year's course together with University Diploma students.

Students studying design, playwriting and administration work mainly in the department and university theatre, though all diploma students join together for seminar classes and productions.

Finally, common ground for all students — both undergraduate, diploma and those studying for such higher degrees as M.A. and Ph.D. — is established through the existence of Studio Group, a loose organisation run by the students themselves, which presents anything from a "happening" to a full length play, often written by the students themselves, on Monday evenings. The only condition imposed upon this truly creative work being the minimum use of scenic elements other than the adaptable rostra, lighting and sound equipment of the studio itself.

The department was re-housed last year in premises immediately adjoining the university theatre. All offices, lecture rooms and seminar rooms are located in this building, thus leaving the old church for purely practical purposes. This has enabled us to provide a small additional studio, as well as housing our wardrobe and design department within the building.

Hugh Hunt

Living on Borrowed Time

Drama as a main subject in the Initial Teaching Certificate

When John Allen first joined the Department of Education and Science there were recognised only a handful of colleges who undertook specialist courses in drama in teacher training. Now, some eight years later, there are over one hundred and twenty main courses in the subject. In the intervening period, officially recognised training of teachers in speech and drama has escalated. At first sight this may seem like very healthy progress; although many schools are still without teachers qualified and able to undertake teaching of this area of education, it would appear that at long last drama is seen as a subject worthy of attention and specialised training. Each year there are more and more students leaving more and more colleges, equipped, qualified and eager to undertake drama teaching. But before we begin to rejoice too loudly, before we begin too vigorously to pat ourselves on the back and enjoy this new awareness, let us pause to examine in more detail this state of affairs.

Each time another college offers a specialist course in drama there is a call for experienced and highly trained personnel to undertake this guidance and training of students. So over a very brief period of time, more and more people leaving colleges have found it easier and easier to obtain quick promotion. At first sight, again, we might rejoice but is this state of affairs so healthy? Anyone recently who has found a vacancy existing on the staff of a College of Education must have realised that something is happening to the quality. While there are still many people sending in applications for jobs available, a quick glance at the application forms reveals how soon people deem they are ready to undertake the training of others. Most of the candidates for drama lecturer posts are offering as little as one, two and three years teaching experience and in some cases (mainly graduates) no teaching experience at all. Few have more than a very elementary understanding of the nature, purpose and value of the subject. Only a handful have anything like a rich background of myth, story and other literature from which to draw and hardly any appreciate the complexity of teaching skills involved. And perhaps the most alarming fact of all is that the candidates are blissfully unaware of their shortcomings. Two years ago the new principal of Bretton Hall was interviewing, with the head of drama, people on a fairly extensive short list. The Principal, who had over the years taken trouble to brief himself on this area, found himself better informed than the candidates. The head of department desperately wanted to offer him the job.

Perhaps because the interest in drama teaching has grown so rapidly, it has not been adequately supported by deep thinking, careful research and adequate appreciation of the need for a varied background and a plentiful supply of ideas and material. The skills of drama teaching are different from the skills required for most other kinds of teaching. In drama greater demands are made on the teacher than in almost any other area. Heads of schools are recognising that there is value in active drama work and so, because the number of trained personnel in drama is few, it is easy to obtain quick promotion. It is possible to become head of a drama department after one year's teaching. This kind of mushroom growth has led over the last few years to a weakening of the roots of understanding, appreciation and skill. Those with little training and less experience are beginning to pass on their elementary knowledge to others. As time goes on the material is spread thinner and thinner over a larger and larger area.

DIFFICULTY OF STANDARD

This state of affairs is perhaps both the cause and effect of the wide diversity of practice in the colleges offering drama as a main course. In some courses, all too few unhappily, main course drama includes a very thorough understanding of play and its value to education and of the way in which the child and the teacher can work together in a joint enterprise, discovering many facets of life through acting it out. There are courses which take adequate appraisal and cognizance of the way drama can be used in therapy, in understanding literature, in social activities, in religion, and the contribution it can make in the general growth of confidence, skill and ability, in the development of personalities who can make a constructive contribution to society. But there are others where the course amounts to little more than theatre-going, the writing of a few literary essays about traditional texts and a rapidly acquired summary of the main developmental features of theatre form. There are courses in which projects deteriorate to the collection of theatre programmes and comments or diaries about a weekend visit to London or provincial theatres. It is all too easy to see drama work of the school diary we-rose-at-six-caught-the-bus-to .... type of approach. Some prepare dreary prompt books, transposing a simple playing text into a French's acting edition. Some offer stimulating courses on broad aspects of decor, but others go no further than training in elementary stage management or the theory of construction of flats and the box set. A great many of our courses still base their central work upon the school play and its ancillary activities. There are those leaving colleges of education, having taken main course training as specialist teachers of drama, who really have little more understanding than will make them rather inferior amateur play producers. Others see drama as an adjunct to the teaching of literature and are not really prepared to extend it further.

HOW MUCH TIME?

Besides the variation in training and experience of the tutorial staff, two other factors contribute to this disparity of approach. The first is the allocation of time in different institutes and colleges.

Some colleges are expected to develop all that is required within the space of a few hours a week; others have as much as two or two and a half days a week, while the specialist colleges have their students for as many as four days a week in the first two years. The problem is that drama is not an area in which cramming can take place. Time is needed where individual growth and understanding are concerned. It is not possible even to begin to find one's way around the drama of the past and equate it with the needs of the present and future in a few hours of lectures each week. Many discoveries have to be made through practice and first hand experience. It is not possible to develop human skills in speed and movement quickly. A drama cannot be created or produced without a great deal of preparation and painstaking practice work. The art of working with others, drawing out their ideas, observing their needs, coordinating their efforts cannot be arrived at overnight.

We are striving towards maturation of understanding and towards both mental and physical assimilation. Individual change is often apparently slow but we should not lose sight of the fact that in many instances we are attempting to overcome bad traits, faults and insecurities which have been set up over as long as eighteen years. It all takes time. We have to learn not to look for quick results. Work in drama needs adequate hours each day and week and ample opportunity for continuity throughout the years. Most of us find that an hour is the very minimum time in which we can approach effectiveness and most of our activities require a whole morning, afternoon or evening for progress. Furthermore, if the present position is to be rectified we all need at least two full days each week for the main drama work and as often as possible this should extend to four full days a week.

NEED FOR A UNIFIED COURSE

The time factor is related to the second process, namely that of the integration of the work in drama with that in education. Drama is still seen by most education departments as an area of extra-curricular activity, and they cannot understand the interdependent nature of drama with the whole curriculum. An irate librarian once rebuked a drama lecturer for ordering John Holt's 'How Children Fail' for his drama students. "How long have you been an education lecturer?" she demanded. This is perhaps a problem not confined to drama but seen more acutely here. We cannot and should not attempt to divorce theory from practice or essay to divide up the subject matter into "for the class room" and "for the student" categories. Perhaps the day will come when education departments will realise the full potential of drama as a learning method and accept its relation to play, theory and theatres. Perhaps the day will also come when drama departments will be fully aware of the difficulties of teaching drama properly without finding themselves deeply involved with educational issues, psychological issues, sociological issues and all that concerns the whole life and development of the child.

SPECIALIST COLLEGES

But signs are that the move is in the opposite direction. Up to the present time, specialist colleges like New College of Speech and Drama and Central School have had the opportunity to put into effect this kind of integration. Now, however, the bureaucrats of Curzon Street and no doubt other streets have decreed that all teacher training students must undergo the "Intellectual rigours of college of education practice". So out has gone the baby with the bathwater. For sure, the psychological and sociological and other "educational" aspects of some of these special courses needed attention but the principle of integration was a good one. Because improvement was needed in part of the course it seems foolhardy to ignore the potential benefits. Now we see "education" and the "main course" thoroughly separated, in most cases by several miles of city; education is undertaken in one college and main course in another. For two years the student is based mainly in one

71

college; for the third year he moves to the other. And this is a move brought into effect, not by those practising in schools or colleges but by those with tidy administrative minds in government offices.

But this only hints at the general need throughout colleges of education — the need for drastic re-thinking from within all courses and their inter-relationship.

For the most part our time-tables are as fragmented as any school curriculum. We have separate areas of working, and generally separate thinking areas too. Frequently departments of education carry out one set of policies and the remaining departments another. There is almost everywhere inadequate understanding of how and to where the two sides of the work are progressing. Too much of the work is unrelated to the needs, interests and concerns of the students themselves. Courses ought to be planned through discussion between departments so that, in main courses, fuller use could be made of studies in education and, in education, more use could be made of other materials, methods and approaches which would help any teacher in his communication. Such central understanding and the pooling of ideas is essential if a student is to feel that his course has an element of unity and the certificate of education he receives at the end of the course is not like a G.C.E. or C.S.E. qualification, but represents a course of training which is relevant and related to the individual for the job he is going to take.

WHAT KIND OF COURSE?

This is not to suggest that the only concerns of certificate training in colleges of education are to be immediately related to the classroom. In training drama specialists we are concerned with developing the teacher as well as the skills the teacher undertakes. Because we are concerned with developing the creative individual in drama as well as the understanding of methods and means for the classroom, we need to be working both at the student's own level in the enrichment of his powers and at those levels which will immediately find practical expression in the classroom. The drama teacher, like every other teacher, is better in his relationship with his students and in his contribution to the school if he is himself a person of rich cultural understanding and of adequately developed powers of expression. He needs to realise that the certificate enabling him to teach is not the end of his training but the beginning. What we should be aiming to infiltrate into college courses is an awareness of how to go on developing skills and finding material, rather than a feeling that once college is left behind all the exploratory work, all the thinking, all the quest for material is ended.

In a sense, college courses should set out to open up the road, to make students aware of uncharted areas and to help them find techniques of exploration as well as train good habits of thought and clear habits of expression.

Basically, College of Education courses need to be less structured to teach the method and more structured to enable the students to discover the basic principles and to learn how to formulate the questions. We do not want a standard, approved course, but we need greater parity amongst the different approaches. Standards must not be set by the lowest common factor, but we all have to aspire towards the highest and it is up to those working in the field to see to it that they guide and formulate the policy. Every drama main course needs to work out its own balance between the demands of the basic essentials. These are opportunities for:

1. extension of personal and individual qualities and powers of expression
2. development of particular teaching skills where movement, noise and space are involved
3. acquisition of an expanding fund of material and a growing appreciation of its qualities
4. capacity to develop, modify and explore a range of methods
5. understanding the different uses of drama, so avoiding confusion of aims and values.

THINKING TIME

Drama teachers have still retained a reputation for being amongst the more lively members of the profession and it is up to us to make sure that this reputation is enhanced rather than diminished as the years go by and the demand increases. So to ensure continuity of good drama teaching there needs to be a very clear programme of research thinking and a greater awareness of what other people are doing. And above all a readiness to share.

It is to be hoped that we can seize present opportunities for re-examining the function and the place of the College of Education. College staffs must be given more sabbatical leave for thinking and writing, reading and practising their own skills. They will, after all, be expecting their students to be practitioners as well as theorists of the drama. We as tutors and lecturers need to see our function as a personally expanding one. We have to look to the future, not as a further element of patchwork, surviving from the days when colleges for teacher training were the government's answer to supplying a training to people who could not afford University opportunities.   In the welfare state of the 70's colleges must be recognised as undertaking a job which while it has parity of esteem with the university is also an opportunity for the undertaking of a different kind of training and education.   In main course drama work we have a special contribution to make within this framework.   There is, if not a frightening, at least an awe-inspiring opportunity ahead.

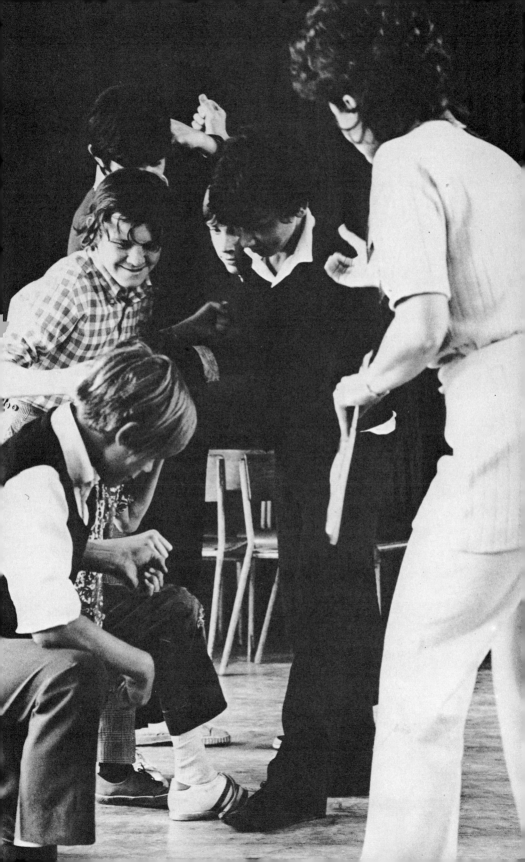

What's It For?

The Bachelor of Education Degree in drama

Drama is now firmly established as a main subject in a large number of schemes for the Bachelor of Education degree in the United Kingdom. This is a logical extension of the place of drama studies in Certificate courses in education, and a recognition, that does not have to be laboured in this book, of the great importance of drama in education. But within the various schemes offered and approved by the Universities (under whose guidance and prestige the B.Ed. schemes have grown) there are almost infinite changes to be rung in terms of syllabus, status of the degree, method and approach. One immediate point is that in some Universities the B.Ed. is an Honours degree, whilst in others it can only be awarded as a Pass degree. This seems a somewhat arbitrary distinction according to the temper and persuasions of the sponsoring Universities, and clearly leads to an anomalous situation whereby graduate A from University X may get a second class Honours degree in B.Ed. (Drama) whilst candidate B from University Y — no worse intellectually, perhaps better — will merit only a Pass. As we all know, this has practical repercussions throughout the candidate's teaching career. Surely there is a basic case to be made here for standardisation? Again, some Universities (and Colleges of Education) appear to approve of tacit acceptance of students at the beginning of a Certificate course with the assumption that they will go through to the B.Ed., and bend, if not structure, courses and hurdles to that end. Others still regard the final B.Ed. year as a prize to be won, as the exception and not the rule, and are consequently stern in their assessments. Here again the candidate needs to look well, and be well advised, before selecting his College of Education. One should also note at this point the insistence of some Universities upon matriculation, which causes clear abuses of natural justice in disqualifying students who, through three Certificate years, have proved themselves academically and professionally.

Little of this confusion is deliberate (though some of the restrictions have without doubt grown from the entrenched prejudices of some Senates towards "professional" degrees, or more imaginative subjects and schemes). Most of it has apparently arisen through the manner in which the B.Ed. was conceived, and the disgraceful failure of Government (ours and theirs — take it which way you will!) to support it in a proper manner financially. This means, in effect, no proper financial provision for staff for B.Ed. teaching in Colleges or Universities, but a general direction to "absorb" the teaching in the duties of the present staff. This has led to less than satisfactory schemes planned to fit within the available staffing situation, and to not unreasonable criticism that the academic standard is often dubious. Which really is having your cake and eating it. A basic requirement of a developing B.Ed. programme is generous finance for staff, and in the field of drama this is particularly so. Many College drama departments are working under quite improper stresses in order to fulfil B.Ed. obligations — and in a subject based upon practical work these stresses and strains are a great deal more obvious than in some more traditional subjects, where teaching and instruction can be confined to the lecture room or the tutorial.

We have opened with some of the complaints. We believe them to be real in substance and in urgent need of attention, but they are shared over the field of B.Ed. teaching to a greater or lesser extent. Our present concern, however, is to look at the question of our particular subject, and to try and suggest the kind of work that should properly go towards the B.Ed. in drama.

THE NATURE OF THE BEAST

Let's start with a few basic facts, working on the assumption that the B.Ed. is a vocational degree. (In the previous chapter we discussed an alternative view.)

(a) the degree combines two subjects, drama **and** education
(b) it is intended specifically as a degree for teachers, and generally assumed to be mainly for teachers of children between 5 and 18
(c) it is structured in such a way as to continue after the student's satisfactory completion of Certificate work.

Various points arise from these three assumptions. Take (a) — the combination of drama and education. The B.Ed. is widely regarded by Education Departments to be **their** degree, and as a consequence the education content of the course is high — at least 50%. Now it is clear that a student with a Certificate in education is a long way away from knowing all there is to know about education, either in practice or in theory. But it is also presumably true that he knows enough about it to satisfy the Education Department that he is fit to be a teacher. If this is so (and if it isn't there is an obvious answer!) then is there not a case for saying that in this extra B.Ed. year, courses dealing with education theory should play only a small part in the total work, and that such education content as is there should be related directly to the teaching of the main subject? The development of the student's knowledge of education theory can be left in appropriate cases to a higher degree. That is what the M.Ed. is supposed to be for. This is not an arrogant attack on the place of education as a subject, but a plea for a realistic assessment of what is possible and what is desirable in the one year (in reality eight months) which turns a student from a Cert.Ed. to a B.Ed. The main emphasis in the B.Ed. year must be on drama, but what "kind" of drama? Some Universities have insisted upon very "academic" syllabuses in drama — ie theatre history, dramatic literature, criticism, and so forth. These approaches are familiar to the Universities through subjects such as English (with which it is widely assumed drama is closely associated) and have the apparent advantage of being examinable in traditional ways. "You must have a three hour written paper" the planning committees are told, apparently because that is the only form of assessment most subjects are capable of. Or is that being uncharitable? But what is the drama teacher going to teach? Surely not a syllabus for thirteen year olds centred around dramatic literature. That may quite properly fall to the English teacher in some cases or be only a peripheral concern of the drama teacher. Again theatre history — one of the most stimulating, informative and delightful of subjects — may be utilised by the imaginative teacher, but is not central to his concern.

The central part of the drama teacher's programme will be creative work at one level of sophistication or another. Thus there will be imaginative group creations with young children, developing to detailed creative reconstructions and explorations with older children. The work will be based on movement and improvisation, speech and song, construction and manufacture, ideas and imagination. Surely, therefore, the logical drama B.Ed. syllabus, whilst not neglecting options in fields such as theatre history or dramatic literature, should be based around the actual teaching situation — its demands and opportunities. Thus we should not have a degree with two parts — drama and education — sometimes garnished with a ludicrous "linking" paper which suggests two parallel subjects with occasional bridges — but a degree in one obvious part, drama **in** education. It may be argued that that is exactly what the Certificate is about, but that, surely is the point. The B. Ed. only makes sense if it continues and refines the central purpose of the Certificate of Education, and in the case of our subject that is to make, exercise, stimulate and inform, a good drama teacher. Which point has carried us on to and through point (b), that this is a degree for teachers, that there is nothing to be ashamed about in that, and that it must clearly be seen to produce people skilled in a way relevant to the demands of the teaching situation. In many of the syllabuses constructed around traditional subjects and traditional methods there is a very regrettable hangover of that school of thought that denied any connection between education in the arts and its application in practical situations. A reticence not found in educating doctors.

A SYLLABUS

A possible B. Ed. syllabus in drama in education, therefore, might consist of three elements:

i) various options within education theory and drama/theatre in which the student might wish to be better informed. To be examined in an appropriate manner, and quite reasonably by a written paper

ii) a long study (**not** a thesis, **not** a dissertation — postgraduate terms beloved of B. Ed. syllabuses!) on a subject selected by the student and his tutors, and selected so as to be relevant to his work and interests as a teacher. (For instance, a study of a movement of vital interest in the contemporary theatre; a study of the uses of drama in particular educational situations; a study of the work of a stimulating and important individual in theatre or education.) The kernel of this might be a written presentation, but evidence could be presented in the most appropriate form, which might well include visual demonstration

iii) practical, investigatory, exploratory work with children in schools or other "real" situations, under guidance and tutorial advice.

This has brought us on to point (c), namely that it is academically irresponsible to "tack on" a "university type" year to a Certificate, and think that anything meaningful has been achieved. Self respect and confidence are undermined from the beginning for what is seen to be a rushed and unsatisfactory job. Here the Universities have to accept the fact that the Certificate schemes which, through their Institutes of Education they supervise and give approval to, represent a purposeful and carefully (and professionally) designed programme in education, which it is quite appropriate to refine with good candidates, and which does not need a para-academic gloss upon it to turn it into a decent degree. Quite the opposite happens in this case, and the significant number of qualified candidates who choose not to proceed with the B. Ed. at present is evidence of this.

In drama we need to be confident of the value of our subject, and insist upon its being taught and examined in a proper and meaningful manner. Otherwise we shall have fallen at the first hurdle, and, as we all know, we are only just being admitted to the starting post.

NOTE

B. Ed. Drama is offered at the following colleges

Alsager
Bakewell
Barry, Glamorgan
Bedford
Bingley
Bishops Stortford, Hockerill
Blackburn
Caerleon
Cambridge, Homerton
Canterbury
Cardiff
Carmarthen
Chorley
Clacton-on-Sea
Coventry
Crewe
Doncaster (2 colleges)
Durham (2 colleges)
Enfield, Trent Park
Exeter
Exmouth, Rolle
Hertford
Kingston upon Hull
Leeds, Trinity and All Saints'
Leicester
London:
    Avery Hill
    Coloma
    Digby Stuart

London (continued)
    Froebel
    Furzedown
    Goldsmiths
    Maria Assumpta
    Maria Grey
    St. Mary's
    Southlands
    Whitelands
Loughborough
Manchester:
    De la Salle
    Didsbury
    Sedgeley Park
Middleton St. George
Newcastle upon Tyne (2 colleges)
Ormskirk, Edge Hill
Ponteland, Northumberland
Portsmouth
Reading
Sheffield, Totley Hall
Sittingbourne
Sunderland
Wakefield, Bretton Hall
Warrington, Padgate
Watford, Wall Hall
Winchester, King Alfred's
Wrexham, Cartrefle

Training Needs for the Future

Dorothy Heathcote, whose work in education is becoming increasingly renowned, has doubts about the "conventional" courses in drama. In the following notes she presents some debatable alternative ideas

PRESENT TRENDS IN COURSES IN COLLEGES OF EDUCATION

1. Tendency to teach conventional drama areas — eg
    a. study of text (academic and practical)
    b. theatre experiences — visits, bringing text to life for others
    c. theatre skills — lighting, sound, make-up, interpretation, production, design (architectural and costume),characterisation
    d. theatre history — architecture, style, zeitgeist, personnel etc, plays of period
    e. children's theatre studies — usually practical and child-orientated.

2. The relationship of all the above to the teaching situation.

3. Improvisation and child-orientated drama and its ramifications throughout the age and ability range.

4. "Education" tends to cover play, processes of learning, skills of teaching, historical aspects of school drama — if any are taught.

RESULT

Students acquire a basic knowledge and experience of the above areas and some discover a flair in themselves. Many acquire an interest in the classroom application of their special courses.

D.E.S. and colleges say that main courses "are for students' own development", but headmasters appoint, expecting main subjects to be taught in their schools. Not only applied, but thoroughly understood. Most heads do not understand drama — its use has grown rapidly and many folk still apply theatre convention to their thinking of it anyway — what else can they do?

WHAT MORE IS NEEDED?

No-one can deny that "theatre understanding" is necessary in classroom practice, but not the elaborate "game" element which the professional theatre must employ. Teachers must understand it at the deeper levels of cause and variety of manifestations (both personal and group) rather than its methods and elaborations. Its primitive heart and driving power to release energy rather than its "slave" areas of architecture, lights and make-up. There is, for example, a great dearth of knowledge of how theatrical tension is created, of the understanding of the difference in the experiences of (a) dramatising for others, and (b) making drama serve the needs of those who create it, while they are creating it. Teachers require to understand their unique positions of "witch-doctor, Guru and restless spirit" when working in the medium. To obtain progression in their work they must not only understand the linear development in play-making, ie the unfolding of events in true dramatic form, but also the necessity of achieving volume-development in the children so that experiences are personally meaningful.

Most drama teachers spend years of classroom practice fumbling to discover their own ways of achieving internal growth and experience for children. Very few ever succeed in successfully using the art form without resorting to variation and corruption of it in order to bring it within the capacity of children. Many teachers emerge with the skill to teach 5% of the school population, yet they could emerge capable of teaching 95% — for it is not their youth or their inexperience which holds them back. It is the bias we give to their training. Many teachers of drama emerge with too little academic background to their work and also too little experience of thinking and talking with precision about their job.

A POSSIBLE NEW CURRICULUM

An experimental course would include the following areas of study:

Academic study and experiences
(not in order of importance)

1. Birth and origins of saga, myth, legend, folk-lore and varying attitudes to and uses of it in different societies.

2. Differences in dramatic form, eg Tragic, Comic, Didactic, Absurd, Dramatic play.

3. Group dynamics.

4. Anthropological studies of the place of theatre and drama.

5. Understanding of play and elaboration procedures.

6. Child development. The stages of "drama growth." Individual and group needs.

7. Motivations in learning.

8. History of educational drama in formal learning situations — not only Western schools, but, say Aborigine hunting training.

9. Analysis of types of confrontations which create tension.

10. Mental health.

11. Sociology — particularly in the areas of groups and methods of communication.

Practical experience
(not in order of importance)

1. Production without "producing" — text, novel and play.

2. Self-discovery of teacher-type and strengths and weaknesses.

3. Harnessing children's drama instinct to the classroom group situation.

4. Handling groups of all sizes in all sorts of spaces.

5. Skills of using tape-recorders creatively, lighting creatively, filming creatively.

6. Understanding relationships between movement, language, architecture, sculpture.

7. Collecting sources and resources.

8. Relationship of drama and other "subjects."

9. Learning to "focus" for groups.

10. Studies in observation and analysis of self and others.

11. Ability to classify in the ongoing situation.

12. Grasp of and skills in the total signalling process in teaching.

13. A delicate understanding of verbal signalling — skill in the spoken word — choice of language, volume, modulation.

14. Skill in tension and confrontation.

15. Skill in making plans which allow opportunities rather than creating rigid frameworks.

16. Learning to receive and listen.

17. Skills of recovery and rehabilitation.

Dorothy Heathcote

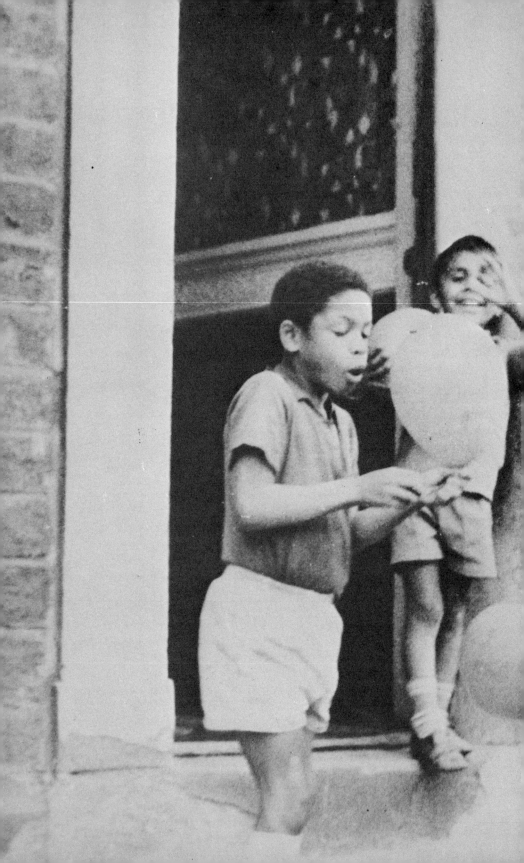

3. Drama Inroads into Education

First Steps in Theatre in Education

For some years after the war Esme Church ran the Northern Theatre School in Bradford. In this interview with Drama in Education she tells of some of the events and ideas behind this enterprise

ESME CHURCH: When I was working at the Old Vic in the war years with Guthrie, I noticed that there didn't seem enough work to keep the younger actors happy. So I had a word with Tony. "I think we're going to have trouble on our hands; the younger end of the company are so bored that I believe you are in danger of losing some of them." It was very difficult to get good actors in the war years. He asked me had I anything to suggest. The actors I had in mind were about eighteen, nineteen or twenty and mostly army rejects. I said, "What about a children's theatre?" At first Tony wasn't very interested in "childish things" as he thought them! But he said, "Yes, I think you've got something there. Let them write their own stuff for a start and we'll have a children's variety entertainment. Let's get hold of a director of education." So, we began. They wrote their own material and we put on a show which lasted between an hour to an hour and a half. Our first performances were at the Old Vic in Burnley, Lancashire. The director of education was there and the house was full of kids. It was a riot! Most of the kids hadn't seen any theatre before. The older ones had perhaps been to the odd Macbeth, but there was nothing for the little ones. Then Tony said, "What are you going to call your company?" I said, "The Young Vic." So, the Young Vic it was called and off we went on tour to mining villages and places like that. Wherever we went the miners' kids used to flock in to matinees and enjoy themselves. Then the air raids became rather bad and suddenly the dictum went forth that you weren't to gather children together in one place, especially in the larger towns we went to. So the Young Vic project had to be put aside until after the war and by that time I had left the Vic.

DRAMA IN EDUCATION: How long had you been there?

ESME CHURCH: I worked for Tony for ten to fifteen years.

DRAMA IN EDUCATION: Did you run a training programme?

ESME CHURCH: That was the Old Vic School. It began the year before
the Young Vic. There had been a sort of tentative school at The Vic
for a thousand years, but nobody did much about it. They used to
take students and dear Beatrice Woodson, who spoke more beautifully
than almost anyone, used to take them for voice production. I think
the odd actor used to take them and make them fence and do the odd
play, but they were called students and really nobody taught them
anything. Then Murray went to Tony Guthrie when he was at the
Vic, not his first year at the Vic, but the first year when he really
took hold, and said, "These students are really being exploited because nothing is being done for them." So Tony said, "All right, take
it over." He had a way of doing that; if he wasn't interested himself,
he would say, "It's a good idea, get on with it." When Murray left
to go to the West End, Tony asked me to be assistant producer and
master of students. I reorganised the students and a lot of my Vic
students turned up from time to time to join in the training.

DRAMA IN EDUCATION: How did you organise it?

ESME CHURCH: By setting up a proper rota of teachers. I got a
wonderful man to teach singing and another to take movement. His
name was Gibson Cahan. He taught those boys and girls to walk up
the side of a wall and fall, even to fall backwards off a 6ft rostrum.
There was Beatrice Wilson, of course, and the singing teacher, who
was very good for their voices. One of the Sadlers Wells Ballet
people came in to take dancing classes and then we had fencing. It
was a very full time programme. Then when the school was bombed
we went on the tour I spoke of in industrial areas and mining towns
in the North. We took the bulk of the school with us as crowd. Lewis
Casson and Sybil Thorndike were doing Macbeth at Burnley and all
went well for a time, but the audiences were tough. The kids were
wearing clogs and on one occasion the boys got bored at some point
and there was a solid front to the dress circle which they kicked with
their clogs. For a time Lewis Casson took it. Then he put down his
sword and buckler, walked down to the floats and said, "You boys,
if you don't stop doing that I shall come up and personally take your
clogs off." Well, they had seen him commit two murders and that
was all they needed. When we went back to London because the Vic
had been hit we went to the New Theatre. We took students out to

87

Toynbee Hall and had the classes there. That was thanks to Joe
Hodgkinson of the Arts Council, which was then C.E.M.A. This all
went well for a time – a couple of years or so – however, later the
air raids became worse. I was sent for by H.M. Tennent who wanted
me to go to Edinburgh and Glasgow to run a season between the two
theatres, the Lyceum and the Grand. So off I went, but I wasn't away
more than six months when Tony Guthrie whistled me to come back,
so back I came. C.E.M.A. had sent us to Durham, Northumberland
and all the mining areas. There we did start up the children's
theatre again because they were pretty safe places. We went everywhere by bus.

DRAMA IN EDUCATION: What sort of plays did you do then?

ESME CHURCH: We did a play by Cecily Hamilton called 'The Beggar
Prince', which was founded on the Princess and the Beggar Maid, and
we still had our variety programme for a time. We refurbished
items and wrote fresh material. Then we started going back to the
big cities again, and so had to pack up the children's theatre once
more. At places like Liverpool, for instance, anything in the nature
of children's theatre was out of the question for all the children had
been evacuated. It was about this time that the Arts Council, (still
C.E.M.A. I think) sent me on a fact finding tour to see directors of
education about children's theatre. So I went off fact-finding and I
only found one director of education against the idea. This information I took back to the Arts Council, though they weren't prepared to
back children's theatre at that stage. Not because they didn't see the
sense of it, their charter was for adult (so-called) education. I left
the Old Vic then because it had become stationary at Liverpool and
there was very little left for me to do. The school was closed and
John Moody was sharing productions. We weren't doing much
Shakespeare and I said to Tony I thought I'd like a change. So I went
to Bradford, to the Civic. It was there that this bug about children's
theatre bit me again. The war was now over. By then I had seen
David Giles, Bernard Hepton, and a clutch of young North country
lads and lasses who had neither the money nor the opportunity to go
South to get training but they all had very obvious acting talent.

DRAMA IN EDUCATION: Where had you seen them?

ESME CHURCH: I'd seen them playing at the Civic, which as you know

is an amateur organisation. I then had the fight of a lifetime with the
Civic. I had some very powerful allies to back me. When I said I
wanted to start a school for these young people they supported me.
Before we knew where we were we had more applications than we
could deal with, (including Dorothy Shot, who later became Dorothy
Heathcote). I arranged a three year programme, two years training
and a third year with children's theatre, and that's how Northern
Children's Theatre, and The Northern Theatre School began. By then
the bulk of the Civic decided that we had become too professional so
we split away into a separate organisation. About this time I went to
do a weekend course for the West Riding at York. During one of my
off periods I sat watching some work done by a man whose name at
that time meant nothing to me, Rudolf Laban. He was doing this
wonderful movement work. When the opportunity came I spoke to
him. I said, "Quote me a figure. You have got to come to teach at
my school." He said, he'd like to very much. He worked with our
students from then on – he was worth his weight in diamonds. The
students adored him, they called him Uncle Rudi.

DRAMA IN EDUCATION: When you were arranging the programme for
the students were you conscious of having any specific philosophy?
It seems that your students have gone perhaps into more spheres of
work than students from many other areas. They seem to be able to
cope with education more readily than most.

ESME CHURCH: All our students had to take both education and the
theatre. (Rose Bruford to some extent developed her school from
some ideas we had been using. She came to see us before she set up
her College. She is still a great friend of mine – I also taught for
her when I went South.) Here we were taking on some of these young
people, taking them away from secure jobs. They were keen to go
into the theatre, and we were encouraging them. We felt, therefore,
that we must give them a second string, so that we arranged that
they had a teacher's training as well as that of an actor. Leeds
University helped over that, thanks to Bonamy Dobrée. He said that
we at Bradford would be the last bulwark of civilisation in the North!
I told him that he must be the one beyond since he was at Leeds.
Barbara Williamson, who trained at Central School, took speech with
them; Winifred Hodgkinson, (the wife of Joe Hodgkinson the Arts
Council Drama Director) did the ordinary dancing and Uncle Rudi
(Rudolf Laban) did the extraordinary dancing. There was room for

the two of them. We got a local man to do the fencing, but these classes were very spasmodic. However, out of this situation emerged a first rate swordsman and a first rate movement person in every way, Bernard Hepton.

DRAMA IN EDUCATION: How was all this work organised?

ESME CHURCH: Like any other school we had a schedule and a very full one at that. The students started at 9.30 in the morning and finished at 5 at night, with an hour's break for lunch.

DRAMA IN EDUCATION: They all took both sides of the course?

ESME CHURCH: They had to. We had to say to some of them that they ought to specialise more in the teaching side while others would give more attention to the acting.

DRAMA IN EDUCATION: What were the main things you worked for with your Children's Theatre?

ESME CHURCH: I wanted everything to be good. If there was slapstick it had to be good slapstick; good, not silly. Uncle Rudi had a gift there. With kids you can go from slapstick to dire tragedy but you can't do that with adults. They would still giggle. Not the kids. At once they take it and at once they reject anything false. Another thing I was keen on was that we should take them all over world literature; we should give them the plays of all sorts of different countries, so that they would see that emotion was the same whether you were Japanese, Greek, German, French, Belgian or Italian. That "If you prick us do we not bleed, if you tickle us do we not laugh." I thought that was very important. Another thing I gave importance to was that the play should be well written. I wanted them to listen to good English. I tried to get people who wrote our plays (in the main I think they did) to write not necessarily literary but good standard basic English. I wanted the plays to be presented with a lot of colour, too, because that gives enormous pleasure. Starting as we did in the North, the towns are pretty drab, and I thought that they lacked colour in their lives and so needed more colour in their theatre. I wanted the actor to show the amateur where the professional had it and I think the professional had it in clarity of speech, and in movement. I wanted the actors to learn that complete and absolute control goes with fine acting. I felt, too, that there was a move to more theatre in the round, not necessarily in the total round like Circle in the Square in New York but in the semi-round. I thought if that was going to happen it was very important that every bit of the actor should speak because at some time part of the house was going to lose his face; sometimes part might lose his voice and perhaps get nothing but his back. So the way he stood must speak, everything about his physical being had to be eloquent, and that was where Laban and his movement were a godsend.

DRAMA IN EDUCATION: What about your acting theory?

ESME CHURCH: When I was just leaving R.A.D.A. I was in a play by Arthur Wing Pinero. Somebody had fallen out at the last minute and my guardian angel sent me to take up this part with only four days' rehearsal to go. Now Pinero was rather a frightening man. He had big black eyebrows that shot out in such a way that they used to call him Satan. He was, however, a very kind man in reality and after the first rehearsal he said to me, "You're very nervous aren't you, lady?" I said, "I'm terrified, I've only got four more rehearsals." He said, "Look, wait for me when rehearsals are over and we'll go back over lunch and I'll talk to you about the part." Well, we met, he read through the play and said this and that and the next thing, then suddenly threw the book down and said, "What are we fussing about? I'll tell you what you ought to be concentrating upon. Never think, this will make them laugh, that will make them cry, this will make them angry, that will make them angry. Think with the brain of the character you are playing and you'll never go wrong." That I think has remained my philosophy every since, though it took me a long time to really learn what he meant: leave in the dressing room the bits of you that aren't the character you're playing. Take with you on the stage the brain of the character acquired through years of training and experience. You can't teach anybody to act. You can teach them how acting is done, about the basic equipment. You can teach them what not to do and you can teach them the disciplines and controls but only the actor himself can develop this into genuine acting. We each have to do it in our own way.

Blazing a Trail

Drama in Education, in an interview with Rose Bruford, investigates some of her early progress in developing training

ROSE BRUFORD: While I was working at the Royal Academy of Music as director of the drama course for teachers I also taught at the Royal Academy of Dramatic Art — a course which was exclusively for actors. In both fields I found there were students who wanted to be able to do both jobs, actors who wanted to teach and teachers who wanted to act being attracted by the supposed glamour of stage and screen. So I decided it was worthwhile trying to build a training on the integration of these two sides.

At the beginning I think the parents of the students who came were very sure that they wanted their young people to be able to teach and have the security of that profession and I think this had something to do with our initial success. But amongst the points I always made was that if their intention was to go into the theatre they probably didn't know enough about it anyway when they were eighteen. I emphasised, however, that they were not to treat teaching as a second string and this was pointed out all the way through the training. The two sides, as far as we were concerned, were equally important and I have found again and again that many individuals don't know until the end of the three years what they really want to do. Some, of course, were absolutely committed to the theatre and said they must get it out of their system. Some were absolutely committed to teaching. Many of them who never thought they would, I found, grew by their experience in the classroom, to like teaching. They began to realise what the theatre really meant and what teaching really meant, so they changed their minds as they went through the course. I am aware that some people in teaching are worried by the fact that they think some actors are using teaching as something to fall back on, but I've always tended to disregard this because my experience was rather that they didn't know what they wanted. What sometimes happens after they leave is that they go

93

into the theatre for a while and some succeed and go on; others succeed and still change their mind after a time. They realise they want something more. I've had several instances of ex-students saying "I've enjoyed my work in the theatre but I want to do something more worthwhile. I want to teach. I know I said I would never teach, but you will be surprised to hear I am now enjoying it". I found there was a strong link between the two sides of the training. I found almost always that the best teachers were also the best actors and vice versa. I've proved this year after year because we used to have a prize (it now sounds rather old-fashioned) among others for the best potential teacher and the best potential actor and on many occasions the same person received both. Gripping and holding an audience is very much like gripping and holding a class. The required qualities are the same: timing, pause, variety, change of pace, surprise, sincerity and truth. It is, after all, holding your class and getting something back from them. I think the two sides go hand in hand. I've had many students say by having the discipline of classroom, their acting has improved and vice versa. The knowledge of the creative work in the teaching has made their acting work creative too.

The teaching programme at Rose Bruford College grew out of many years of experience. When I first went to the Royal Academy of Music I was brought in to teach mime to a class of singers and then I taught the drama class as well and finally said, "They need a full time course". So the principal gave me a chance to employ staff and build a course. This experience gave me considerable insight which I later extended in my own college.

DRAMA IN EDUCATION: In planning your first course were you aware that this was a new departure?

ROSE BRUFORD: I would not have opened another College unless I had felt there was something different to offer, and that to me was worthwhile, and I was very conscious of R.A.D.A. students asking me to find them teaching posts, and R.A.M. students wanting to enter the theatre; this was a reason for planning such a course, but I was not conscious of personal originality. We learn from everybody, don't we? I had a very good training myself at Central School under Elsie Fogerty. We all draw ideas from every possible corner and put them together to make them our own I suppose. I obviously built on what I'd learnt in the past and what I thought was good.

DRAMA IN EDUCATION: How did you ensure that the students kept

94

the balance between the teaching skills and the acting skills?

ROSE BRUFORD: I asked for advice; I knew what they needed on both sides, but certain points had to be observed because of the then Ministry of Education, so I asked Arthur Dean who had just retired from Goldsmiths College to come and advise. We put together a programme that fitted both satisfactorily for the Ministry to give us recognition for qualified teacher status. We learnt that children's theatre could be recognised as part of teaching practice and from the first year we had children's theatre every Saturday morning. Local children came in even before we had a theatre. This, I think, was very valuable experience for all giving such useful contact with children.

DRAMA IN EDUCATION: When you look for students what qualities do you require?

ROSE BRUFORD: To be honest, in the first year, I took anybody who would come, and we had a great mixture. I'm not at all sure we weren't better off. The educational qualifications then didn't have to be what they are now. We looked obviously for what we called a good background of education, but not specific examinations. For instance, there was a boy who had been on newspaper rounds. He found writing very difficult, and had poor speech, but he worked remarkably hard and became a leading student in the year. He wrote a good essay at the end, developed good speech and became a very good actor. He's still in the theatre. It is no longer possible for that sort of person to gain admission because now they have to have five O-levels and several Advanced levels too. I've always kept as flexible as possible in my approach to entry so as not to miss talent. I think we tried very hard to get a variety, a cross section, because it helped the students to mix in their working together. I think we did a lot of good team work and one of the things that brought this out more than anything else, I think, was their annual London Show in which every student took part. I believe in this very firmly because it doesn't matter how talented they were individually, they all had to do something towards it, including all the back stage work, scenery and costumes. They were divided into groups and there was a tremendous team spirit. After the show, the next year was so different — as if they sensed they were all working together, for one thing.

95

DRAMA IN EDUCATION: Having devised a programme, how did you appoint your people for aspects of education and teaching? Were these always people with some knowledge and understanding of the subject?

ROSE BRUFORD: If they came from education I did see to it that they knew something of our work and were interested in drama, though they might not have what we would call professional knowledge. I mean starting off with Arthur Dean, he was terribly interested in acting and had acted as an amateur himself. I think all the people we've had since probably have had that sort of feeling. Avice Allchin was a great help in the early days with Arthur Dean, in making the local schools interested. She wasn't herself an actress, but she was well qualified. She gave the students practical material for the classroom. We certainly owed her a great debt in going round to the schools, who were quite suspicious of us at first, and saying these people aren't as bad as you think they are. She established a good liaison which has remained. I don't think we could have done it without her. Now those same schools praise the vitality and energy of the students, welcome them, and offer them posts.

DRAMA IN EDUCATION: How do you tackle such things as the teaching of drama in the class and in the hall? Did you expect your students to apply the way they have been taught themselves, or did you give them specific help?

ROSE BRUFORD: That was one of the difficulties I've found because they were always apt to try and apply what they'd been given. Many times I've said, "You must realise it's different. We are teaching you slowly and steadily all the basic things that children, because they are not going to specialise, won't necessarily need". Of course the school practice tutor gave further direction about this and they were observed in the classroom as anyone else is and helpfully criticised. But I think this is a fault of many students when they first begin to teach, and not only drama students.

DRAMA IN EDUCATION: Did you see them as being teachers who would be expected to make some contributions through what might be called English areas as well as through drama?

ROSE BRUFORD: Yes, to some extent. I would never want them to take charge of the whole of the English. I don't think most of them had enough background. We had some graduates amongst them as it happened. If they were capable, they were given that opportunity in school, but they were very varied in their ability in this direction. Indeed, some of the schools asked them to teach other subjects as well, which they had to do. But I was always sorry. Latterly I used to find this was a growing trend, and I was certainly very distressed when we were sending them to schools where they weren't teaching speech and drama at all. This to my mind wasn't practice in our subject at all.

DRAMA IN EDUCATION: Did you specialise in the secondary level as teachers or were you thinking that your training was for primary and secondary?

ROSE BRUFORD: I've always maintained that if they can teach at all they ought to be able to teach any age, which I know is quite an unpopular theory. A few have been teaching in primary schools, but the majority, in fact, are teaching in secondary education, Colleges of Education, and many other fields of work, such as Drama Advisors, Teacher/Actors, etc. I know the feeling is now that they should be trained for an age range. I don't agree with this. I have myself taught an age range in most types of school, and speech and drama can so easily be adapted to them all. Some of the specialists must, of course, teach in Colleges, or from where will specialists grow?

DRAMA IN EDUCATION: Since you have been involved in it, the subject has grown enormously. Has this made any difference to the kind of training one is giving?

ROSE BRUFORD: I suppose the training has moved with the times; inevitably it's changing all the time, because you find better methods and some of those methods must come from development that is going on all around as the need seems to arise. I don't think it's a conscious thing, because the whole thing is creative from the beginning.

DRAMA IN EDUCATION: Do you see any difference in the calibre of students?

ROSE BRUFORD: As far as I am concerned with my limited group of students, they are different nowadays, because they have to be educated to a certain level. I sometimes find them duller, too. You can no longer have the ones that have the spark and no exams, and this

97

can be a pity (though I see the reason for it, of course). The teaching of drama is an art in which they have to learn two important things: one is freedom and the other is discipline, and these go side by side. There was a time when one had at all costs to free them from their inhibitions. Now there are not so many inhibitions, they are so free that you have to spend more time helping them in their control. I used to start off with freedom, that was the first thing. This took quite a long time; then I used to say, "Freedom and control must be learnt at the same time". Now it has got to the point of control being the first need. The present training period isn't long enough for all that could be achieved. I don't think three years is enough to do it all, and I never have thought so. If we could have four years it would be admirable.

DRAMA IN EDUCATION: Would you like it to be four integrated years?

ROSE BRUFORD: Yes, I would. Although, of course, it is much easier to teach them their skills if you haven't to spend so much time on learning to teach these skills. But I don't believe what people say of one subject destroying the other. I'm quite convinced of the truth of the opposite point of view: that one discipline aids the other. Indeed, I can think of no student who has not, after completing the course, agreed on this point.

DRAMA IN EDUCATION: Since you began your college this whole phenomenon of theatre in education teams has grown. Were you aware of this and how aware were you of actually producing people or being the only person producing people trained for that area?

ROSE BRUFORD: I don't think I was aware of it at all. I have noticed that when I am looking around for lecturers on the subject I find that quite a number of my old students are working in this field, and have valuable information to give. Originally, when I was training actor/teachers it was because I thought that at seventeen or eighteen they didn't really know about either job. It wasn't until they had had three years training in it that they really thought they knew which way to go and even then they ought to be able to change. I suppose it has become more conscious over the last years.

DRAMA IN EDUCATION: We've suggested that you have led an area of thinking — however intuitively — you have nevertheless pioneered it. Looking back, would you want to change anything or the way in which you've gone about things?

ROSE BRUFORD: The time factor was the thing that worried me most. I wanted to put so much in and there was never time to do it. A four-year course would have made it easier. On the other hand there is something good about being pressed, I think, when you are a student and it might become too easy with four years. I think, too, there are points when I was too strict, in my anxiety to get discipline and because the college was larger than I wanted. Although I did know them all quite well it would have been better if I could have had time to give more personal help to each student, though against that it is not good to spoon-feed too much, they have to learn to stand on their own in the end.

DRAMA IN EDUCATION: What about the future? What do you hope will be the future of the Rose Bruford College? What do you hope to be the future of this teaching area?

ROSE BRUFORD: It is very difficult to forecast today because it is all in such jeopardy at the moment. I shall be very sorry if the specialist colleges are given up, because I see no future for the subject without them.

DRAMA IN EDUCATION: Would you like to see more colleges working on the lines that you've worked and more of the training coming together like that?

ROSE BRUFORD: I think it's the right line. A lot of people disagree with me and say you can't do both. I think I've proved by the result that it is possible. They are better actors and better teachers. So many of our teachers go into our schools knowing only teaching and if they have something like acting and a link with theatre and its vitality, they have an enormous amount to give. I think it's the training of the whole personality. I think it develops the person and gives them that control and discipline and freedom altogether that makes them into much more interesting people in whatever profession they find their future.

Force of the Future

A survey of the development of Theatre in Education teams

Of the many strongholds of conservatism (nothing to do with the party), two especially stand firm against the winds of change – education and the theatre. Paradoxically, however, each has something for the other and when they invade each other's territory each brings hope of renewed vigour and relevance to the other.

Even just the fact of kids going to see a performance of a conventional play, at a traditional theatre, does something for the actors. In an interview with DRAMA IN EDUCATION at Stratford, Judi Dench spoke enthusiastically about performing Shakespeare to school parties. Even though she recalled the girl who sat through 'The Merchant of Venice' eating a Mars Bar and ignoring the play, she felt that, generally speaking, young people were quicker to reject false acting and phoney direction than most adults. And similarly, players on tour arriving at a school tend to upset our educational complacency. They give and demand a fresh kind of response. They bring a lively teaching method; they tend to have little respect for timetables and they work as a challenging approach to relationships. It seems well nigh impossible to move either of these institutions by working solely within one or the other but a combination of the two forces seems to be opening up hope and opportunities.

POOR ACTOR/POOR TEACHER?

At the outset, of course, there are problems. Those who work in each of these fields have their own protective frameworks. Pay structures in teaching, though basically poor, are better than the pay structures for the theatre. Training programmes are different for workers in each and each remains jealous of any intruders. Oddly enough, training for both teachers and actors is something which has grown up comparatively recently and in both cases there have been attempts to make science out of an art. We are perhaps, still too reluctant to recognise that elements of both actor and teacher are born and not made. To be a teacher in a state school requires Department of

Based on sections of an article contributed by John Hodgson to Theatre Quarterly 1

Education and Science recognition. To be an actor in a professional theatre requires the coveted Equity card. What kind of personnel, then, can develop this new force of Theatre in Education and Education in the Theatre? Opportunists who lack the necessary lead into one or other of these fields can see it as a way in, short cutting the usual steps. It might become a refuge for those who can't cope in the classroom or those who can't make it on the stage. It could become a dumping ground for poor teachers. But it doesn't have to if those responsible know what they are about and keep clearly in mind the opportunities.

FROM THE BELGRADE - FIRST IN THE FIELD

The whole idea of a Theatre in Education team was born out of vision, idealism and a sense of community. And it was crystallised in Coventry, that city which boasts that it dares to be first. In 1962 Anthony Richardson was appointed Artistic Director of the new Belgrade Theatre (opened in 1958 – the first new theatre since the end of the second world war). Richardson was a man with an unusually keen social sense and he was eager to involve every area and aspect of the community – civic, industrial, artistic, recreational and educational – in theatre activities of some kind.

Richardson built upon useful foundations already laid at the Belgrade. Soon after the theatre's opening Derek Newton had been appointed with special responsibility for young people. He set in motion theatre holiday sessions which were held at weekends in the Christmas and Easter school breaks and included activities designed to show how the theatre works and to give insight into the nature and development of drama. He also included practical groups on playwriting and sessions called 'Rock and Rhyme'. It was no casual approach – the scheme was linked with the Gulbenkian Foundation and Derek Newton wrote a report for them on "Youth and the Theatre." Derek Forder continued this work when he took over. With a group of actors from the theatre company he devised a programme called 'Theatre as Entertainment' and toured schools with it. There was also the organisation 'Young Stagers' which allowed those in full-time education to purchase cheap seats for the theatre and take part in a growing number of activities.

When David Forder resigned, it was some time before his successor could be appointed and some of the interest which he had stimulated had begun to fall away. But after Anthony Richardson became Director of Productions, Gordon Vallins was appointed for youth work and his immediate brief was to re-establish the educational links and

generally to encourage young people to come to the theatre. Gordon
Vallins took careful stock of the situation and soon produced a memorandum which he put before the Belgrade Trust. Of his nine recommendations the most important seem to be: 1. involving the young people
in organisation and decision through participation on committees; 2.
revival of theatre holiday sessions but with more participation by the
youngsters; 3. more regular drama sessions which young people could
attend; 4. establishment of a permanent children's theatre company at
the Belgrade. There was at that time no money available for the setting up of the children's theatre company but with the co-operation of the
College of Further Education and nearby schools the recommendations
began to be implemented. So began a very useful and important liaison
between Coventry education and its civic theatre.

In September 1964 Gordon Vallins and Anthony Richardson produced a paper on "Theatre and Education" and a further stage in co-
operation began. A meeting between the authors of the paper and a
group consisting of the Chairman of the Belgrade Theatre Trust, the
Chairman of the Education Committee and the playwright David Turner,
took place. The outcome was very encouraging. The councillors
reckoned that a penny rate would produce the £50,000 needed. The
scheme was that of visionaries. Richardson and Vallins knew that they
wanted every aspect of the community involved and had indicated ways
in which the local authority and industry, the cinema, art gallery,
library, cathedral, and working men's clubs could also be there. They
envisaged links with local press, Midlands TV and radio.

Looking back on it Gordon Vallins feels that they did not perhaps
have time to work it out in detail. As it stood, some of the scheme
was too unwieldy and somewhat impractical. Frustration followed.
More memoranda and more meetings. The Local Education Authority
officials were less enthusiastic about the idea. The sum mentioned
dropped to £28,000. An advisory committee was set up. Local head
teachers and the city treasurer were brought in. The scheme was
modified. What they now wanted to do was to offer an inspirational
teaching service to the teachers and schools of Coventry. The advisors
saw that it would be necessary to draw together a team of people who
could work with children in schools and also be able to work with actors
in the theatre. They would need to be actor/teachers. In the first
instance four people were appointed with Gordon Vallins as head of the
Theatre in Education Department. Estimates were worked out and the
sum suggested became £15,000. But at last the scheme passed all the
negotiating stages and personnel could be assembled to implement their

ideas. The team set out to explore the values of drama in the development of the child's personality, to experiment in teaching methods using drama and theatre techniques and to stimulate an interest in theatre in adult life.

FINDING THE RIGHT PEOPLE

With such bold aims it is vital to find the right people to make up the team. They obviously have to be exceptional personnel. Should they be trained teachers with an interest in acting or trained actors with an interest in teaching? Or should the balance be divided equally between the acting and the teaching sides of their talent? Certainly things were not ideal at the beginning. The team encountered personality problems, so that when the Trust came to appoint a new leader of the Theatre in Education team in 1966, they seemed to be looking for someone who would consolidate and build the strength of the enterprise. Rosemary Birbeck was appointed in April of that year, a trained teacher with a diplomatic, unobtrusive personality. Rosemary, employing considerable sensitivity and understanding, gradually evolved viable methods and techniques of working in this new form of education and theatre service which were to become influential. She built up the team to nine in number and effectively used the talents of her colleagues in creating programmes which were taken into infant schools, junior schools, secondary schools and youth clubs. And all the while they were using material based on local events and forging important links with local industry, library and church.

A couple of years ago the Coventry Theatre in Education team hit a crisis when the Local Council decided to make economy cuts and slash the service. The actors and teachers found themselves involved in local politics in order to save what they were working for. When the crisis was over and the grants maintained, they used their experience as a topic for improvisation and called it, 'Running Local Affairs'.

SOME PROJECTS

As their experience increases, their handling of both teaching and dramatic situations becomes more confident. They have become skilled in ways of involving young people in dramatic situations. In one year they may have as many as twelve teaching programmes using different approaches. With infants they may tell a story through the use of simple puppets or "projected play" objects; with juniors they may involve the children in the dramatic reconstruction of an historic event. Or they may work with seniors or adults as they did with their

Emergent Africa Game based on the Penguin book 'State of Emergency'.
Here they were concerned with political and world events, graphically
presenting facts and stimulating the audience into decision-making.
This programme was most successful when played to a group small
enough to take part in improvisations, for example queueing for jobs
and arguing with the terrorists.

Another important area the Coventry Theatre in Education team
have begun to develop is social drama, originally designed to bring
plays to the less mentally gifted children. A simple situation is acted
out: a teenage lad is seen carrying out the everyday tasks of his job
as milkman, and finds that a host of petty irritations build up to a more
or less uncontrollable frustration which leads him into a punch-up in a
pub where someone gets hurt. Those of us watching the build-up of
events, became very involved and were soon arguing the case from all
sides debating the question of responsibility. Children see it differently from adults of course – many even approve of the violence. But
they begin to see that there is more than one viewpoint. They learn to
appreciate which reasons are valid and which will stand up most to
counter-attack. The play is entertaining, but it is also educational in
that it presents different points of view. (For the script of this play,
see Part 4)

THE TEAM'S FUNCTION

A theatre in education team of this kind has many advantages. Because
they are actors and teachers, they bring a liveliness of approach with
a spontaneity of communication which is refreshing in the classroom.
With more teams of such people – skilled in the arts of communication,
able to use technical aids but also able to structure, shape and pattern
material with a human centre, a happier emotional response to the
word "education" may emerge. There is an opportunity for the future
to grasp. Through such teams, educators could break right away from
the desk-ridden, cerebral, silent, dominant approach and see education as taking place through heart and mind and body, catching, harnessing and extending imagination. Teacher and taught could be seen
in a fresh working relationship engaged in a series of active projects
primarily concerned with people. Education could be entertaining,
diverting and (we should suddenly discover) instructive. Similarly,
in the theatre, these teams could bring a more spontaneous response,
a closer link with audiences, and a really creative approach to acting
and production. Whether they were working on established texts or
original group material, theatre companies could be ensured of more

actively interested patrons.

These actor/teachers are in touch – in a way in which ordinary actors are not – with the people they serve, constantly adapting and developing material. Because of the feed-back from the community, they are able to bring to the theatre the kind of flexibility which will give it continued life.

ARTS COUNCIL REPORT

The Belgrade scheme in 1966 was on its own. The Arts Council Enquiry "travelled to Coventry where the unique Theatre in Education team was presenting a programme." Then several recommendations were made and money became available, notably to help "adult non-profit distributing theatres with approved schemes to enable them to engage an extra member of staff to organise and promote activities for young people at their theatres". The Arts Council cautiously ventured encouragement: "The Committee also feels that 'Theatre in Education' and similar projects are of value, and urges the need for professional drama experience in the people employed." Professional teaching experience and training were not urged, but they would seem to be equally desirable.

After this report, everyone wanted to be on the bandwagon. Some theatres saw this as a way of augmenting the permanent company on the cheap; others looked at it in a more creative manner. Some took the Arts Council's financial assistance and appointed one man to be a kind of organiser, P.R.O., and general factotum; a few saw the need to follow Coventry's lead and enlist the help of the Local Education Authority. So other theatre in education teams began to form – at Bolton, at York, at Watford, at Liverpool, at Leeds, Sheffield and Greenwich. Naturally enough new teams look to Coventry for their example and many have drawn personnel as well as ideas from the Belgrade teams.

LIVERPOOL, EVERYMAN

In Liverpool at the Everyman Theatre, founded in 1964, the policy has always been that of producing theatre primarily for young people, and under Peter James's direction the company survived several lean years while maintaining a lively programme. They were not "educational" in the Coventry sense but the Arts Council Young People's Theatre Panel (notably John Allen) recommended them for a grant. Expecting to have their estimates slashed, they asked for the moon and got it! This enabled Peter Lover to be appointed (he had worked

previously with the Watford Theatre in Education team). Now the new
director, Alan Dosser, is building up a team which, while still being
concerned with performance in the theatre, will have special responsibility for work linked with school and young people.

AT SHEFFIELD

Colin George became Director of the Sheffield Playhouse in 1965 and
soon began the Pegasus club – a Saturday morning venture for young
people. This attracted the attention of many theatre people and led to
John Neville inviting Colin George to launch a similar project at the
new Nottingham Playhouse.

Colin is one of the few directors to recognise the two way traffic
possibilities of theatre in education. He acknowledges how his own
work with young people has led him into a more flexible approach to
play directing. On several occasions in these early days of developing
work with young children he found himself advertised to take an open
rehearsal and then on the day there were none of his regular actors
available. He therefore had to ask for volunteers from his audience.
With these enthusiastic but inexperienced youngsters he realised traditional approaches were inappropriate so he tried out other methods
based on improvisational techniques. They worked and brought a
quality of response that he sought for in his regular company. So he
took back into the theatre a freshness from these young people.

When the Arts Council founded their Young People's Section, Colin
George became a member of the committee and was later given a
special bursary to make a year's study of Theatre for Young People.
In January 1967, the Sheffield Playhouse started a pilot scheme to
demonstrate the possibilities of a theatre in education team in the city.
This, under the title of Theatre Vanguard, became a full-time company, financed by the Arts Council and local education authority grants.
The team was under the leadership of Glyn Walford until the summer
of 1970. Now a team of eight works under Ed Thomason as manager.

Theatre Vanguard go into Infant, Junior and Secondary Schools
with programmes which are designed to involve the children in active
participation. They also work with Youth Clubs and periodically
present formal and experimental productions at lunch and other times.

The publication of the Arts Council report and their financial
support made possible several other theatre in education teams in
1968. Although at Watford young people's work had all along been
thought of as an integral part of the theatre programme, it was not
until 1968 that the Education Authorities accepted a five point brief

and made enough money available both for plays for children to be given at the theatre, and for a team of seven or eight personnel to devote their full time to it.

OTHER GROUPS

At York, things have developed less easily and without quite as much local support. Nevertheless, Tom Spencer has created a programme with a fluctuating team of around six people. Generally speaking, they tour to schools for the younger age range and work in the theatre with older groups. They began by studying the Belgrade scheme.

The Octagon Theatre at Bolton opened at a fortunate time and Robin Pemberton-Billing, the theatre director, appointed Roger Chapman as Director of Theatre in Education. Roger Chapman aimed to build a children's theatre company, explore drama as a teaching medium, and extend the imagination and personal development of young people through drama. At Bolton, in fact, they are building a special theatre workshop for this work.

In 1969 the Greenwich Theatre opened. Ewan Hooper, the theatre director, established the Bowsprit (the name given to their theatre in education team) which began its activities at Easter and was therefore functioning before the theatre company. By a link with the Greenwich Youth Theatre they are able to call upon seven actor/teachers for work in the schools. In the first year, Bowsprit ran six projects which were taken into schools, each built up with the children during a day or a half-day visit. The team also act in the theatre with the parent company.

The new Playhouse at Leeds has appointed as Director Roger Chapman who comes to them from the Bolton Octagon team via the Belgrade team. He formulates his basic aims:

1. To extend the imagination and personality of the child through creative drama.
2. To be the nucleus of a children's theatre company.
3. To work with young people in their leisure time and through creative drama develop an appreciation of theatre as an art form.

It is not difficult to discern influences from Peter Slade, Brian Way and others. But at this stage there is enough experience amongst the existing teams to ensure that most teams are led by someone who has a great deal to draw upon. One can only be encouraged by the fact that Stuart Bennett now in charge at Coventry, is beginning with his new group on a re-examination of first principles.

EARLY STAGES

There is still a long way to go, however. Throughout the whole range
of theatre in education work there is usually more skill, imagination
and intelligence employed with projects for children of primary school
age (5-11) than with youngsters of thirteen and fourteen. Two of the
projects we saw taken by the Watford team amply illustrated this. The
one for infants involved baking a pie and hunting for berries to put in it.
The team ingeniously absorbed everyone in the activity by carefully
building up the detail of each aspect of the story. In spite of the elementary nature of the business, even the adults present became
engrossed and unselfconscious. The situation for the older age group
(13/14s) was appropriately more demanding but executed in a much
more superficial and perfunctory manner. Through a device entitled
'Big Mother's Discotheque' the young people were invited to imagine a
situation in which they took over the whole town and ran it on new lines.
What an opportunity − but the youngsters were rushed from one activity
to another with impossible speed. Concentration and belief in the
situation were never allowed to develop. They were expected to take
part in reforming a community with less attention than had been given
to pastry making!

Fortunately the Watford team, if not very experienced actor-
teachers, were at least critical and caring individuals. They knew all
was not right and they readily began to discuss and sort out the problems involved. In spite of the failure on one level there remained both
theatrical and educational value. There was team involvement and
examination of the work of a kind a teacher in a school or an actor in
a theatre is rarely able to achieve.

EDUCATION AUTHORITIES' INTEREST

Now at last local authorities are beginning to wake up to the value and
potential of groups and one or two are setting up their own team based
on an arts centre or theatre club. Under I. L. E. A. drama advisor
Geoffrey Hodson's inspiration The Cockpit is forming its own team.
When the Cockpit opened in September 1969 there were two members
of staff − a director and a music tutor and they were joined by the
drama tutor in December of that year. Gradually a pattern of work
evolved.

1. Theatre Events − including art and sculpture exhibitions.
2. Exploration Groups − the youth service side.
3. School Projects and teachers' courses.

4. Special vacation ventures and outreach.

Cockpit now has seven full time teaching administrative and technical staff and offers a wide range of facilities and team teaching to the schools in the Authority. They see themselves as "an urban resource centre for imagination with many of the advantages of a field centre: a theatre plus a workshop environment which can be transformed into what-you-will with visuals, noise and action – a triple arts approach". They see "the social aspects of the work as important as the creative and academic".

On the South Coast there has for some years been a group running calling themselves the Brighton Combination and a team using some L.E.A. facilities but running largely on its own initiative.

In the county of Flintshire they have established a drama in education scheme on different lines. Four specialist drama teachers were appointed in September 1970 to be permanently timetabled in Secondary Schools for three and a half days each week. For the other day and a half they were responsible for a drama project which was taken to Junior Schools in the county. They enlist a range of interest and help. From teachers in both Primary and Secondary Schools a research team was formed to compile material for schemes involved. This contained information to form historical, geographical, artistic, cultural and religious background and a dossier was issued to the schools. Working as closely as possible with the class teacher the actor/teachers prepared the children for a "dramatic event". Members of the drama in education team visited the schools on two occasions preparing the children through improvisation, movement and speech activities. Then came the "dramatic event" which was a play with participation. There was follow-up work and a continued liaison with the teachers in the school.

In September 1971 the team was enlarged to six and the proportion of the time changed to three days on normal timetable and two days in other schools.

Rumour has it that Alsager College of Education will shortly establish its own drama in education team and Bretton Hall is hoping to do the same in the not too distant future.

Some will argue that such teams need to be based on the theatre where there is a regular company. Others maintain these teams should be centred on the Local Education Authority. But why should we limit such an enterprise at all? Surely what really matters is that those teams should be and that they should have the resources, the facilities and the freedom to be able to experiment and develop? The more starting points, the better. They could all help to spur on each other.

BBC Children's Television - A Cosy World?

Norman Tozer, who contributes this article, works extensively in children's television for the BBC

Everyone, including children, watches a vast amount of television. We are only beginning to discover its many effects but for the children it is a most important influence in their lives along with family, school and friends. How highly placed is this fourth force depends on the attractiveness and strength of the other three but all four are now responsible for giving a child the information and attitudes which will see him through the rest of his life. If even two fail him the others will see him through, but if more than two don't match up by the time he is in adolescence, both he and society will suffer. Any of these four factors can be the roots of sickness or revolution.

Children lean heavily on television; on average they watch it for three hours a day — only slightly less than the time spent on school-work, perhaps less than the time spent with parents or friends. The very fact that they wish to spend so long in its company means that it has a great deal of use for them. However, at this time the values of society in the Western world are being intensively re-examined, so that the three traditional components of a child's life are coming under scrutiny. The barriers of parental and teacher authority are being called into question (and parents and teachers feel inhibited in exercising the old authority). The child's peer group is assuming a greater importance, though in its isolation from traditionally cherished and balanced culture, its values may become extreme or distorted. In such an upheaval it seems necessary to ask: Is the fourth force in question? Can it too be challenged? Are television's values possibly false and, if they are, what will our children do when all four of the main forces in their life get increasingly out of step with what they observe and believe to be reality? It may not be the Revolution but it will be a revolution. And of course this is not a prediction — it is happening.

Is this not ludicrously to magnify television's role in the lives of our children? Surely a medium such as television can only reflect an existing (ie true) situation — to accuse it of playing a part is to argue

that the telephone, say, is an instrument of bias in a telephone call?
Yes, this is my argument: that television is very important to children;
it does not necessarily reflect an existing situation; it is biased. In
these circumstances surely television will be as responsible for revolution (as accelerated change) as the failure of the education system or
the ineffectiveness of parents or the peer group.

THE IMPORTANCE OF TELEVISION

Children under the age of 11 or 12 spend about three hours per day
watching television — as much time throughout the year for school age
children as might be given to play. So much time would not be given
over to an activity which the child did not find useful in some way. This
is an argument developed in the American study 'Television in the Lives
of our Children'. [1]

> "It seems clear that to understand television's impact and effect on
> children we must get away from the unrealistic concept of what
> television does to children and substitute the concept of what child-
> ren do with television."

It went on to outline the currently accepted uses of television as
sources of entertainment, incidental learning and social utility:

> "A child is growing up ie learning social skills, customs, acquiring
> the knowledge currently thought to be suitable for life in his own
> society. Television supplies the information for this process."

The Nuffield Foundation study [2] showed us that young primary
school children who watched television arrived at school with a bigger
vocabulary. There tended to be little difference at this age between
bright and dull children. The informing process for this age group can
be very fast; you don't have to learn to read to absorb the information,
and the incidental learning is considerable.

But, for the younger segment of the audience (say, up to 9), the
learning process remains incidental. The child cannot choose either
the time or the pace at which he can receive the information and, as
the authors of the US study point out:

> ".... the language of television is real, not abstract as print is,
> so this means that abstract ideas get lost in the concreteness of
> the language — it's easy to focus attention on the reality and not the
> abstract meaning."

The Nuffield study noted: "There is an optimal age for responsiveness for each attitude or topic." If the child is too young the cues
are not taken up. If the child is too old he already has fixed attitudes
or has gained the information in other ways. And further:

"Responsiveness depends on emotional and social maturity as much as mental age."

The consensus was therefore that younger children used television not for information or "reality" but as a source of fantasy. In many ways, I would hazard, as they use play – especially if you accept the McLuhan idea of television as an incomplete communication because the degraded electronic picture means that the imagination must fill in the visual and aural "gaps."

'Television in the Lives of our Children' lists the uses of fantasy as wish fulfilment, distraction and "experience free from control, so that problems can be solved in a non-risk environment" and added that "Fantasy outlets are usually chosen where effective real life solutions are lacking." To corroborate the theory that television was used as a fantasy source, the authors noted that viewing time replaced time previously given to cinema-going or reading comics.

Fantasy, we know, is a serious business. The Nuffield study seemed to draw attention to the fact that no-one's feet left the earth because of it:

> "Nor has it (television) blunted the older children's ability to differentiate between fact and fiction. They do not become more gullible: indeed, in certain respects they become more sophisticated. Much exposure to adult plays and to documentaries influences many of them to reject the comforting black and white philosophy of childhood tales. This is an interesting finding, particularly since television writers and producers always give children's programmes happy and just endings."

A final note on television's current importance for children comes from J. D. Halloran in 'The Social Effects of Television'. [3] He writes of times of social change: "A situation may now exist in which there is considerable scope for television to play a part in the formation of attitudes," and again:

> "If the conventional sources of learning process are not available or are not felt to be adequate, then other sources including television are more likely to be used."

However, as young people progress in their secondary education they tend to use afternoon television much less. Despite the pleasure their parents may get from 'Blue Peter', 'Search' or 'Animal Magic' (audiences for these programmes are composed of approximately 40% adult viewers) they are moving on to so-called adult programmes or not viewing much at all. Only the duller children of secondary education age tend to be heavy viewers.

We assume adolescents, especially the bright ones, now wish to be regarded as adult; that there is a conscious rejection of childhood

or childishness – certainly there would seem to be a rejection in the
adolescent of values which may well be returned to in adult life. But
if television had anything of use for these young people I suggest it
would be used. It is used by duller children and those whose adjust-
ment to the world around them is difficult. But, for most adolescents,
television loses credibility in some measure. Is it that fantasy, perhaps television's biggest use up to now, is no longer necessary in
adolescence? Certainly the American researchers I have quoted
believed that there was at this age a search for greater "reality" and
noted an increase in reading in this age group. This would suggest
that in some informational fields, books and newspapers were regarded
as a more reliable source. However, that television is no longer used
as fantasy is not true, as P. Musgrave pointed out in 'How Children
use Television'. [4] His survey of Scottish children aged 11-15 found
that the most watched programmes were quoted as Pop, 'The Avengers',
'Batman' and 'The Man from UNCLE'. Perhaps what are no longer
regarded as valid by young teenagers are the values purveyed by television. Have they seen through them or is the rejection an automatic
and necessary part of growing up? How you answer that may depend
on your attitude to those values and attitudes. What is not in dispute
is that television's values and attitudes are sectional and often biased.

TELEVISION AS BIAS

"Television influences the way children think about jobs, job values,
success and social surroundings" said the Nuffield Foundation report.
It then went on: 'It stresses the prestige of middle class occupations:
the professions and big business. It makes essentially middle class
value judgements about jobs and success in life." (my emphasis)

That was published in 1958. A decade later a former Controller
of BBC Television, Stuart Hood, wrote:

"The dangers which beset children's television are ... a certain
detachment from life and a middle-class assumption that everyone
is interested in ponies and lives in the Surrey Hills. The relevance of many children's programmes to the life they actually
lead is minute. "   (5)

In 1969 in 'New Society' Christopher Williams wrote:

"About young people we have a loaded rhetoric: potential, opportunity, the future ... and a practice which doesn't match up. The
painful contradictions which this produces in real life aren't
allowed to seep through on the box; but the falsity of so many programmes makes one constantly aware of them. "   (6)

Last year J. D. Halloran in 'The Social Effects of Television' gave a warning example of bias:

"There is a good chance that deviant behaviour will be presented by the media out of context and in a stereotyped, negative and possibly sensational manner. It would be unwise to ignore the possibility that these presentations may intensify the problem by, amongst other things, helping to produce ill-informed public attitudes, social policies, and perhaps even legislation."

The fact that television can and does present stereotypes has been noted by Melvin De Fleur in his studies of occupational roles as portrayed on US television. In one instance he concluded that these portrayals lacked reality and were stereotyped. [7] In another that much superficial and misleading information about the labour force was provided by television. [8]

In passing it may be worth noting that the use of stereotypes was one of the five conditions outlined in the Nuffield survey as a condition for affecting the young viewer. One further point should be considered when discussing bias, although it does not affect my argument here. It is that the very medium imposes a bias. It is only imperfectly understood but the very act of conveying information by electrical transmission of images and sounds can in many circumstances proscribe the nature of the information.

That television has been catalogued and criticised for over a decade as presenting programmes which are lacking reality, stereotyped and sectional in attitude surely cannot be an example of a self-perpetuating myth. These examples I have given come from differing sources and have arisen from different circumstances. Yet that they all operate today I am in no doubt from my own experience. For approximately two years I presented a children's programme on BBC television intended for the 10 to 13 age range – the age range which begins to be more interested in concepts and is capable of absorbing information as such, with less of the dramatic element necessary (which the Nuffield study showed was an essential ingredient in having an effect). As presenter of the programme I was rarely in a decision-making position. Consistently, the criteria used for judging the suitability of the material to be included in the programme seemed to be of stereotypes. Just as the press asks whether material can be made to measure up to one of its stereotyped patterns, so the production staff of the programme tended to look at the suggested raw material. Much as I believe in intriguing an audience and arousing its curiosity, time and again I have found the "Oo! Ah!" factor at work: if the editor does not believe the subject will surprise or confound, it is assumed not to be of interest. Such coarse screening of ideas, damaging as it is for adult press and television, must further degrade children's television in the young viewer's eyes.

That we lacked reality sprang, I would think, partly from the use of stereotypes (wrong or unsuitable ones) and partly from the BBC's desire to appeal at some level to all the potential audience – in this case children from 5 upwards. Although we were to use a magazine format (ie short items, not necessarily related) and confine ourselves mainly to descriptive treatments of our material (how a technician achieves success with a specific process, the method used by sportsmen or artists which results in being able to do something) we were often dealing with concepts and implicit social roles. We had often to assume in our audience a knowledge of job structures which the younger ones could not have had. If we are to believe the Nuffield study in its assessment of young audiences as being interested primarily in visual information and not influenced by the world of work that they are shown, and as not responding to values, then if we interested the older children we could not have held the attention of the young viewer – or vice versa.

That the values of BBC children's television are middle-class can be deduced by taking a wider view than personal experience.

Almost without exception all decision-making posts in the BBC are advertised in terms which say that a university education is desirable or necessary. In lower production vacancies, evidence of a form of further education is sometimes acceptable. Apart from severely limiting the number of people that could be called upon to fill these posts this must mean that decision-making posts (especially policy makers) would by definition be overwhelmingly middle-class. By this I do not mean to infer that all the people originate from the middle-class but that by training and association they will have had to adopt these mores and values. And, as they owe their positions to an understanding and acceptance (in some measure) of these mores, it is extremely unlikely that they will act (or cause others to act) in a way which is outside them – even if they any longer understood other values as being morally valid.

At their worst the values show in the programmes as an undue attention to ponies and riding techniques, at their best as a genuine social concern over collecting for victims of famine. My argument is not that middle-class values are good or bad but that they are sectional and, by being so, do not square up with some children's experience of life – a further reason for supposing that television lacks credibility with many youngsters.

But if today's programmes are the result of a present sectional structure they are also the result of history. The origin of BBC television's children's programmes is even earlier than the BBC.

SUMMARY OF BBC CHILDREN'S PROGRAMMES

A. History:

> Between the dark and the daylight,
> When the night is beginning to lower,
> Comes a pause in the day's occupations,
> That is known as the Children's Hour.

This quotation from Longfellow's poem 'The Children's Hour' (and you couldn't get more middle-class than that!) appears in the very first 'BBC Handbook' for 1928. The section on programmes for children shows that the Corporation had inherited from the Company the responsibility for, and acceptance of, separate programmes for children. In 1926, it says, when the company was broadcasting only on the London & Daventry stations it received 54 thousand letters about these programmes. (It doesn't record whether the letters were complimentary or hostile but, either way, that's not a bad post.) The purpose of the Children's Hour, records the Handbook, was "mainly recreation and not instruction or moral improvement". Thereby demonstrating that, at least for the Corporation, you couldn't mention recreation without calling to mind instruction or moral improvement — certainly a "sectional" attitude.

That philosophy of purpose is still held today. In a statement dated March 1971 the head of BBC Children's Programmes wrote:

> "For some of the time available each day we try to provide relaxation and refreshment through laughter or excitement ... Most of all we want to nourish children so that they can be active and full of enthusiasm to learn and do things for themselves." (9)

The first children's television programme seems to have been a junior edition of 'Picture Page'. This was a magazine programme which originated before the second world war and was continued after it. The junior edition started in 1949 and was introduced by a popular announcer of the day, Mary Malcolm, with Max Robertson.

Regular programmes, however, started the following year. In May 1950 the first transmission from the Lime Grove studios was 'For the Children,' an hour's programme which was broadcast weekly and it introduced the first famous television character for children, Muffin the Mule, a puppet whose human partner was Annette Mills.

In July 1951 another puppet, Andy Pandy first appeared. A big success in 1952 was the re-creation of that famous (middle-class)

schoolboy 'Billy Bunter'. Gradually the amount of children's programming increased until in 1956 it was eight hours per week instead
of the original one. The classic serials had made their appearance,
in this year it was 'Children of the New Forest'. There were 8 plays
about 'Jesus of Nazareth' and simple conversation was explored with
'Bobby in France'. In lighter vein, 'Crackerjack' had emerged and a
travelling show called 'Children's Caravan'. Young viewers were
invited to 'Spot the Tune' or join 'Sketch Club'. 'On the Rails' had no
apparent moral connotation, it showed how to build up a model railway –
just as 'Our Port' showed children making a scale model. Also in the
field of information the 'Children's International News Service' showed
films from various overseas television services. Pre-school children
continued to be catered for. 'Toytown' was a current offering and
'Watch With Mother' had started in 1953.

From now on the number of hours' programming was to remain
fairly constant – 400 hours in 1957/58, 397 hours in 1960/61. True,
there was a sudden decrease in 1963/64 when "Children's programmes"
were merged with "Family programmes" and the entire department
only managed 290 hours but, by 1967/68 they were back to 416 hours.
The last published figures were for 1969/70 when Children's programmes was again a separate department and showing 445 hours.

Programmes come and go as in other departments and I wonder
who remembers those "participation" programmes like 'Thrash it Out'
(good middle-class title) a series of debates or 'All Your Own' a programme on hobbies. Most people would recall the classic serials (not
part of Children's programme department) or the monoliths like 'Blue
Peter' (started 1958) and 'Play School' (started 1964). What is certain
is that these programmes were watched by very large numbers indeed.
By 1968 'Blue Peter' had on occasion achieved audiences of 8 million
and the Sunday puppet programme 'Pinky & Perky' of over $5\frac{1}{4}$ million.
(If you take the 8 million 'Blue Peter' audience and discard half the
total, on the assumption that it is adult, and compare that with the
figure of 4,200,000 which is the population of the UK between 5 and 9
years old, the target audience, its success would seem phenomenal.)
In 1970 its February audience was quoted as approximately $6\frac{1}{2}$ million.

By now the variety of programmes and the number of hours
seemed to be able to substantiate the claim by Miss Monica Sims, the
current Head of Children's Programmes that they were "a microcosm
of a complete television service". [10]

B. Current Programmes

The pre-school children's programmes begin at 11 a.m. on BBC-2 with 'Play School', an entertainment sequence presented by a young man and woman who are usually in their twenties. It features the date and a time each day and concepts like floating and sinking in water. It examines the outside world through film of places like the seaside or the desert. It has songs or stories and inevitably animals and pets. There are resident toy animals who are spoken to from time to time. It is a simple, direct programme and its unaffected activities take place in a visual environment inspired by Abbatt or Heals.

On BBC-1 at 1.30 there is 'Watch With Mother', basically a puppet series.

The main children's time, however, remains as just over an hour before 6 o'clock. At 4.40 there is the daily story telling programme 'Jackanory' which is aimed at the 5-9 year olds. There follow two programmes of 25 minutes' length which may be topical information magazines like 'Blue Peter', natural history programmes like 'Animal Magic', entertainments like 'Vision On', quizzes, cartoons ('Wacky Races'), drama ('The Flashing Blade') and documentaries ('Search' or 'Behind the Scenes'). Last of all and before the News there is a five-minute story for the very young like 'The Magic Roundabout' which often ends with the hopeful line "Time for bed".

In addition to these weekday programmes there are week-end serials and series which are produced by the Drama department and not by Children's programmes. They are not meant only for children but for viewing by the whole family. In this category come the serials like 'The Last of the Mohicans' and the series like 'Dr. Who'.

Everything on children's television is grouped into a series – just like adult television – in the belief that the audience prefers familiarity. Much as this might be true it is equally true that, as the BBC is in the battle for audiences, the pre-packed programme helps not only the audience to identify what it might want but the BBC to "sell" programmes with the minimum publicity effort. To be fair the packages are certainly capable of embracing a wide range of material but every so often comes a subject (just as in adult television) which producers might like but must turn down because it won't make a series of its own and there is no existing "slot" for it.

But to return to the current programmes. I would rate 'Vision On' highly. Originally it was a programme for deaf children but it is now a fast-moving, sophisticated visual comedy programme. It has a wide range of gags which range from corny to nicely inventive and it is not unduly cluttered with "presenters". Its personnel are well integrated into the show's fabric. It employs a good selection of visual techniques from live action film to cartoon and studio sequences. It seems to owe some of its humour to 'Monty Python' and some of its pace to 'Laugh In'. The studio environment is once again Heals influenced, but it is not noticeable.

A series for older children is called 'Search' and it is one of the few cases where a whole programme is given over to one topic. The BBC recognises that this is a tricky area because they believe it very difficult to hold the attention of the viewer growing into adolescence. This is the problem outlined in earlier sections of this survey. Nevertheless it usually tries to present one programme with older viewers in mind – at the time of writing it is 'Search'. Despite its desire to examine one subject – eg the News or Exmoor – it often tries to do too much. The programme on the News was a good example. Young people who had made a special study of the News (like a school project) were faced with the Editor of BBC Television News. They brought complaints about specific stories. This was a programme of no appeal to children, only to emerging adolescents. It was a good idea so long as you assumed an interested audience and didn't try to hedge your bets and attempt to popularise it. In what I take to be an attempt to keep it moving too many points were made. The film-example to studio-discussion ratio was too high. Therefore the audience was whizzed along till nothing registered. It was a prime example of trivialisation through perhaps poor planning and lack of faith in the ability of an audience to concentrate. It is precisely this sort of programme that must lose the BBC its young, serious adolescent audience.

Unless it be 'Score with the Scaffold'. This is an example of what the department calls "easy entertainment", I think. It really is difficult to believe that young people would enjoy this example of the "children's party" approach. A visual equivalent of false gaiety is provided as a framework for the Scaffold to use weak material played in a half-hearted manner. The approach is an uneasy compromise between the humourous and the funny. Regrettably it is neither. The programme consists of sketches straight, sketches with a deliberate mistake, Scaffold songs (illustrated with acted sequences on film), a song from a guest singer sung straight and a long quiz sequence which is incompletely integrated into the show. There seems to be no real effort to involve the young studio audience in the proceedings – it is an irrelevance. It would be difficult to imagine any child chosing this programme in preference to red-blooded entertainment.

121

Another programme which involves young people in its proceedings is 'It's your Word'. Jonathan Dimbleby presides over a general knowledge quiz between two teams of three children. It is extremely difficult to get children to relax in the highly artificial atmosphere of a television studio and only a particularly precocious talent would flourish easily in it and produce (in adult terms) watchable television. I have a feeling that this sort of competition without the motivation of money is an antique survival of the age of the Mechanics Institute and a desire to improve the working classes through middle-class competitive education. No doubt the form is acceptable to some, but intellectual quizzes have to have firmer mental structures; otherwise 'Top Town' or 'Jeux Sans Frontières' is a lot more exciting.

Everyone has heard of BBC children's television pièce de resistance, 'Blue Peter'. It manages to preserve some of the innocence of 'Play School' within its three-presenter magazine format. It is intended for the 5 to 9 age group and therefore its items do not concern themselves with concepts but are mainly descriptive of places, things and activities. Its presenters, a young woman and two young men in their late twenties, are always seen to be involved in either the film or studio pieces in a way appropriate to their personalities. As they appear to be agreeable they suffuse each topic with this quality and thus make "palatable" a wide range of subject matter. The danger of this method could be to reduce all the material to only one of three flavours – imparting a 'Blue Peter' blandness or agreeableness (or wholesomeness) to any subject. This could account for its popularity. However, its film reports, especially, can have a pace and sense of excitement.

I have outlined only a few of the current offerings from BBC children's television. I have not mentioned the almost daily cartoons, for example, because they seem to be typical of the genre and well within the "easy entertainment" definition. Of the filmed adventure serials, it is difficult to be fair because they are so diverse. They usually originate from non-English speaking countries and have either to have a narration spoken over the original soundtrack or be dubbed into English. Both processes seem to be technically effective. Of the two French serials running at the moment I prefer 'The Flashing Blade', a straightforward swashbuckling adventure of 17th century France. Less swash or buckling than a 40's American movie but well mounted. 'Belle, Sebastian and the Horses' I find less attractive. Its horsey setting may well go a bomb in the Surrey Hills but I'm not so sure about the young (7 year) hero. His tearful, slightly sentimental,

personality might seem a little "cissy" for the audience. I just think
he's a neurotic!

In trying to give a fair, if colourful, picture of a number of BBC
children's television programmes I find myself again and again aware
of a blandness in programming. That the desire for series and stereotypes is creating a mesh which allows sharp, sour and above all distinct
flavours to escape. In 1964 Edward Blishen wrote of all children's
programming (both BBC and commercial):

> "The over-riding aim appears to be to keep abreast with what is
> known to be the lowest common denominator of young needs: to
> follow taste, rather than attempt to create it: to echo activity
> rather than to set it going. There is so little that is original or
> experimental ... Of course a restlessly radical and experimental
> service would be intolerable. But it is the conservative side of
> children's natures that appears on the whole to be catered for: the
> other, progressive side is left out of court. Anyone who works
> among children knows how easy it would be to become infected by
> childish conservatism. This happens at times to whole schools --
> a condition that leads in the end to bad behaviour, rebellion,
> because the experimental side of a child's nature cannot bear to
> be forever starved. I would think that children themselves should
> have far more to do in, and with, television than they are allowed.
> What a feeling of thwarted energy one gets when listening to BBC's
> 'Junior Points of View'." (11)

And again,

> "After fifteen years of teaching I came to the firm conclusion
> (and it wasn't **cosy** teaching) that we underestimate the spiritual
> stamina of young people everywhere. We feed them, in too many
> fields, according to mild old formulae. We give them too little
> to bite on. We lay too little on their shoulders. We **involve** them
> too little."

That an attempt to summarise existing programmes in 1971 leads
me to agree with a criticism written seven years earlier also argues an
atrophied attitude to programme making – at least in BBC television.
Yet the present head of the Children's Programmes department, Monica
Sims, has been in the position for only three years. How does she see
her responsibilities? Does she see any need for experimentation?
Does she feel that the programmes do aim at the lowest common
denominator and are they "cosy"?

PRESENT POLICY

> "All of us who make children's programmes believe that because
> our viewers are at the most receptive and impressionable period
> of their lives we have to give our programmes even more careful
> consideration than producers of programmes for adults. If we
> are to use our opportunity to influence children to expect pro-
> grammes of high quality we have a duty to introduce the best
> literature, drama, music and art presented by the best actors

and performers and must find ways of making such programmes comprehensible and attractive to children." (9)

Miss Sims' statement went on:

"One way of persuading children to watch programmes which at first sight may seem to require too much concentration is to make them regularly in long series. Children need security and familiarity in their viewing and one reason that 'Jackanory' has been successful in presenting the best children's books from all over the world is that it is on the air for fifteen minutes every day.

"Television is sometimes accused of stultifying the imagination by showing pictures when words and sounds are in themselves sufficient stimuli, but we have to remember that the visual stimulus is also imaginatively enriching, and to provide this we need to seek out the best designers and artists. Pretty or amusing decoration is not enough — children need strong pictures to illustrate strong stories."

These were the two points made when dealing with "quality". Concerning the range of children's programming, Miss Sims wrote this:

"In the competitive situation of television in Britain, children's programmes producers have no captive audience and there is no question of giving children what parents and teachers believe to be good for them unless the children themselves make a positive decision to watch."

In an interview with Monica Sims in July 1971 I asked her if she regarded her department as being in hard competition with commercial television.

"When they just simply copy things that we're doing, then I think we are in competition with them. Where they are providing something different I think this is a healthy choice."

But, I questioned, didn't her statement about children making their own decisions to watch mean that she would be making programmes for the lowest common denominator?

"Whatever we do children must enjoy it. It actually makes us work to a higher standard. I think that children expect the highest professional standards. They see a lot of adult programmes and they expect the programmes made for them to be every bit as good and mostly they have to be better, because children won't put up with people just talking as adults will. Children require something a bit more exciting and stimulating."

This led us on to talk of experimentation and that took us immediately to costs and money. It seems to be a fact of life that all broadcasting organisations put children's programmes very low on their list of priorities where budgets are concerned.

"This is understandable" said Monica Sims, "when one considers the total size of audience available at off-peak transmission times."

She went on to state that producers of high-budget evening programmes
are delighted if their programmes are seen by a third of the available
audience, whereas children's programme producers take it for granted
that the programmes are seen by at least half their target audience.
What she did not mention was that often more people (in absolute
numbers) watch children's programmes off-peak or not. 'Blue Peter'
at $6\frac{1}{2}$ million (appr.) audience beats 'The Wednesday Play', 'The
Tuesday Documentary' and 'Braden's Week'. 'Tom Tom' with $4\frac{1}{2}$
million audience beats '24 Hours' and 'Omnibus'. [12] It would seem,
therefore, that the "audience argument" for keeping these programmes
low on the budget priorities list is just not tenable.

I asked Miss Sims: if you had more money what would that enable
you to do?

"It would enable us to make more experiments and to take on more
people, because good programmes come out of good producers
and good production teams. But limited funds mean that our
teams do not get the chance of experiment and change.

"We would certainly do more drama and light entertainment. They
are not done as much as we would like now because they are the
most expensive forms to produce, because of union agreements
and the costs of visual effects, scenery, costumes and so on."

We talked about the US programme 'Sesame Street' and whether
that sort of experiment was needed here. Miss Sims thought not. In
America there was a need to spend some money on children's television
programmes and, although in both countries there was a need for a pre-
school programme – especially where there was a shortage of nursery
schools – we already had one which had done most of the things which
'Sesame Street' was now doing. This didn't mean that there was not
more room for pre-school television programmes, just that it would
not be the right style for our programmes. Miss Sims was critical of
the people in this country who extolled the programme without having
seen it or who had only seen one programme.

"It's great fun for adults and older children. Half of it is totally
beyond the comprehension of 3 or 4 year olds. It is not getting at
the disadvantaged children in the negro ghettos for whom it is
intended. It has been much enjoyed by children from middle-class
homes whose parents want to abdicate the responsibility of helping
their children. We don't believe that a television set is a substitute either for nursery schools or people."

To see how far BBC Children's television might stray into unorthodox paths I asked if they would ever feature details of either the
schoolchildren's protest movement or the Little Red Schoolbook? Not
the Little Red Book, said Miss Sims because, whatever its wrapping,
she considered it as a book concerned with sex education. She believed

that was what a child would go to the book for. Because the age range of the audience was from 3 to 13 it would be impossible to devise a treatment suitable for such a wide age range. As far as "Kids Lib" or children's protest was concerned she saw no reason why there couldn't be children in a discussion programme like 'Search' talking about it. "I don't see any reason why we shouldn't do it in that way — but it will be utterly boring to about two thirds of the rest of the audience."

I wondered if the world as presented through BBC children's programmes wasn't too cosy?

Monica Sims replied:

"I don't think that's true. A child may be watching alone with no other child or adult about. Television, we know, can be very disturbing. It can provide very frightening images to haunt a child. We have got a responsibility to those children who are watching alone, without any adult around, that we should not do anything — either that would cause the child to get into danger through imitation or that could damage it psychologically by too much upsetting its security. We also have to remember that there are always six and seven year olds as well as the tens and elevens watching. I don't really think it's true if you look at the range of stories with which we deal, which are not always cosy at all. The other thing is that I don't think — I suppose I shouldn't say this — that it matters terribly what programmes the children from good homes see because the home influence is so much greater than anything children can do. The children will grow up with the help of interested adults and teachers and so on. Where television can be dangerous is with children from very deprived homes where nobody helps them. One of the things that they actually need from television is some security, and they get that in children's programmes through the regularity of the programmes and through the familiar people and the familiar programmes they see. It can give them some little oasis of security in the day. If you give them the security you can also give them the sense of adventure. You give them a base from which they can start finding things out for themselves and being extended and stretched and excited. But you must give them the security first. I think there's a great difference between doing programmes for children and for adults in this way. This might be true if we were doing programmes for adolescents because they have rejected that security. But, for the age group we are dealing with, I don't think we can do things that are going to be too disturbing — although we have got to get them to start thinking."

More than that, the department wants to have the participation and involvement of children. "We set out to encourage children to make, shape and contribute to them whenever possible," said Miss Sims.

"We are not interested in providing moving wallpaper to keep them quiet and we do all we can to stimulate individual thought and action. 'Play School' directors always try to view their programmes with young children and are disappointed if a child does not join in a movement item or try to make something suggested in the programme.... About half the items in 'Blue Peter' are suggested by the children themselves."

For the children's department the 'Jackanory' Story Competition was also a success, attracting many hundreds of stories – mostly conventional, about witches and wizards, but a good many not.

However, quantity doesn't always mean success. At our meeting Monica Sims told me of a weekly serial where children were invited to suggest how the next episode should go: "Quite honestly, most of the things that the children suggested we couldn't use because they were too bloodthirsty and too violent for the majority of the audience.

"Of course we do have children doing things in the programmes but we do not think it right to exploit them, just to have them there because they are children. We only want them there if they are doing something interesting and good."

Although children, especially in the drama serials, identify with other children, Monica Sims did not see this as a case for presenting plays acted entirely by children or children's drama improvisations – children also like to identify with heroic adults, she said. Much as such an idea might make a single programme, say a competition, it was hardly the basis for a 26-part serial. It was not bread and butter television.

POLICY IMPLICATIONS

It becomes difficult to summarise, on this evidence, a policy for BBC children's television programmes. There seem to be contradictions which only raise further questions.

The department is considerably stretched not only in money terms but in having to devise programmes which will appeal to the greater part of the age range. Children aged seven are not the same creatures as children at twelve and it is very difficult to interest them simultaneously with the same material. The department is all too aware of this. Because of the shortage of air time at its disposal it is also stretched in trying to cater for all sorts of interests and interest levels. This results in the fragmentary treatment of material in magazine programmes, often at a rudimentary level. It is true that in certain specialist areas adult programmes can be, and are, watched but both transmission time and the different levels of comprehensibility may mitigate against their full use by young viewers.

I am somewhat puzzled by an apparent contradiction over whether programmes are, or are not, made to supplement parental influence. Monica Sims in talking about 'Sesame Street' seemed to be critical of parents who abdicated the responsibility for helping their children educationally: "We don't believe that a television set is a substitute

either for nursery schools or people. " But later, when she talked
about children viewing alone and from deprived homes, she spoke of
the television programmes and personalities as providing: "an oasis
of security in the day". In other words, a substitute for some of the
functions of the parents or home life. I realise that the context are not
the same but they are similar, they are overlapping areas and I suggest
that there is a dichotomy in the thinking on this problem.

So, too, on the question of frightening children, although Miss Sims
agrees that children like violent action and believes that one of the
pressures that her producers have to resist is the pressure to be over-
protective, she again wishes to remember the child alone and that
programmes should not show anything which would put it into danger
or upset it psychologically. And when she recalls the children's
suggestions for the serial the reason why they were not used was:
"they were too violent and too bloodthirsty for the majority of the
audience. " But these were the children's own suggestions, so who
was being horrified? Who was protecting whom? I am reminded of a
quotation from the child psychologist, P. M. Pickard:

> "Children are innately capable of anger: this anger can appear in
> the earliest months; during anger, thought is phantastically
> horrible and far more fierce than during anger in adults. If we
> accept these findings of modern research, then some of our diffi-
> culties are cleared away. The argument that we have to condition
> children to horrors is now seen as fallacious; there is no question
> of introducing them to horrors, because the horrors already known
> to them are far in excess of anything we experience as adults. " (13)

On the question of participation there is also an unresolved dilemma.
Participation is seen by the BBC as desirable in children's television
programmes. To date that has usually been seen as letter writing and
responding to competitions – a somewhat restricted dialogue. There is
now a feeling inside the BBC that this might not be all they could do, and
indeed it is not. The idea followed logically could mean, ultimately,
decision-making. But even if we stop short of that and accept that
children may only contribute to programmes, not overtly shape the
policies, then many thoughts occur. Competitions might be **judged** by
children, as well as entered by them. Programmes might be **edited** by
them, instead of adults screening children's suggestions. Programmes,
or sections of them, can even be made by them. (This has been done.
A film competition originally organised by the 'Tom Tom' programme
resulted in one whole programme and large sections of several others
being given over to show the films, which in the first year were of a
high standard.) It is now within the bounds of possibility to have a

genuine series of junior reporters and directors who could contribute films to programmes. Surely it cannot be long before they discover how easy it can be to make videotapes on the Local Education Authority television equipment. Far from disturbing the children's security I think it will disturb that of the BBC Television Centre — not to mention Equity and the Association of Cinematograph and Television Technicians!

CONCLUSIONS

So far I have argued that children use television so extensively because it fulfils needs. I have tried to show that BBC television is biased because not only has the medium its own inherent bias but the BBC is sectionally biased by being run by the middle-class. This situation has its roots in the history of broadcasting but it is perpetuated by, amongst other things, current staffing policies. I have further attempted to persuade you that the current programmes for children not only represent sectional values, because they are the outcome of the organisation, but also are often stereotyped, bland and even atrophied. This may be due not only to the perpetuation of traditional policies but to the inhibitions imposed by unresolved problems in the present programme-making system and philosophy.

I regret that I have only hinted at a whole area of study concerning the incidental learning of visual material. What values are there, for instance, implicit in the images children see via television — what visual vocabulary are they learning? It is quite clear to me from my experience with the 'Tom Tom' film competition programmes that the great majority of those who submitted films had absorbed a basic film or television grammar — why should they not, since it is a part of their daily lives? It seems equally true that little conscious teaching goes on concerning that part of children's daily lives, either. Stuart Hood had some tart words on this subject:

> "Education in television appreciation is more or less non-existent. It is possible to argue that it is more important and more relevant for a very large proportion of school children to know what is a good and what is a bad television programme than to be able to read a novel. Of all the mass media, television is the one which will be most closely integrated into their living habits; it will — for the majority — be their main source of entertainment and information. Unfortunately educationists have not yet dealt with the problem in any systematic way."   (5)

I suggest that the growing child loses faith in BBC television children's programmes not only because he puts aside supposed childishness but because the reasons I have given above may make him

129

believe he sees through the programmes. It may not simply be that adolescents have a tendency to reject all previously held values but that for many youngsters the life they lead — and that their family and peer group lead — has little to do with the sectional values in the BBC programmes. This may result in a strong reaction against the BBC and the middle-class but, where contacts with the family, the school or even the peer group are bad, that reaction might go further than switching to another channel. From a search for an alternative culture it could change — in certain special cases — to anti-social behaviour.

For reasons like these, I see television and its values as of prime social importance, to be studied alongside family, peer group and school. But far from wishing to see a greater watch kept on television to restrict its offerings to children I see a necessity for us to seek out and use different values in addition to those now employed. I want to see the good, but restricted, BBC children's television programmes widening their horizons, focusing and utilising conflicts and effectively adopting a less protective attitude to its audience.

Always in our thoughts about children's television we must question our motives: who are we protecting, our children or ourselves?

Norman Tozer

NOTES

1 'Television in the Lives of our Children' Schramm, Lyle and Parker. Stanford University Press 1961
2 'Television and the Child' Himmelweit. Nuffield Foundation, Oxford University Press 1958
3 'The Effects of Television' Editor James Halloran. Panther Modern Society 1970
4 'How Children use Television' P. Musgrave. New Society 20/2/69
5 'A Survey of Television' Stuart Hood. Heinemann 1967
6 'Children's Television' Christopher Williams. New Society 13/3/69
7 Melvin de Fleur in 'Public Opinion Quarterly' Vol. 28 No 1
8 Melvin de Fleur in 'American Sociological Review' Vol. 32 No 5
9 'BBC Television Children's Programmes' Monica Sims, BBC TV A statement dated March 1971
10 Based on 9
11 'The Children are Watching' Edward Blishen. Contrast (published by BFI) Autumn 1964. Vol. 3 No 5
12 Audience figures from 'BBC Handbook 1971'
13 'I Could a Tale Unfold: Violence, Horror and Sensationalism in Stories for Children' P. M. Pickard. Tavistock/Humanities Press

Feeling the Discomfort on the Other Channel

An interview on the problems of producing ITV children's programmes

MIKE SEGAL: Do you want to divide it into the strictly "educational" side and the more "entertainment" side? I know more about the entertainment side because I worked in that area for a number of years. I have, though, done some investigation on the educational side and have talked to the people involved with BBC, Weekend and Thames TV.

DRAMA IN EDUCATION: How can you make such a distinction?

MIKE SEGAL: The distinction is clear-cut. It affects the budget; it affects the facilities; it affects to a large extent the quality of the personalities involved. Educational programmes are still going out in black and white while everything else is going out in colour.[1] It is certainly true that anything done for children on television is done either in terms of a gross sentimentality which denies children their humanity or because it has to be done. Or perhaps it would be more correct to say that there is a feeling that it has to be done. I think it is the BBC tradition which still lingers most on the education side, and on the children's entertainment side it is the re-think tradition that is most strong. The difference in attitude is again reflected in budgets and quality of staff, although there are on both channels people who are dedicated. They may not be dedicated in the right way but they are dedicated.

DRAMA IN EDUCATION: Yes, but what is the difference? How do you tell what is "entertainment" and what is "education", in inverted commas?

MIKE SEGAL: Well, I imagine the best way of showing you the distinction is by looking at a television set. You will soon discover that the educational programmes are the dullest. Where you find it the more didactic, the more official, you've got your inverted commas. It is almost as if (possibly due to pressures from educational authorities) anything that is enjoyable is automatically not educational.

DRAMA IN EDUCATION: You mean education is what does you good and entertainment is that which can't possibly have any lasting effect!

MIKE SEGAL: That might be something of a working definition. What springs to mind is a music programme I saw on TV the other week. They were taking folk songs and totally ruining them by the way they were trying to teach kids to sing them or play the music for them. As far as entertainment drama is concerned, the BBC and ITV have a different approach. BBC children's department don't do it. It is done by the drama department and the result is what tends to be called family entertainment. Which tends to be either a classical series or a science fiction piece like 'Dr Who.' The drama department have better facilities and their programmes go out in colour. In fact, a lot of the entertainment drama programmes made on film are in colour merely because where possible they are going in for co-production. It is obviously cheaper if you can get Bavaria or somebody else to co-produce with you. The rest tend to be show business in short pants. There is a series on London Weekend called 'Jamie' – a fantasy story in which a little boy has a magic carpet and goes back in time to meet Nelson or whoever. Though it's on a higher level in execution and concept, its association is with the run-of-the-mill, day-to-day serials. The result is still inadequate. It's inadequate in many ways as entertainment, it's inadequate as drama, it's inadequate because the writing is so third-rate. One of the things that's always astonished me is that more of children's literature hasn't been dramatised for television. Some of Leon Garfield's stories have been dramatised very well. One of Alan Garner's was dramatised by Granada, very badly. A very good novel but a very bad television series. On the whole, it is cheaper to use hack writers, even if you have to put up with hack dramatic dialogue, than to pay a good author for their rights.

DRAMA IN EDUCATION: What's the reason behind this low-budget thing? Is it that they expect their public to be less critical, or that they expect it to be a smaller public, or just that children are thought to be less important?

MIKE SEGAL: It is very difficult to work out any kind of philosophy behind any of the material shown to children. If it doesn't sound too arrogant, I was one of the few people in children's television to have some idea as to why I was doing what I was and to have thought about the effects I wanted from it. I think most people are doing children's TV because they are there. In Weekend for example, the man who runs the children's section is also running further education and adult education and religious programmes and documentaries and Uncle Tom Cobbleigh and all. He's a Jack of all trades. He's also a nice guy and a pretty good producer working with what materials he has to hand.

DRAMA IN EDUCATION: How much scope is there in children's TV for free drama work?

MIKE SEGAL: There have been some attempts to do improvisational drama on ITV. Marjorie Sigley and Gwyneth Sirdival both worked through improvisation. Marjorie Sigley was put into the religious slot, so she had to do all her drama around religious ideas. But the programmes were found to be upsetting. The kids she was working with were upsetting adults by their rather irreverent approach to God and the Bible and the various stories that they were acting out. Although "Siggy" is a strong teacher (and in the end is probably stronger than the man who sets out to direct more formally,) there remains a certain amount of spontaneity, for it was never finally rehearsed. People liked it because it was cute, but they hated it because in fact it was subversive. If you give children their head they tend to be subversive. Unless you are prepared to accept that and to work within it, you are not going to be able to do spontaneous work. Gwyneth and I, in 'Stage One', probably achieved the most spontaneous programme you ever came across. Of course it frightened the technicians who were working with us to death because they were so used to a set place to go and a set angle from which to take things. The minute you say "Well, look, take it as it comes", they are totally lost. They are not trained for it, so they don't want to do it. It's a pretty difficult technical job in any case, and to add spontaneity to that without ever having experienced it before is asking a great deal. Nevertheless I think 'Stage One' was pretty successful in achieving what it set out to do. It was great fun for us and great fun for the kids in the studio, though I don't really know how much came out of it either as education or entertainment or both.

DRAMA IN EDUCATION: Are such improvisational programmes meant to be educational or entertainment?

MIKE SEGAL: 'Stage One' was in the entertainment slot. Marjorie Sigley's was in the religious area which you might say was even duller than the educational. 'Stage One' was meant to be entertainment and that's why we worked very much towards a completed form during the half hour take of the programme. In fact a lot of the work was done in rehearsal the week beforehand, so what you had on television was a fairly finished process – always allowing for a certain amount of finishing while finally working with the kids. One of the things that put us into entertainment was of course that we used a pop song or a pop star of one kind or another as an added draw, because at that time kids were very much more interested in the pop scene than they are now. (Some people we gave their first acting part to and have regretted it every since.)

DRAMA IN EDUCATION: When you speak of the success of a programme like that, do you mean it had a bigger viewing public?

MIKE SEGAL: An interesting thing about 'Stage One' was that it wasn't very successful from the ratings point of view and we had irate advertising department people coming round and saying, "What the hell are you doing?" They were interested in selling advertising during that space and we were getting small ratings. With television, however, a "small audience" is a nonsense phrase, since a small audience is something just under a million people. A million kids is a marvellous, even a fantastic audience for anybody to have. There is always a pressure to keep ratings up and the competition between BBC and ITA leads not to a better programme but to repetition of the same kinds of programme. There are something like five magazine programmes at the present, three on BBC and two on ITA, all going out about the same time. They have much the same kind of Central School presenter, same kind of items about Princess Anne or animals, same kind of interesting bits of information and so on. It's a lazy kind of programme!

DRAMA IN EDUCATION: Do you think that this state of affairs is any better than with the more educational programmes?

MIKE SEGAL: On the education side, drama from the improvisation point of view is done occasionally. They present much more of the straight play. Sometimes their drama is in extracts from plays or sometimes a play is broken up and goes out in three programmes. They make very great efforts.

DRAMA IN EDUCATION: Presumably they are working on smaller budgets.

MIKE SEGAL: They are done on very much smaller budgets than would be expected in the main drama department. And they are working with less able directors, less able actors and all the rest of it. Probably they are on smaller rehearsal times, too. The "in" thing of course is dramatisation of documentary material. I think that the use of dramatisation there is to make what are essentially very dull programmes, worth looking at. The approach that you get in the kind of documentary that goes out at nine o'clock in the evening isn't used. This is partly because a major documentary will spend something like £12,000 on an hour's programme. (Particularly if they are going abroad with it, taking cameras and camera crews and the whole paraphernalia of filming.) Education programmes just simply don't have that kind of facility and have to rely on stills, old bits of film and the montage technique – which remains a fairly poverty-stricken effort. Dramatisation is a way of making a more interesting effect for all concerned.

DRAMA IN EDUCATION: What is to stop them making a good documentary which could be repeated? If it is a good documentary it will have more permanent value.

MIKE SEGAL: I don't think that kind of consideration enters the head of the budget makers. There is a budget for the education programmes and you keep within it. Granada have a programme for schools which in fact consists of repeating documentaries that have already been made for other reasons. This seems fair and works very well.

DRAMA IN EDUCATION: Is there anything to choose between the commercial companies as far as children's work goes?

MIKE SEGAL: No, I don't think so. As far as educational material is concerned it's almost identical. The education department is the only area where there is a certain amount of discussion and avoidance of the same kind of treatment and programmes. There was none at all at one time but it has now become formalised.

DRAMA IN EDUCATION: This ought to lead to something more interesting in the way of broadcasting?

MIKE SEGAL: Yes, I think so. The people working in the education programmes are serious and serious minded and obviously want to do their best to attract schools to watch their programmes. But they labour under enormous difficulties and increasing pressures. And this is not just in primary education, even in further education such pressures are felt. Recently two guys have been sacked because of programmes they were making about Marx and Mao. Not because they wanted to plant Marxism or Maoism into tiny minds, but a great row blew up as to whether these were suitable subjects at all. Another further education programme was stopped – this was on race relations – which was being treated in a very lighthearted, even flippant way.

DRAMA IN EDUCATION: In a way, until you can start laughing about subjects like race relations you are not going to be able to take a really balanced view towards them.

MIKE SEGAL: Yes. Too often education material ends up being dour as most of the teaching.

DRAMA IN EDUCATION: How do you feel ITA entertainment programmes compare with those of BBC?

MIKE SEGAL: On the straight entertainment materials there is a tendency for the independent companies to follow the lead of the BBC. The fact that 'Blue Peter' is a very successful programme meant that 'Magpie' was born a pointless carbon copy of it – two 'Blue Peters' are enough for any child. The other difference is, I think, that children's programming on ITV is a bit more vulgar. It's less middle class orientated. It doesn't, for example, do what the BBC does, which is to show foreign children's movies with either bad dubbing or a commentary in English over the top of people talking in Spanish or Yugoslavian or whatever. I find those films dreadfully dull. There is something to be said for the fact that the

commercial product is the unofficial product. It relates in a curious
kind of way much more directly to children and their need for fantasy
and so on. It's like Flash Gordon always really wins over Rin Tin
Tin. That's not the right comparison but anyway the most garish
things happen. Which I find preferable to programmes like 'Junior
Show Time' in which a lot of stage-struck girls are trying to be Judy
Garland and all the boys trying to be – I don't know what! The
imitation of Judy Garland in these kids is pathetic.

DRAMA IN EDUCATION: There seems to be a sort of feeling that
children will accept the second-best and the second-rate.

MIKE SEGAL: At about the age of four or five I think children are
indiscriminate in their viewing. I think there has been a progressive
lowering of the age range at which children's material is seen (except
for a captive audience in school with educational programmes). Once
they have got past that, they begin to discriminate and once they've
got past ten or eleven they stop thinking of themselves as children in
any case and don't watch it.

DRAMA IN EDUCATION: Do you really believe that kids are as dis-
cerning and discriminating as all that?

MIKE SEGAL: It's a very complex subject, I think. Certain inferior
material is marvellous.

DRAMA IN EDUCATION: Enlarge on that.

MIKE SEGAL: I can't immediately think of anything in terms of television but there is an Italian film I saw recently with my boys which
was so badly made as to be marvellously funny. It wasn't intention-
ally bad but nevertheless it was a very enjoyable experience. Certain
vulgarities work better this way. It happens in comics. Batman in
the end is essentially better than 'Eagle'. The 'Eagle' set out to be
a comic, became essentially a middle-class one and failed miserably
while Batman is still going strong one way or another. I think the
fantasy there is better, truer to children's minds than that of the
'Eagle'. There isn't anything in ITV children's programmes which
measures up to that because they are too bounded by all kinds of
fears about what the result of anything outside the conventional might
be. When I was with ITV we were doing a play and I simply wanted

to do a piece about mythical animals – the dragons and the phoenix. All was fine until it came before the lady who sits and vets all programmes for legal problems. The fact that the phoenix rose from the flames terrified the life out of her because she thought that if you mentioned this or tried to act it for very little children, they would all start walking about on their electric fires and central heating and set themselves alight. Really, it took an enormous amount of argument before we could convince her.

DRAMA IN EDUCATION: Did you in fact use the phoenix as a symbol?

MIKE SEGAL: Yes. And nobody complained about it. It went by like a lot of television goes by. But at the time there was a huge amount of fear that if only one child is going to fly out of the window because he's seen Batman, you don't show it. It's all very curious because there have been as many reports of kids trying to fly after seeing Peter Pan as seeing Batman but it is Batman that gets the complaints – it's unofficial and not middle-class. It is extraordinary that the difference in attitude and feeling in approach is still so often on a class level in this country. Standards still seem to be those of a Boy Scout.

DRAMA IN EDUCATION: Is there much research being carried out with regard to television's influence on children?

MIKE SEGAL: The amount of research is very limited and it is always conducted under conditions which I think tend to limit its value. Television research tends to confine itself to asking people questions, which is very dubious. There was a report very recently in America on the effect of children being exposed to violent programmes and being exposed to boring programmes. The people exposed to boring programmes afterwards got much more violent in their behaviour than those exposed to violent programmes. But in most of this research you can find what you want. And you can nearly always find one piece of research which counters any other investigation.

DRAMA IN EDUCATION: Are there any ways in which it can all be improved? Would you start with parity of budgeting?

MIKE SEGAL: Parity of budgeting would be one important area but you don't want to go to the other extreme. We don't actually need as

much as most people use simply because we've got it. You can make
good programmes on quite small amounts of money by television
terms. What you need, obviously, is the amount of money which is
appropriate to what you are going to do. With ITV if I wanted to put
more money on something I used to cut it from somewhere else. As
long as the departmental overall budget was the same, it was all
right. We need better technical facilities but the way to ensure
improvement here is to get people in television to be much clearer
about what they are doing and why they are doing it. On the educational side, they are told that their work is meant to extend or expand
on what the teacher is doing. They are not there to replace the
teacher in any way. We need more feedback with teachers about what
they are doing and providing. More work, too, on how kids are
reacting to it. My own kids led a revolt against doing television
stuff and said, "We prefer to sit and do mathematics than watch all
this." They found it boring and the whole of their school found it
boring and in fact it was dropped almost totally because they pre-
ferred to have real relations with real people. There is something
frightening about a lot of technical equipment going into schools and
replacing the one thing which is the most valuable experience to
children, a direct relationship with a person who happens to be
called a teacher.

DRAMA IN EDUCATION: But I am afraid the opposite is also possible.
Kids can become so used to being bored that they would rather be
bored than meet people. An equally frightening situation.

MIKE SEGAL: I think many kids prefer to be bored by television than
by a teacher. The problem is one of the quality of teaching in the
schools and what that teaching is about. Once we have got that
sorted out we can more easily sort out what educational television
programmes are going to be about. With entertainment programmes,
too, I find it extremely difficult to know why they are there except
that they fill up the time reasonably cheaply and help to build up an
audience later on in the evening for people. Television ought to be
some kind of a tool; it could be used that way. Then it's the basic
philosophical question really: what are you trying to do? If you are
trying to expand a child's imagination, if you are trying to encourage
its curiosity, if you are in fact trying to make the kid work, then I
think most of the material that is at present offered ought to be
scrapped because it does the opposite. Some material of general

interest is OK but it seems, having reached that level, everybody
has sat down and said, "That's it! " As far as I can tell, 'Blue Peter'
is going on for the next two hundred years, and nobody is really making much attempt to introduce programmes which have any kind of
experimental quality. There has never been a straightforward documentary service for children. Something I wanted to do (which is
not all that experimental) was to present schoolboy football matches
in much the same way as other football matches are covered by adult
television. I'd like to scrap most quiz programmes, which are very
boring and make assumptions about the value of facts as sheer facts.
Instead I'd like to see kids handling cameras and kids directing.
There is now very cheap video equipment and given the resources of
television companies, there is a lot that could be done that might be
fed back on to the screen. Fed back or not it would be nice and would
be one of the ways of improving discrimination. The older children,
there is no reason at all why you shouldn't give them the studio to
play with and see what happens. It really means devoting enough
resources to it. The technical side is not so difficult – mainly you
need to do it for long enough. The camera director's box is not that
difficult, an intelligent child could work it.

DRAMA IN EDUCATION: When you were working with television what
sort of brief did you set yourself?

MIKE SEGAL: I set myself several briefs because one was faced with
several different sets of people to relate to. My first brief to myself
was to produce programmes which were of an expanding character
which attempted to broaden both kids' imaginations and what they
could do for themselves. My other brief to myself was to make
enjoyable programmes that I liked doing, and worked in relationship
to the kids. As far as the company was concerned I had to maintain
ratings. Although 'Stage One' had very bad ratings, all was forgiven
because we won the international prize with it. It was the first time
we had ever entered a competition from the commercial channel and
won. They did not want to repeat any further experiments of that
kind but nevertheless the whole thing almost justified itself in their
eyes. I quit eventually because I wouldn't take a programme which
was being forced on me – a programme that's still going I think –
'Tingha and Tucker.' It seemed to me to be the epitome of all those
approaches to children which are grossly false: sentimental, un-
imaginative, bland and really sickening. Compared with children's

literature, especially that for young children like 'Little Red Riding Hood' or 'Hansel and Gretel' which has a real psychic quality, the stuff is skimmed milk, and I think a total denial of a child's dignity. Too much of the television stuff approaches children as small things from another planet, as if they are not human at all. If children watch for a large number of hours, they watch programmes much later on at night and the one bit of real solid evidence there is about children's viewing is that their favourite programmes are the ones which are on about 8 o'clock. The kind of melodramas that are made for adults. It's not terribly good stuff but at least it's exciting or it tends to be exciting and of course a lot of money is spent on it. If you tried to do the 'Manhunt' kind of programme in children's television, everybody would scream at you because it isn't quite nice enough. But that is in fact what kids are watching.

DRAMA IN EDUCATION: Which of the programmes you were involved in, do you think, worked out best?

MIKE SEGAL: Well, I did a programme about kids writing plays which we had acted by a rep company. I think that was worth going on with for a while. There are always ways one could work with music – and particularly music, drama and documentary together – that will produce something that hasn't been seen. I think with more experiment we could get to a situation where you wouldn't be able to disentangle the educational and the entertainment process.

(1) Editors' note
At the time of writing, Mr. Segal was right. But now (February 1972) most educational programmes are made in colour. Of course very few can be being **received** in colour!

142

Let's Pretend

Caryl Jenner, founder of the Unicorn Theatre, outlines the growth of what has become one of Britain's major theatres for young people

In 1948 a borrowed Civil Defence van set out from the Amersham Playhouse in Buckinghamshire with the first company of what is now known as the Unicorn Theatre for Young People. After ten years of intermittent experiment and research at the Playhouse, this company was formed to bring a true experience of theatre to young people which would last long after the performance was over. The majority of performances in these early years were given to audiences who had never experienced theatre before. No books or guidance on the subject existed and the work was like a voyage in uncharted seas with new discoveries being made at every performance. Programmes of plays were presented for three age-ranges: 4-7 in arena form, and for 8-11 and 12-15 in semi-arena form.

From the start, the aim was to establish regular performances throughout the year in a purpose-built theatre. However, in 1948, the time was not ripe to gain interest, encouragement or support for such an idea and so the only way to operate at all was to take the theatre into schools. The co-operation and enthusiasm shown by a large number of Education Authorities all over the country were the main factors which enabled the development of the work to occur and much strength was gained through frequent discussions with teachers and educationists.

GROWING INTEREST

By 1957 there were four companies on the roads playing for over 50 Education Authorities. In that year Sam Wanamaker invited Unicorn to provide children's theatre as a regular feature of his New Shakespeare Theatre in Liverpool. Interest was increasing and it was realised that it was only a matter of time for major developments to occur. Unicorn recognised that its four companies, who battled their way through fog, snow and floods day after day to innumerable schools, were pioneering and that the time would come when this touring work would rightly be passed on to regional centres. The time was ripe, therefore, to sow the seeds for the establishment of a permanent theatre for young people in London and to plan a gradual withdrawal from the touring work.

At Christmas in 1959, a play was presented at the Rudolf Steiner Theatre to enthusiastic audiences and another in 1960 when audiences trebled and there were vociferous demands for more than just plays at Christmas. Meanwhile, the touring companies continued their work, with Malta and Northern Ireland added to their schedules.

WORK IN LONDON

In 1961 the Arts Theatre in London became available at Christmas and, with performances at Toynbee, Questors and the Lyric, Hammersmith as well as regional theatres such as Salisbury Playhouse, Coventry Belgrade and the Yvonne Arnaud at Guildford, one company was able to devote itself to work in theatres only. In 1962 a play was presented at Easter as well as Christmas and in October of that year the Unicorn Theatre Club for Young People was launched with just on 500 members. With the Club in being, demands for more plays grew insistent and the first week-end performances were given at the Garrick Theatre.

During these years Unicorn kept up continual pressure through Press, Television and Radio for the formation of a Junior Arts Council with its own funds.

In August, 1964, the first permanent London company of Unicorn was formed. However this company still had no home and had to move in and out of theatres of varying sizes, often in incredibly difficult conditions and frequently unable to have a dress rehearsal in a theatre prior to the opening performance. In addition the entire operation was carried out from a one-room office and a backstreet Parish Hall where all scenery and costumes were made and where all rehearsals took place.

ARTS COUNCIL AND YOUNG PEOPLE'S THEATRE

These were the crisis years when audiences were growing, costs rising, time was short, staff were few and standards could only be improved with the help of hard cash. It was in this atmosphere that hope came, with the news that the Arts Council of Great Britain had set up an Enquiry into Young People's Theatre with a view to the possibility of grant-aid in 1966. This grant-aid was delayed for a year and so Unicorn reached a major crisis in June, 1966. Closure was only averted at the last moment by emergency grants from the Arts Council of Great Britain, the Calouste Gulbenkian Foundation, the Leche Trust, the John Spedan Lewis Foundation and the young Unicorn members themselves.

Grant-aid mercifully arrived in 1967 and, at long last, after nineteen nomadic years, in July Unicorn took over the Arts Theatre in London for the remaining 6 years of its lease. In September 1967, therefore, the first season was launched and Unicorn set out to prove the viability of running an all-the-year-round Theatre for Young People.

In the four years since then, the membership of the Club has increased to just on 5,000, largely between the ages of 4 and 14, with approximately 50% from the London Postal districts and 50% from the Home Counties.

THE BUILDING OF THE FUTURE

The Arts Theatre, with its intimate auditorium seating 350, has at least provided Unicorn with a temporary home but the physical limitations of its small proscenium stage and Dress Circle militate against the fulfilment of the basic aims of the work. Unicorn has therefore had a new building designed for the future which will contain two auditoriums – the first a small area to take about 200 children from 4 - 7 seated on cushions on raised steps around a square arena; the second a semi-circular auditorium to seat up to 500 8 - 11 year olds with a space stage. The ages mentioned and their needs were the basis for the planning of each theatre – but both theatres are adaptable for various uses and for age-ranges 3 to 25. Together they create the possibility of presentations ranging from a play with 3 actors and one symbolic scenic unit, leaving imaginations free to create what they will – through to a full assault on the mind, the emotions and the senses – with every possible marvellous effect of which the theatre is capable – from the space stage.

The use of the word "assault" does not mean "attack" or "overwhelm" nor does it imply any desire for a sense of "power" over the audience. It is intended to imply that all the means at one's disposal can be used to lift the mind, emotions and senses away from automatic re-action, automatic thinking and automatic emotional response and to lead each individual child towards a sense of total awareness – something of which the child is even more capable than most adults who have been educated and civilised out of this possibility.

In addition to the two theatres, Unicorn plans a communal "baby-sitting" room where the youngest member of a family may be looked after while the rest of the family watch the play, a restaurant, a book and magazine stall, and many other amenities.

Society changes and technology develops with increasing rapidity – it is therefore necessary to look all the more to the universal and eternal values – to gain from the past and to think in terms of the future, but not to be diverted by fashions that come and go.

Unicorn's continual study since 1948 of age-ranges, actor-audience relationships, other theatre buildings both here and overseas, leads to the belief that the two auditoriums will meet the needs of the aim to stimulate the individual imaginations and emotions of young audiences and so lead them to a fuller inner life. With an ever-increasing population and the growth of mass influences and herd instincts, Unicorn seeks to speak to the individual, to stimulate mental acrobatics, to explore inner space and to create a situation in which young audiences will retain and develop the ability to think for themselves. Unicorn seeks also to offer impressions which will, individually and imaginatively, extend the range and richness of expression for creative dramatic play in the home and in the school.

WHY A THEATRE BUILDING?

To achieve this Unicorn presents plays in a theatre. Unicorn does not believe that this is the only way to create theatre for young audiences. It just happens to be the way it thinks it can do it best. In a strong and healthy young people's theatre movement every company or group should have its own face and the greater the variety of approach the better. Unicorn studies and watches and is aware of the many developments in this field and is always ready to learn, to be stimulated by new ideas, to select, to adapt and to incorporate what will help in the development of fulfilling the needs of the audiences.

The new building does not exist yet and so, for the time being, work must continue in the Arts theatre. At this theatre the resident company presents 9 plays each year ranging from plays specially written for Unicorn to translations from abroad, from conventional folk-tales to avant-garde experiments. Performances are given on Saturdays and Sundays and in holiday periods for the normal public, and mid-week for school parties. In addition about 100 sessions for creative dramatic work by the young people as well as concerts, films and visiting Puppet Companies are provided.

INTERNATIONAL OUTLOOK

Over the years Unicorn Theatre has sought to develop and extend the international aspect of its work in conjunction with its efforts to promote Young People's Theatre as a whole. It is not insignificant that

the first presentation by the company in its residence at the Arts was
the translation of a play from Sweden. Through the auspices of the
British Council and similar organisations, Unicorn is pleased to receive the many colleagues and interested visitors from abroad who
come to observe and experience the Company at work. In addition to
these opportunities for dialogue and discussion and the reciprocal
mutually beneficial exchange of scripts and ideas, Unicorn intends that
the projected new theatre should provide for this country the focal
point for the work of Young People's Theatres from abroad.

Unicorn is not highly subsidised and has chosen to have a small
but experienced company of 9 actors rather than a larger but less
experienced group. They are an ensemble company and the majority
have, as with many overseas groups, worked for many years for young
audiences. Whether they achieve it or not, they all believe in Stanislavsky's reply when asked how an actor should play for children – "as
for adults – only better" – and work incessantly to develop as artists.
They aim to create for their young audiences that true experience of
theatre which is like falling in love – except that it lasts longer!

In the present restricted circumstances the only kind of participation which can occur is the natural, logical, vocal and mental participation stimulated by the action of the play. In the future theatre physical participation will occur in varying forms for small numbers of the
youngest age-range.

VALUES

A great deal of emphasis is placed on the work for the very young.
Psychiatrists state that the main influences on a human being occur
before 6 years old. The Jesuits said "Give us the child until he is 7
and we will give you the man." For Unicorn the very young are the
most intelligent. Here then lies a great responsibility and a challenge.
In fact theatre for young people from 4 to 14 is a continual challenge
and it is necessary to keep one's ear to the ground in order to be aware
of rapidly changing needs and demands and attitudes.

KINDS OF PROGRAMMES

For all ages the main concern is with the scripted play and the main
problem lies in finding good plays or good playwrights willing to write
for young people. In searching for plays Unicorn always looks for
plays which have something of value to say – but whatever a play says,
however valuable its contents may be, it is valueless to us unless it is
a good play. We do not seek to educate or moralise or act as a political

platform – we are concerned first and foremost with the art of the theatre: if what we do also educates or moralises or puts forward a political attitude it is the by-product of the experience of theatre but not the experience itself.

The form in which the plays are given is of necessity conditioned by the physical circumstances of the theatre building in which we work. A proscenium arch is a proscenium arch. However, sound and light out in the auditorium are frequently used to heighten involvement and break down any barrier; the actors work towards a great clarity of thought and a high degree of sensory communication.

The style of presentation varies considerably according to the plays – in some cases a symbolic setting may be used, in others something more realistic, yet others using shadow play and projections – in general, simplicity and suggestion are the aim, leaving each individual to extend imaginatively in his or her own way.

The common denominator in all this is the attitude of the actors, their approach to their work, their study of and consideration for their audiences, their flexibility in tackling many differing styles and their sensitive adaptability to each and every audience – in addition their physical stamina, because in plays for young children the characters never seem to sit down!

LOOKING AHEAD

Unicorn has plans to take on extra accommodation in the Autumn of 1971. Apart from providing much needed office and rehearsal space, this will also make it possible to treble the number of creative dramatic sessions which, at present, are always over-booked and to carry out some experimental work for 3 to 6-year-olds in conditions somewhat similar to those planned for the small studio theatre in the new building.

It would require a book to go into the specialised detail with which the actors rehearse, the results of periods of research into audience response, the creation – through going to the theatre – of better parent-child relationships, the way in which audiences relate ideas from plays to their own lives, the study of the emotional effects of colour and sound, the discussions with teachers and educationists, the discussions with the children themselves ...

In the end, for all the detail and research and discussion, Unicorn's main objective is that the young audiences should enjoy themselves – that they should laugh and cry and gasp and know moments of silence and stillness as well as of sound and action – and that they should go away with something new added to their inner life.

Caryl Jenner

Let's Put on a Show

A student of drama at Birmingham University gives her response to a range of productions for young people

Plays for children presented in a theatre can be absorbing for the adult observer as for the children, provided the standard of acting is high. The Unicorn Theatre presented a play called 'The Prince, the Wolf and the Firebird', an adaptation of a Slav Legend. The Prince encountered a number of adventures and trials in order to achieve his heart's desire and no child would find difficulty in following the plot as each adventure depended on the last. The technique, though simple, was effective and the children were gripped by the action. They responded emotionally to the Prince's troubles, and the use of theatrical effects, coloured lights and music heightened the response to the spectacle. The "magic" of the theatre held them rapt. Too much reliance on visual effect is dangerous, of course; it is easy to get children's attention by effect, but it is far less easy to get them to listen to words, which the Unicorn also tries to do.

James Saunders' play 'The Travails of Sancho Panza', presented at the Old Vic, relied more on the spoken word than on visual effect, perhaps too much, for the children were often restless during much of the action. But they responded with shivers of excitement at the marvellous theatrical effect of the "real" knight's entrance towards the close of the play.

The great limitation of this kind of theatre for young children, as Caryl Jenner has repeatedly said, is the lack of good plays for children.

THE STOKE VIC AT THE COCKPIT

The Victoria Theatre, Stoke, presented one of their theatre in education productions for younger children at the Cockpit Theatre in London soon after it opened. The programme was called 'Jupiter 13' and involved two actors, an actress and about 20 children. Although the programme entailed total involvement on the part of the children, it was fascinating and rewarding for the adult observers secluded round the walls of the theatre. The children were asked to become the passengers on the first passenger space ship to Jupiter. Soon after

take-off the Captain told them that Earth had asked them to volunteer
to make a detour into outer space to pick up vital supplies of uranium,
without which the Earth would perish. The Captain and first officer
put the pros and cons of making the trip to the "passengers" and after
discussion a vote was taken to make the detour. Everyone on board
the ship was put to sleep for the duration of the journey. They were
automatically awakened from their suspended state as the ship neared
its destination. Years of space travel thus passed convincingly in
minutes. The ship was then taken over by an alien presence who spoke
to the ship's company through the medium of the lady lieutenant. The
"passengers" were again offered a choice, of returning to earth with
the vital uranium or of travelling on to a promised paradise on Alpha
Centurius. The children asked the "presence" questions about her
country and had to decide whether they could trust such a mysterious
voice. The Captain and first officer were ready to remind the "passengers" of the moral issues, but this particular group of children
showed a ready grasp of what was at stake. Finally they rejected a
trip into a potential Eden, partly because they could not trust the voice
and partly because Earth was relying on them to bring the vital
uranium.

In this work of the Victoria Theatre there is a close association
with Brian Way's work and the value of such programmes is multi-
faceted. The children experience total involvement, emotionally,
intellectually and physically in the drama in which they participate.
In addition they learn about human and moral dilemmas by experiencing
them.

This production had a satisfying dramatic unity which made it as
rewarding to watch as to participate.

A COVENTRY PROGRAMME FOR JUNIORS

The work of the Belgrade Theatre, Coventry's Theatre in Education
team is of a different nature. One of their programmes for younger
children, called 'The Box-Inventors', involved a classroom full of
children aged between seven and eight running amuck with cardboard
boxes. To an adult observer there was little of interest to watch. An
audience was totally irrelevant to the action. If you were not participating the event was of no value. The value for the children, however,
was real. The Coventry team fill a significant gap in the schools.
They exploit drama as a teaching method in the schools. The relationship between teachers and actors is good and co-operation between the
two has some rewarding results. 'The Box-Inventors' was not a

particularly successful experiment but it did encourage the children
to use their creative imaginations and left the teachers with something
to work on. One striking aspect of this type of work is the stimulus it
gives to the less intelligent child. When the group gave the same programme to a class of backward children it produced a more imaginative
response than with the brighter children. An actress with the Oxford
Playhouse schools team also told me that the children the teachers
themselves despaired of contributed the most exciting ideas in this kind
of drama in education. Clearly this kind of work has a great deal to
offer.

For older children, and young adults, many theatres are producing
good work. Often the plays themselves could appeal to any adult, the
problem being to attract the younger people to the theatres. The
Liverpool Everyman Theatre's audience is composed mainly of eighteen
to twenty-five year olds. They present all kinds of plays under difficult circumstances. Scene-shifting in Chekhov's 'Three Sisters'
becomes a major operation, for example, but the standard of acting
is good.

SHAKESPEARE FOR SCHOOLS

The Liverpool Everyman also presented a programme for older school
children on 'Henry IV, part 1' in the theatre. The course was designed
to look at the main themes of "honour", politics and humanity in the
play through the medium of Falstaff. Peter Lover, the Educational
Director, discussed the play in broad terms and the children in the
audience were asked to contribute to the discussion at times. A team
of actors backed Peter Lover up and illustrated the points he was
making in several key scenes from the play. The obvious and real
value of this type of course is not what has been said about the play,
but what is seen to have been said when the actors play out the scenes.
For a child studying the play in the classroom this type of course must
be both a real help and a pleasure. The advantages of seeing actors
play the scenes are obvious, and seeing them done in an informal
atmosphere with discussion before and after reveals the mechanics of
the play to critical view. The children have time to stop and consider
the effectiveness of certain aspects of the play.

This is to take but a few examples of children's theatre in performance. It does however indicate something of the variety of the work
available yet even so, children's theatre has much more to offer in
many directions.

Rosemary Jervis Smith

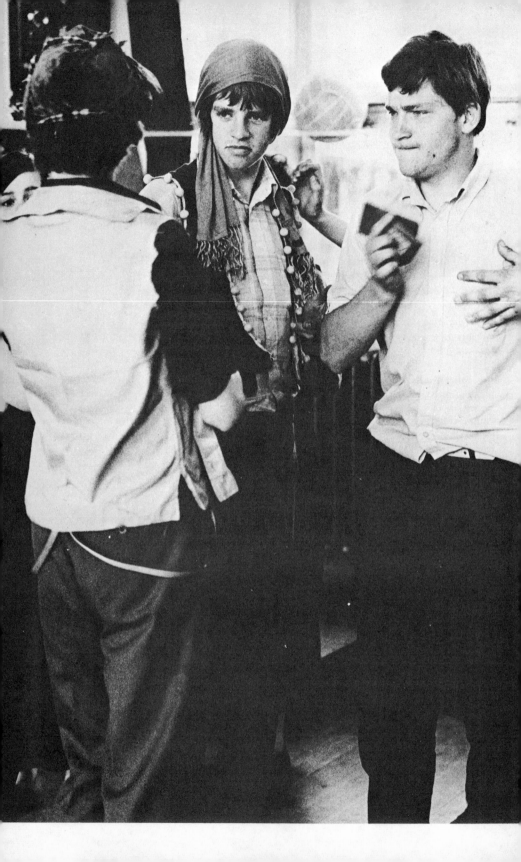

The Fight for Recognition and Co-ordination

Gerald Tyler, a pioneer in the Children's Theatre movement, gives a personal view of the growth of Children's Theatre organisation in an interview with Drama in Education

Coming back from the war at the end of 1945, directly I could get turned round I called together a meeting of people interested in children's theatre in 1946. At the beginning of that same year I moved house and job and came to Brighouse. From here we started the Leeds Children's Theatre and then in 1947, after I had been in Brighouse for a time, I started the Brighouse Children's Theatre. We had our first meeting in the summer of 1947 and our first production in January of 1948. In March 1949 we held an International Exhibition of Children's Theatre with material drawn from America, from France, from Belgium and from Germany. I wrote to Russia because I had been there before the war and seen children's theatre in that country, so we also had some pieces from the Theatre for the Young Spectator and the Moscow Children's Theatre. I had heard of Celia Evans and her work and had been in correspondence with her in South Africa and she sent material from there.

FIRST LINKS WITH I. T. I.

There was a notice in the paper in 1952 that the I. T. I. (International Theatre Institute) were holding discussions on children's theatre in Paris, at their conference. John Allen's name was mentioned so I wrote to him. He at that time was running the theatre at Toynbee Hall in London which was known as the Glyndebourne Children's Theatre. So the outcome was that I joined their discussions, which were chaired by John Allen. Leonard Chanchorelle took the professional children's theatre side and John Allen was leading the side concerned with theory and creative dramatics. From these meetings came the decision that 'World Theatre', the magazine of I. T. I., should carry articles about children's theatre and that one whole issue should be devoted to children's theatre work. While at the Paris conference, I had heard about a certain Mr Michael Pugh from England. I did not see him except at a distance, and never actually spoke to him. He was, however, at the next conference at the Hague where we again had a variety of discussions

about children's theatre. There Michael Pugh and I talked together.
He had just come out from spending an advanced year of sabbatical
leave at the Rose Bruford College and wanted to work in Yorkshire
where there was some children's theatre on the go. He got himself a
job through the Divisional Educational Officer in the Barnsley area and
began teaching at Darton Secondary School. From there he formed the
Harlequin Children's Theatre. Then Michael Pugh moved to Leicester
as a peripatetic teacher of speech and drama, so for a time he moved
away from us. However, during his time in the West Riding of Yorkshire he had taken an active part on the children's theatre committee
which met at County Hall. This committee brought together those
people who were working or interested in children's theatre and from
our deliberations we produced a series of papers on the function and
value of children's theatre – such questions as: What constitutes a good
children's theatre play? Whatever is going to make a play interesting?
What should one do to promote children's theatre? What in fact is a
child? Also at this time Michael Pugh and I must have been talking
about the possibility of forming a National Association. But Yorkshire
being at the North East corner of the North East island, we felt it a
long way from London to start up something. So we hung back for a
while although we were still working on the basic material.

When the Young Vic finally had to close because of the failure of
the Arts Council to support them financially, George Devine was for a
time without a post. So I wrote to him suggesting that we needed a
National Children's Theatre Association to bring people together. I
pointed out that though many people work in the field in different ways
it was difficult to keep in touch and exchange ideas and that some kind
of organisation was needed, "You, " I said "are the man to start it. "
He replied that while it was very nice of me to say that, he had a living
to earn now and would have to concentrate on himself. A few months
later, Michael Pugh wrote to me and said, "What about this National
Children's Theatre Association? If you're not going to start it, I am. "

BRITISH CHILDREN'S THEATRE ASSOCIATION

The two of us then had a meeting and decided to bring together all those
people who were actually engaged in children's theatre. This took place
at the Institute of Education in Leicester in 1959. I remember a number
of people who were there. John English of the Arena Children's Theatre,
Peter Slade who was running a children's theatre at that time, Margaret
Faulks, Caryl Jenner and I believe Gerald Bagley. As a basis for discussion we used the West Riding documents. The outcome of the

several days' conference was the forming of the British Children's
Theatre Association. Michael Pugh was General Secretary and I became the Chairman. Membership was open to anyone associated with
a children's theatre. Caryl Jenner put forward a motion, which was
carried, that while professional children's theatre companies might
belong they would do so only as associate members. A professional
group was defined as a group recognised by Equity and subscribing to
the Esher standard contract. At that time this was understandable but
after one or two years it became evident that some of the better children's theatres were not in Equity and some of the not so good ones
were. So, in time it didn't really make sense to use Equity recognition
as a bar for membership of the professional section of British Children's
Theatre Association. About 1960 or 61, therefore, we dropped this
distinction and though we were now able to include people like Bertha
Waddell of Scottish Children's Theatre, groups like those under Caryl
Jenner and Brian Way withdrew even from associate membership.
People like Brian and Caryl had been working all hours that God sends
on a shoe string budget. They had high standards in their work and did
not want to associate themselves with a number of people, so called
professionals, who were not rising to the proper standards. There has
always been, and still is, this desire for children's theatre to be recognised by the whole profession as equals and not as half or just as
distant cousins. They wanted to be seen to be fellow actors and co-
partners in the whole business of professional theatre.

AN INTERNATIONAL CONFERENCE

As General Secretary, Michael Pugh in 1962 said that he was getting
a number of Commonwealth and other groups from abroad interested in
joining the Association. He felt it would be worth while bringing out in
association with our usual directory, a Commonwealth directory. He
also felt it would be a good idea to have a Commonwealth Conference,
so that any people from the Commonwealth could come and join it. We
felt such a Conference would need careful planning and that 1964 would
therefore be the year for this. In arranging the Conference, Michael
Pugh was most energetic. At that time other meetings were also on
the go. There was one in Paris, largely sparked off and influenced by
the Puppetry Association, to which Michael Pugh went. They were
talking about people getting together internationally and several people
expressed interest in attending the Commonwealth Conference which
we were planning. At a further gathering, also held in Paris, Michael
Pugh acted as chairman to a discussion about international co-operation

and association. At that meeting they even drew up a basic constitution. From then on we had so many more people from so many different countries becoming interested in the Conference to be held in Britain in 1964 that we decided it had indeed grown into what would become the First International Conference of Children's Theatre. That Conference was opened by Sir Edward Boyle and Michel Saint-Denis, as British Children's Theatre Association president, was in the chair. About forty countries were represented, including India, Japan, Russia, USA and many Commonwealth groups. During the conference a public meeting was held to consider the forming of an International Association and from this large gathering a steering committee of twelve countries was selected. It was agreed to hold a meeting of this committee in Venice in the autumn (about five months later) to prepare the constitution and make other preparations ready to bring the findings to a conference which was to be held in Paris the following year. Acceptance of a constitution came in 1965 and the first assembly, when the International Children's Theatre Association was really properly off the ground, came the following year in 1966. From the beginning there has been a constant link with the ITI – no move has been made without consultation with the general secretary, and the offices of the Association were properly at the same address as ITI.

SORTING OUT DIFFERENCES

The struggles and complexity of drawing up an acceptable constitution at Venice and Paris are history in themselves. Three important points of argument are worth recording:

1. Language and recording procedure
2. Performance and creative dramatics
3. Clarification of what is meant by youth and child.

We argued for a long time about the language in which proceedings should be conducted. Clearly the fewer the better, unless expense was to mount – our resources were small. We thought at first to follow the line of ITI and use French and English but it became clear that we ought also to include Russian. So finally we decided that conferences, publications and proceedings should all take place in three languages: English, French and Russian.

We also had a great deal of disagreement about our terms of reference. Many were concerned with the performance of plays by young actors and actresses in professional companies. Some were prepared to accept members of amateur companies as well as professionals and a few were interested in including dramatic work done

by the children themselves – what the Americans call creative dramatics. The problem was complicated by the fact that there were also
troupes of child performers around. From children's theatre in Paris
at that time we knew there were some of those little companies where
children were sharpened up to do variety turns and solo acts – a sort
of drama school for the professional variety stage. These kids looked
pushed and somewhat scared and what we did not want was what the law
wouldn't allow us to have in this country. Unfortunately out of the same
window went creative dramatics, which really ought to have had
separate discussion and attention. Since that time I have attempted on
several occasions to bring up again the creative dramatics question. I
did base a presidential address on this subject in the Hague but I
suppose this takes time. The A.S.I.T.E.J. conference in America
next year will perhaps be the time for at least a separate sub-section
concerned with creative dramatics to be developed.

This question is also related to that of age range. One delegate
who had worked in Africa said that children from the age of six were
having to serve, work and look after the family: in those terms the
difference between adult and child was difficult to assess. It varied
from country to country but finally I think we asked the French delegate,
who said that under fifteen a person had not had the experience or the
training to give artistic performances of any value and so we all agreed
finally to be concerned with performers over fifteen.

REPORT ON THEATRE FOR YOUNG PEOPLE

The next important development in this country came when the Arts
Council decided to look at children's theatre and produce a report on it.
Earlier the Arts Council had been subsidising the (post-war) Young
Vic, the Amersham Children's Theatre (under Caryl Jenner) and the
Glyndebourne Children's Theatre (under John Allen at Toynbee Hall).
Then they decided that their brief did not really entitle them to give
money to children's theatre and so they stopped their grants, leaving
those three enterprises to go down the drain. (John Allen went to the
BBC, Caryl Jenner carried on touring the schools as the English
Children's Theatre Company, while the Young Vic had to end all its
good work.) Meanwhile, we were making various attempts to get something from the Arts Council. Caryl Jenner came to one of our British
Children's Theatre Association conferences where we were talking
about a Junior Arts Council. Caryl wrote about it and talked about it
and by pressures from all sides the Arts Council eventually decided to
set up a report to take a look at young people's theatre. We, I think,

in children's theatre had high expectations of this. We looked on it as a great move on the part of the Arts Council and felt certain that something good would come from it. We felt that we must not prejudice what they were doing and sort of held fire for a while waiting for the report to come out.

About this time Caryl Jenner was striving to get members of CORT together to form a young people's committee composed of professional children's theatres. It still seemed to me that it was a pity to separate the professional performance side of children's theatre work from the work undertaken within education. We were in East Germany on a conference and I wrote while there, to Caryl Jenner, expressing this point of view. I appreciated that they as theatre companies working for children wanted to be members of the Council of Repertory Theatres but I felt it would strengthen the effect of the work if they would also become members of British Children's Theatre Association. We could not join them in CORT but they could join us. She said she would talk this over with other members of CORT but nothing came of it and there remained a strain between the members of each association.

A NATIONAL COUNCIL FORMED

During this time Jennie Lee came on the scene and took a personal interest in all this. At one of our conferences she said that it was time we overcame our differences and came together. Clifford Williams was chairman of British Children's Theatre Association and we talked this over with him. Then we arranged another meeting with Jennie Lee and Arthur Geddes, the chairman of CORT. As a result of this the National Council of Theatre for Young People was formed. So the CORT members and the BCTA members came together under the chairmanship of the British Drama League at the British Drama Centre. It soon became clear that others should join, so representatives were invited from the Educational Drama Association, Junior Drama League, the National Association of Drama Advisors, National Youth Theatre, Society of Teachers of Speech and Drama and the Association of Teachers in Colleges and Departments of Education. There were observers also from the Arts Council, the Department of Education and Science, the British Council and the British Centre of ITI.

At first the National Council of Theatre for Young People met at the British Drama Centre, but it had no finance at all – all the members paid their own fares and there was not even money to support the secretary. The total income of the Council was about £35 per year.

Then came a visit to one of the BCTA conferences of the wife of the then Prime Minister, Mrs Mary Wilson. She did not stay long at that conference but the upshot of her visit was that there was to be a meeting at No 10 Downing Street in support of Children's theatre. It was a gathering of a wide range of celebrities and businessmen. David Frost, Kay Hammond, Cliff Richard, Felix Aylmer, Michael Redgrave, Laurence Olivier and Joan Plowright and scores of others were present. Apparently, Mary Wilson was hoping to raise many thousands of pounds. We discovered later that the prime object had been to find money to support the work of Marjorie Sigley.

The outcome was disappointing as far as money was concerned for very little was donated – what there was was divided between Marjorie Sigley and the National Council. This did, however, enable the National Council to have for a year a full-time secretary so the work could at last be put upon a much firmer footing.

So, little by little, the work has begun to spread and develop. There is the beginning of useful organisation and co-ordination. It needs now more and more workers in the field of children's theatre.

Gerald Tyler

Playing in the Street

While engaged upon his B.Ed. (Drama) degree at Bretton Hall,
John Marshall undertook a special study of Street Theatre

Western theatre has rarely been renowned for experiment or creative
diversity; perhaps conscious of its sublime purpose, inherent in its
origin, there has been little sympathy for deviance since Aristotelian
plot. Nonetheless, for reasons too complex to divide into their
separate strands of human science here, the past few years have
supplied a volume and variety of experiment to which the traditional
theatre is quite unaccustomed. Part of this experiment follows the
movements of music and art into mixed media confrontations of electronic dependence, hopefully emerging as a twentieth century expression of twentieth century conditions. One important exception to the
dominant experimental direction is the apparent return to one of the
oldest and generally forgotten forms of communal entertainment –
street theatre.

An extensive range of activities is subsumed beneath the collective
term street theatre, which it is necessary to make clear to understand
its usage. There are the travelling troupes who take their mediaeval,
almost minstrel tradition, entertainment to local fairs and into the
streets. They display an implicit pantomime influence and are essentially concerned with a "live" community experience. Others, notably
Inter-Action in London and Interplay in Leeds, work exclusively with
children, offering both performance and participation in drama –
scape projects. They create opportunities for the children to explore
artistic materials and play, in a way which is denied them in many
homes and schools. A more vociferous element of street theatre to
emerge recently is the didactic utilisation of the theatrical form by
politically orientated activists. Often termed "guerrilla theatre", it
has become more than the animated soap-box platform it once was. In
America, where this type of theatre is more prevalent than in this less
politically motivated country, it has taken many directions. The now
defunct San Francisco Mime Troupe, which was originally formed in
1959, began its political side-shows as a series of passive parables.
They were intended, again in a certain mediaeval sense, to bring to

the attention of anyone in the street issues of political and military immediacy. However, the allegorical nature of this "entertainment" declined as political activity, aroused by the "Kent State Massacre" and Black Panther policies, became more positive. At this time the theatre became "guerrilla" in the truest sense as it adopted the style and motivation of guerrilla warfare. It is arguable as to whether these later political forays, despite their use of the noun, have much to do with the theatre which is of concern. This is not to deny their relative importance, it is perhaps more an argument of semantics.

For primitive man, theatre was more than the luxury pastime it has generally become; it existed rather as a communal necessity. And it is this nature of necessity that makes the Bread and Puppet Theatre perhaps the most important and influential of all contemporary street theatre. Under the direction of Peter Schumann in America, the Bread and Puppet Theatre's title is indicative of its purpose. Bread because Schumann believes the theatre arts to have become separated from the stomach in the transmutation of theatre to an entertainment for the skin. For him the theatre is as necessary as the food we eat and consequently he provides both bread and theatre free. And Puppet because it best describes the basic methods of his work. The group of actors perform mainly in masks or within the mould of some gigantic puppet. The early shows were of the allegorical type, performed with the ceremonious simplicity that separates most street theatre from its domiciled counterpart. The themes with which they deal are simple human truths, often within a Christian context, short parables of contemporary politics and social morality. There is no dogmatism, only shows for good against evil.

Much of the present street theatre, in Britain at least, seems to have appeared as a manifestation of a conscious attempt to encourage the unification of socially fragmented communities. In this connection it is an interesting corollary to note that those geographic areas which have retained customary examples of mediaeval street theatre – the Padstow hobby horse, the pace-eggers of the Calder Valley, the Burry Man at South Queensferry – are invariably those communities which maintain some social cohesion. John Fox, organiser of the theatrical complex, Welfare State, of which street theatre is part, achieved this kind of unity, if only for the day, when he ran a festival of participation for the inhabitants of a small Yorkshire village in June 1965. His first major event in the streets was in collaboration with Albert Hunt for the Meyerhold-styled celebration of the fiftieth anniversary of the Russian Revolution. The project, designed for the streets of Bradford, was formulated within the configuration of a game providing a structured context similar to the concert hall or theatre and was to involve about 300 students. The participants, divided into teams of Reds and Whites, were required to capture by their numerical presence certain focal points whilst carrying out given instructions such as, "Unite the workers of the world" and "Go off the gold standard". Whilst the event was not considered a complete success it was certainly remarkable as a venture utilising the streets as a theatrical arena. After the more successful, "surreal pantomime for beach, sea and the edge of both" at Instow in North Devon during July 1968, John Fox concentrated for a while more specifically on street theatre. The delightful show involving a flea circus and superman has since amused both children and uninhibited adults at various festivals and street corners throughout the country. Although the Welfare State now spends much of its energy in mixed media spectaculars with the Mike Westbrook Band, their free street theatre remains an intrinsic aspect of their work.

The recent revival of street theatre as a theatrical expression and the natural appeal it has for children has led, not surprisingly, to its specific use in an educational context. Ed Berman and the Inter-Action community arts trust began as a structure that might make possible discovery into ways in which anyone could participate creatively in the arts in spite of the apparent sterility of their environment. To make contact with the people of Notting Hill, particularly the children, Ed Berman utilised the drawing power of his Dogg's Troupe street theatre. Having managed to involve them in the street performances of moon-men, Batman, Robin and others, the members of Dogg's Troupe set up play projects for the children. One of the first of these "drama-scapes", in 1968, was the building of a fifty foot model of Gulliver surrounded by Lilliput, creating explorative opportunities for the children in drama, music, carpentry, painting and modelling. Berman regarded fun as the only inspiration behind the scheme and only asked of the sessions that the "leaders and the led find it useful and enjoyable".

Interplay, with a methodology similar to Berman's Inter-Action, are based and work in the streets of Leeds. Their general aim is to counteract the increasing insignificance of the arts to large sections of the community and to do so in the community's own environment and on its own terms. They have no overwhelming desire to bring "culture to the masses, " rather they provide opportunities for self expression within the community through improvised drama, participatory street plays, and environmental projects. As with Inter-Action, it is the street theatre that makes the initial contact with the children, not merely as a form of display but as a means for the children to involve themselves actively. One of Interplay's most successful street projects began with a performance of 'Captain Heartclutch and the Little Awkwards' and developed into a month-long Apollo 15 drama-scape. With help from the members of Interplay when needed, the children, using only waste materials, began their construction. They painted their own blueprint for the rocket and mission control, and their star charts, on old wallpaper. The ripped-out tub of an old washing machine became a radar scanner and the smashed entrails of discarded radio and television sets were transformed into mission control's computer. A massive rocket of cardboard and paint also began to rise from the rubble to the accompaniment of rehearsal from the Strawberry Lane Rubbish Band. The ability of Interplay and other child-orientated street theatres to provide new areas of creative experience raises many educational implications, however it is their use of street theatre as a medium which is here considered.

The observable resurgence of street theatre, acquiring even commercial recognition at times, is not easily explainable in the light of other more technically advanced experiment. However its present appearance is significant in the overall development of the theatre. In requiring only performer and spectator, street theatre contains the two essential and primitive elements of theatre, and as such may be regarded as the simplest and purest of dramatic forms. With emphasis upon these elements and a disregard for theatrical artifice, the existence of street theatre is perhaps inevitable when "traditional" theatre in particular and the culture in general reaches some point of saturation.

The dramatic purpose and style of the mediaeval minstrel and storyteller closely parallels the contemporary flourishing of street theatre. After the demise of Greek and Roman drama, occasioned by its final inanity and the ensuing barbarian invasion, no great theatrical tradition was to exist until the development of liturgical and secular drama in the middle ages. For some time it was considered that the two traditions lacked any purposeful link, but this was surely to underestimate the significance and necessity of dramatic expression to man. More credible is the probability that fugitive performers carried the rudimentary seeds of theatre from the exhausted classical style into the street and village festival entertainment of acrobats, jugglers and storytellers. Their existence may therefore be seen as the provision of a catalytic bridge between the two major styles of theatre; for after many early and unsuccessful attempts at suppression the church was finally to adopt and utilise their performance for religious ends.

Indirectly then, and almost unconsciously, the minstrel and the travelling bands of players were not only responsible for the incipient appearance of a new theatrical genre but were also to influence its style of presentation. Although not representing the archetypal street theatre form, the Commedia dell'arte, appearing toward the close of the Italian Renaissance, can be considered to have similarly fulfilled an essential need.

There are many indications that the present style of commercial Western theatre is nearing its own saturation point, and that even the omnipotence of verbal culture, of which it is undeniably a part, becomes ever more questionable. The degree of banality which pervades most of our theatre is alarming, and the apparent, yet consequent, desire for "spectacular" is prophetically reminiscent of Greece and Rome. If these indicators and the continued appearance of street theatre are markings of the transmutation of theatre then it is perhaps in that street theatre where directions may be found. They may point toward the environmental experience that Ed Berman and Naftali Yavin experiment with or toward the "circus for the senses" of the Welfare State. Wherever they finally lead, it is unlikely that many of the audience will remember the man in the top hat, with trumpet and baggy pants, calling the shoppers and their children to Superman and the fleas.

John Marshall

Arts Centres and Other Strange Places

In the last decade there has been a steady growth in the number of arts centres in this country. Leslie Holloway examines this trend and describes some of the centres, in particular the Midlands Arts Centre at Cannon Hill where he has worked for several years

It has been variously estimated that there are between 20 and 80 arts centres in Great Britain at the present time. The discrepancy results from the problem of definition: what is an arts centre?

WHAT IS IT?

In some holiday resorts there are "arts centres" which are really shops, run on a co-operative basis to sell the products of local potters, painters, weavers, and basketmakers. At the other end of the scale, London's South Bank complex consisting of the Festival Hall, the Hayward Gallery, the National Film Theatre, and eventually the National Theatre, is also "an arts centre". Between these two extremes lies a whole spectrum of different ideas and interpretations. It is probably safe to assert that no two arts centres are alike, and that the one characteristic they all share is a resolute individuality.

Nevertheless there is a broad, general theme in the growth of the arts centre movement – even though any chosen example might not conform wholly to it! To begin with, the basic object of most arts centres is to bring several art forms into proximity, with the intention of enriching all of them. The desire to do this may have some connection with the contemporary feeling that the boundaries between one art form and another are blurred and unreal; freedom to move easily from one mode of expression to another is increasingly seen as an increase in potential. Traditional concepts of "theatre", "music", "literature", "painting" are less valid as contemporary artists use mixed-media techniques to express themselves. Even when we are concerned with more traditional arts, where the distinctions are clear, there are good reasons for arranging them in close association with each other. This appears to be equally true in those arts centres which are mainly concerned with the professional performance and presentation of the arts, and in those which are mainly interested in encouraging people to practise the arts themselves.

There are also good economic reasons for the growth of the arts centre idea in recent years. It should always be cheaper – or more cost-effective, anyway – to build and manage one well-designed multi-

purpose centre than a series of separate buildings; a theatre, an art
gallery, a concert hall, a recital room, a cinema, a studio centre.
Any private organisation which has to raise funds, or any local authority making demands on the rates, is likely to be favourably impressed
by the financial arguments for an arts centre in preference to separate
facilities.

These factors, and the benevolent encouragement of Miss Jennie
Lee during her term of office as Britain's first Minister for the Arts,
led to a proliferation of arts centre projects in the late sixties. Few
of them progressed beyond the pipedream stage. At one period I began
collecting newspaper cuttings of announcements about new arts centre
plans up and down the country, and these soon grew into a bulky file
with more than 200 projects listed. It seemed that every town, village,
and rural district council was determined to have its own arts centre;
it had become a matter of civic pride and often, one suspected, for the
same reasons that fountains and war memorials used to be erected.

Perhaps it is as well that the vast majority of these schemes never
achieved anything more substantial than a few paragraphs in the local
newspaper. No arts centre can hope to survive on idealism and good
intentions, still less on misplaced local patriotism. The comparatively
small number of schemes which have progressed to reality in the last
few years have all had, initially, a clear concept of their role in the
community, stemming either from an enlightened local authority, or
from one or more courageous and clearsighted individuals.

DRAMA AND THE ARTS CENTRE

Almost all of these new arts centres include drama among their activities. Some give a home to amateur dramatic societies; others have
facilities sufficient to permit visits by professional theatre companies
from time to time; a handful have on their own staffs people concerned
in one way or another with drama work. Two or three arts centres
run their own professional theatre companies.

It seems likely that the inclusion of professional theatre work in
arts centres will become much more general as the movement develops.
Several of the larger existing centres are exploring the possibility of
running small but versatile theatre companies as a central feature of
their performance programmes.

Another interesting development can be seen in the desire of some
existing theatres to extend their interests into music, film, and the
visual arts, thus evolving into arts centres. Warren Jenkins, director of the Belgrade Theatre in Coventry, has a long-term plan of this

kind which would make the Belgrade a comprehensive arts complex.

The almost endless variations of design, policy, ownership, and management between one arts centre and another make it difficult to forecast how rapidly this trend towards professional theatre might develop. At present there is little contact between arts centres – yet one could well imagine an organisation similar to CORT (the Council of Repertory Theatres) being established to link the various centres, and this in turn might lead eventually to a touring circuit for theatre productions.

VARIETY OF APPROACHES

The diversity of the arts centre movement makes further generalisation impossible, however, and it will be more useful now to examine some particular examples of the genre.

Some of the most comprehensive arts centres have been provided in New Town developments, where the local authority has the great advantage of starting from scratch without existing buildings (or preconceived ideas) to get in the way. Basildon Arts Centre, for example, was opened in 1968 with the expressed intention of providing a cultural heart for its transplanted community. The building consists of two wings, one a studio block with rooms for painting, pottery, and photography, and the other an auditorium seating 476 for use as a theatre, cinema, or – with all the seats removed – an exhibition area. A restaurant links the two wings. Theatre work at Basildon has consisted of a mixture of local amateur and visiting professional productions, interspersed with films.

Basildon is financed and staffed by the local authority. In Devon, a combination of local authority money and the generous private patronage of the Dartington Hall Trustees has resulted in two arts centres which are the envy of less fortunate regions.

Darington Hall itself, partly new and partly converted premises, serves as a college of art and an adult education centre for South Devon. In this role it has a paid full-time staff, who are then, in a part-time capacity, also responsible for the promotion and presentation of its arts centre events. In this way Dartington can mount an impressive programme which includes, in an average year, upwards of 20 professional plays and nearly as many amateur productions; opera, orchestral, and chamber concerts; film performances; and exhibitions. The Dartington theatre seats 200 and its concert hall 450.

The Beaford Arts Centre, established in 1966, is an offshoot of Dartington intended to serve a widely scattered rural population in

North Devon. Grants from local authorities and the Dartington Hall Trust enable Beaford to mount a similar programme to its parent centre, and also to serve as the base for the tiny Orchard Theatre Company, which tours the South West.

Another local authority which has shown great enterprise in creating a rather different kind of multi-purpose centre is Teesside, with the Thornaby Pavilion and the Stockton Pavilion – and not far away, of course, is the Billingham Forum. Some people would say that these are not strictly arts centres, because in addition to auditoria and workshops, they have facilities such as swimming pools, bowling alleys, squash courts, and ice rinks. This seems to me a semantic difficulty rather than a practical one. By using neutral titles like "Pavilion" and "Forum," the Teesside centres have avoided entering this rather fruitless argument and are able to combine the arts, popular entertainment, physical recreation, and community service without apparent friction.

An arts centre of a more traditional type is that at Bristol. Converted from a pair of Georgian houses, it opened in 1964 with facilities consisting of a 126-seat theatre, a workshop, music room, coffee bar, and restaurant. Its principal strength has been a full film programme – like many arts centres, it serves as a Regional Film Theatre under the aegis of the British Film Institute – but it also presents professional and amateur theatre, concerts, poetry readings, lectures, and exhibitions.

THE GARDNER CENTRE FOR THE ARTS

Yet another trend in the development of arts centres may be discerned in the Gardner Centre for the Arts at Brighton. The Gardner Centre is on the campus of the University of Sussex, and receives most of its income in the form of a grant from the university, but it is open to all and seeks to link the university with the rest of the community.

The Gardner Centre has a financial structure which most other arts centres would regard as idyllic. In the first full year of operation, 1969/70, it had a total income of £49,334, of which only £7,411 was taken at the box office, and the rest was in the form of grants. This situation enabled the director, Walter Eysselinck, to mount an exciting programme featuring many well-known actors, musicians and artists. In the year there were 132 theatre productions, 13 ballet and opera performances, 22 concerts, and 26 student events. On the expenditure side of the budget £15,098 went on theatre work and £21,865 on administrative costs. Sean Kenny's circular auditorium at the Gardner has three stages and movable seating. It can be adapted for proscenium arch, thrust, or in-the-round presentations, with a maximum capacity of 500.

Other facilities at the Sussex centre include a group music studio, a group painting studio, and sculpture and painting studios used by "artists in residence."

THE GREAT GEORGES PROJECT AT LIVERPOOL

If the Gardner Centre is the latest word in sleek sophistication, the Great Georges project is a piece of gritty Northern realism. Great Georges is a former congregational church in the centre of Liverpool, an architectural landmark of genuine if grimy distinction. It has a large hall with tiered seating, a sub-basement housing a lecture theatre, and a large open area with catering facilities adjoining. Its organisers, Bill and Wendy Harpe, call it "a centre for contemporary work in the arts, education, and community development." They have also called it "an adventure playground," which perhaps gives the flavour more accurately. The paid (or underpaid) staff of eight are very much involved in their bustling, multi-racial local community. After an initial struggle to be accepted, they have now reached a point where the local kids are prepared to play their "theatre games."

Activities at Great Georges are sometimes difficult to classify. For example, a theatre game called 'Sanctuary,' commissioned for Shelter, could be regarded as experimental theatre, as adult education (for the audience) or as general education (for the schoolchildren taking part). Another theatre game, the 'To Hell With Human Rights Show' tested the allegiance of the audience to the Charter of Human Rights.

Mixed media shows, workshops, discotheques, bingo sessions, lorry theatre – the Great Georges project will use whatever means and methods seem appropriate. They are not particularly interested in performances as such, nor in working with or through the Establishment. They have been asked to co-operate with the Liverpool Educational Priority Area experiment, and they are now receiving an L.E.A. grant for youth work. Despite this, their only real source of finance remains private donations, and this means that all the staff are making a considerable personal sacrifice in economic terms.

THE MIDLANDS ARTS CENTRE

The largest purpose-built arts centre in Britain is at Cannon Hill Park in Birmingham. Its formal title is the Midlands Arts Centre for Young People, but it has become so generally known as "Cannon Hill" that I shall so describe it from now on.

Cannon Hill is the only arts centre in Britain which maintains a permanent, full-scale theatre company, and which regards educational

173

drama and "drama in education" as a major part of its purpose. This
attitude is the result of the centre's carefully worked out philosophy —
which differs considerably from most other arts centres in Britain, in
being basically educational.

The Cannon Hill centre was the brainchild of a small group of
people led by John English (now its director) and Sir Frank Price, a
Birmingham politician and the first chairman of the centre. Their
argument was that the lack of support for the live arts in this country
is not an inevitable fact of life but an accident of social development.
Thus it is possible, they assert, to change the situation by a process
of education — specifically, by introducing children and young people
to the arts in their formative years, not as academic exercises, but
as enjoyable and stimulating experiences.

Although education is undoubtedly the intention, entertainment is an
equally important key word at Cannon Hill. The programme is chosen for
the intrinsic merit of its component parts, judged by normal artistic
criteria; indeed, the centre goes to great lengths to avoid doing the "set
play, " though clearly attention is paid to the school syllabus.

FACILITIES AT CANNON HILL PARK

Before discussing Cannon Hill's theatre work in more detail, it may
be as well to describe the centre's buildings and facilities, and its
financial and administrative structure, so that the present range of
activities can be seen in context.

When the original small group of founders worked out their plans
in the early sixties, they had in mind a comprehensive arts centre
with auditoria of various sizes, galleries for the visual arts, workshops and studios, restaurants and social facilities, a swimming pool
and other athletics areas. Because the object of all this was to house
a new kind of "social-cultural" education, there was a temptation to
visualise it on an existing educational campus — perhaps alongside one
of Birmingham's universities or polytechnics. The arguments for a
more informal and entertainment-biased flavour were considered more
important, however, and eventually it was decided that a public park
would provide the ideal setting.

Cannon Hill Park is two miles from the city centre, well served
by major roads and public transport. It has more than 80 acres of
exceptionally beautiful landscaped gardens, open parkland, boating
lakes, and recreation facilities. On its northern boundary is a strip
of land, bounded on one side by a lake and on the other by the tiny

River Rea, which had never been fully developed as part of the park. Some derelict storage huts and scrubby undergrowth, with a number of mature trees, occupied most of this strip of land, which was chosen as the site for the arts centre.

To acquire the land meant involving the city council in the project. Fortunately the town clerk and the chief education officer, as well as leading councillors, were already interested in the scheme, and when the proposition was put to the full council, to lease 14 acres of the park to an independent body, there was a unanimous vote in favour. Because the land had originally been a covenanted gift, it was then necessary to promote a parliamentary bill to remove some of the more restrictive covenants from the area in question. Observing the democratic processes in this way was undoubtedly a great help in getting ready public acceptance of the scheme in these early stages.

It may be asked why it was – since Birmingham Corporation gave its blessing so generously – that the council did not entirely adopt the project. There were several reasons against this. First, even the most dedicated local government officials and representatives said that committee procedures might prove slow and unwieldy. Second, the Centre was being planned to serve an area much larger than just Birmingham – north Warwickshire, north Worcestershire, south Staffordshire, and the Black Country conurbation. This meant that a working relationship with some 14 local authorities would be necessary, and it was felt that an independent body would have certain advantages in achieving this. Last, and most important, it was considered that an independent charitable trust would be able to seek funds from many sources not open to a local authority. These arguments led to the setting up of the Cannon Hill Trust, as a non-profit educational charity, in 1961. The foundation committee became the nucleus of the Trustees, and set about raising funds to employ key staff and initiate building work.

Two years later a foundation stone was laid, and in 1964 the Trust headquarters, Foyle House, was opened. Immediately a pilot programme of concerts, exhibitions, and other events began. Meanwhile the fund-raising programme had secured a number of substantial donations from industrial companies and charitable foundations, and work had begun on the main workshop and studio building.

Further on in the building programme – there are 21 separate projects in all – were a pair of theatres, the Swan and the Cygnet, providing auditoria of 1200 and 600 respectively; a visual arts pavilion; a concert hall seating up to 2000; a film theatre; and a whole campus of lock-up studios and workshops for group and individual use. Originally it was planned that all these would be completed in a ten-year building programme, but the economic climate of the last few years has made this impossible. Instead, the Centre is concentrating on the completion of Stage 1 of its building programme, in order to reach a state where it can provide a full range of services. This means adding the Cygnet Theatre, the visual arts building, and a studio extension, to the existing part of the Centre.

The second major building at Cannon Hill was opened (by Princess Margaret) in 1965. It houses the main practical facilities – a central Studio Theatre surrounded by workshops, painting and sculpture studios, pottery, music rooms, photography studios and darkrooms, and a coffee bar. Another wing, the Hexagon, opened in 1968. This includes a library and study rooms, a recital theatre, and a games room. Another major project, the athletics wing, is now (1971) nearing completion. This has three squash courts, a large gymnasium-cum-dance studio, facilities for badminton, judo, fencing, table tennis, and other indoor games, a climbing wall and artificial "pothole," and more restaurant space.

PHILOSOPHY BEHIND IT ALL

It can be seen that, like the Teesside "pavilions", Cannon Hill has a liberal and undoctrinaire interpretation of "the arts". John English will say, when challenged about the validity of, for example, dress-making and carpentry in an arts centre, that many people find the greatest outlet for their creative instincts in clothes and home decoration – and why not? Similarly he refuses to draw lines separating ballet from gymnastics, or mime from fencing; the use of body skills is equally a form of personal expression in all of these. He is fond of quoting the story of a UNESCO seminar held at Cannon Hill, when the distinguished cultural delegates from all over the world found themselves agreeing that the experience of watching a football match was akin to that of attending opera, and that a baseball game in the Hollywood Bowl was just as valid a manifestation of the human spirit as a symphony concert in the same arena!

Despite – or perhaps because of – this catholic outlook, John English has always regarded theatre as the central art form, because of its accessibility, its range, and the way in which it can be linked with music, literature, and the visual arts.

For this reason he seized upon the chance of starting a professional theatre company at Cannon Hill – which came with an Arts Council grant in 1967 – even though the Cygnet Theatre was still on the drawing board. Pending completion of the Cygnet, the Midlands

Arts Theatre Company has shared the 200-seat Studio Theatre with
the various amateur member groups who use it.

The company has been able to accomplish a surprising amount of
work in these difficult circumstances. In the 1969/70 season a total
of 523 performances were given to a total audience of 73,354. This
was achieved by using the theatre for three or sometimes four performances a day. Often these are entirely different – a puppet play
for younger children at 10 a.m., an in-the-round production for eight
and nine-year-olds at 2.30, a piece of adult theatre on a thrust stage
at 7.30, and a late night show at 10.30.

Puppet productions at Cannon Hill are the responsibility of John
Blundall, who has developed a natural and direct style, often dispen-
sing completely with playboards and not attempting to hide or mask
the operators. Children seem able to accept the sight of an actor
holding the puppet, forget the person, and identify with the character –
a more sophisticated version of "the willing suspension of disbelief"
than many people would credit to a three or four-year-old child! Yet
these ideas have developed out of children's own puppetry activities,
and the analogy of play with dolls, teddybears, and other inhabitants
of a child's world is very close. There is no doubt that puppet theatre
is often the best introduction to live drama for young children, and it
has certainly become very popular at Cannon Hill. A great advantage
has been the presence of the full theatre company alongside, because
it has been possible to train actors to manipulate puppets, rather than
teaching puppeteers to act.

THE REGULAR COMPANY

For slightly older children the company presents live plays – a mixture of specially written material, sometimes improvised and with
considerable audience participation, sometimes more formal. There
is a dearth of good material for the 8-12 age group, so the company
has eagerly seized upon the rare exceptions like Ken Campbell's 'Old
King Cole.' This particular need has led the Arts Council recently to
award a bursary to Royal Court playwright David Cregan so that he can
work with the Cannon Hill actors in writing a play for children; and it
is hoped that more writers can be persuaded to tackle this difficult (and
financially unrewarding) area of theatre.

For children of secondary school level, the choice of plays is somewhat easier. There is a reasonable amount of suitable adult material,
as well as a repertoire of "key plays from the past" which are considered important in building up theatrical literacy. For those aged 15

and over (adults, as far as Cannon Hill is concerned), there is no restriction and the company has as wide a range as any normal repertory theatre.

Philip Hedley, who joined the arts centre as director of theatre arts in 1970, plans to develop the company's work far beyond conventional performances to non-participating audiences. He is investigating the possibilities of closer liaison with schools, of street theatre, of open rehearsals, and of participation situations. Although an avowed experimenter he is not disposed to throw babies out with bathwater, and sees a long future for plays performed on stages, by actors who have learned (and understood) lines written by an author, before audiences whose involvement is mental rather than physical.

DRAMA BY THE MEMBERS

Active participation in drama by young people is a substantial part of Cannon Hill's work. It begins with the youngest of children in puppet-making groups, leading on to play-making, and to collaboration with other youngsters in music and visual arts sections. Mime, movement, improvisation, and the techniques of sound and light, are explored at weekend and holiday sessions by slightly older children. Drama work of this kind is also part of the special enrichment programme which the Centre carries out for children from schools in Balsall Heath under Birmingham's Educational Priority Area experiment. These eight and nine-year-olds, living in an area of multi-deprivation – what we used to call a slum – spend one day a week at Cannon Hill, using the Centre's full range of facilities in a free and informal way. Paul Clements, the centre's director of education services, has a full-time drama assistant and other qualified staff to help in this work.

By the time children reach the age of 11 or 12 they can join in the regular drama activities – usually improvisations – of Cannon Hill's Junior Club. From this they move on at the age of 16 to the Senior Club, which has a very strong theatre section, and a great deal of contact with the actors and technicians of the professional theatre company. Both scripted and unscripted plays are rehearsed and performed on a five-week cycle (to integrate with professional work going on in the same theatre), and in addition a good deal of experimental drama work goes on which is not intended for performance.

At present Cannon Hill is being used by about 80,000 people a year. Some of these are using the workshops and studios three or four times a week, while others come only once or twice a year to attend performances. All of them pay, even if the sum is nominal, and the

income from box office and subscriptions reached £60,000 in the last
financial year, out of a total running cost budget of £113,000. The
remainder was made up by central government grants of £25,400, a
payment of £6,600 by local authorities for "educational services rendered," and the balance from the Cannon Hill Trust's own funds.

HOPES AND THE YEARS AHEAD

Ultimately the Centre hopes to achieve a more realistic sharing of
financial costs on the basis of one third each from central government,
local authorities, and the users. It would also like to share its capital
expenditure on this thirds system – though in practice, private gifts
and donations have provided more than two-thirds of the £1m so far
spent on buildings, and the central and local government contribution
has been much less than was expected. "There is no future in trying to
provide a public service without reasonable support from the public
purse," says John English. The alternative of charging higher prices
would be self-defeating, he thinks, because it would keep away those for
whom the Centre offers most benefits.

Setting aside these financial problems, which are common to most
cultural organisations, the Cannon Hill Centre has been an outstanding
success in its pilot work so far. As Michael Green and Michael Wilding
commented in their UNESCO survey ('Cultural Policy in Great Britain',
UNESCO, 1970), "It remains flexible and to some extent unpredictable.
Its essential features are an interest in new experiments and a willing-
ness to adapt itself to changing circumstances and demands." These
authors also remarked that "the centre has been widely admired and
will almost certainly be imitated elsewhere when money permits."

Whether such imitation will be possible in the near future remains
to be seen, but it is certainly true that a continual stream of visiting
parties, representing local authorities, private organisations, and
pressure groups of one kind and another, is received at Cannon Hill.
Most of them appear to be impressed by the fact that the place exists
at all, and at the amount of work it is carrying out. They take away
with them, no doubt, varying impressions, and come to different conclusions. But there is no doubt that their interest is symptomatic of
current thinking on cultural provisions. The arts centre, in all its
varied guises, seems destined to become as ubiquitous a feature of
our community provision in the next two or three decades as were the
public library and the civic art gallery a century ago.

Leslie Holloway

MODULAR THEATER

California Institute of the Arts
Valencia, California

California Institute of the Arts and New Directions in the Arts

A few miles outside Los Angeles on a vast campus made available by the trustees of Walt Disney, Robert Corrigan heads the California Institute of the Arts, a huge H-shaped building where training is available for fifteen hundred students in the arts

During a recent visit to Stanford University, I became aware of the contrast between the incendiary sculpture of the campus dissidents and the imposing new art building containing the works of Picasso, Matisse, and other great painters. This contrast revealed anew the tension that has always existed and continues to exist between rebellion and celebration in the arts.

From the beginning of history, artists have celebrated that which is noblest in human achievement and thereby provided a record of such achievement. But, they have sought also to pioneer and explore new "boundary situations" as adventuresome rebels.

In the past, it has been possible to evaluate the artist's rebellious explorations within a relatively stable framework of tradition. There was change, but its pace was barely perceptible to contemporary observers.

CULTURAL BOMBARDMENT: IMPACT UPON THE ARTS

This situation no longer prevails; everything is changing so swiftly that we are having trouble getting our bearings. This is particularly true in the arts. On the surface it appears that artists have tossed out all of the traditional disciplines. In fact, I think that this is not the case. Rather, technological advance has made it possible for the artist to experience all forms of art and cultural achievement – past and present – simultaneously. He is being bombarded by a wide variety of traditions and cultures, and the challenge is to select from among them.

These developments have led to increasing hybridisation of style and form in the arts, which many people find confusing and of questionable value. The product of this hybridisation process is often downright gibberish, I must admit; nonetheless, I sense a tremendous potential for the advancement of art in this confusing time.

HAPPENINGS: THAT'S WHERE THE PEOPLE ARE

My first real awareness of what is happening in the arts came during a
visit to the Venice Biennale in 1966. I was struck by the fact that, while
it was by all odds the most beautiful in the traditional sense, the American pavilion attracted scarcely any interest. Nobody was there! By
contrast, the Argentine and Japanese pavilions (especially the latter)
were thronged with people viewing "paintings" that had no paint on them
and other exhibits which in one way or another demanded **participation**
by the observer. **One experiences such art not by looking at it but by
becoming part of it.**

Now you may say, "That wasn't art, " and maybe it wasn't; but the
indisputable fact is that that's where the people were! And, they were
having a wonderful time!

The "happenings" and the improvisations, the electronic music,
the light machines and the anti-theatre plays, the computer films and
sculpture – all of these are foreign to the world of art that was presented to me in school. And yet, these are not the works of faddish,
undisciplined, self-indulgent kooks but of highly trained artists who
have mastered the traditional forms and moved on into new areas.

The Electric Circus in New York City – one of the most exciting
experiences in my life – illustrates the point I am making. The Electric Circus simply demands participation by young and old alike in an
environment of music, light, and projections. It was largely the
creation of two men, both highly disciplined and traditionally trained.

THE REACTIONARY AVANT-GARDE

It is a misconception to think of these developments as constituting a
radical departure from tradition or simply to dismiss them as products
of the avant-garde. The literature and the manifestos of the avant-
garde reveal in fact a basically conservative and even reactionary
philosophy; they are always trying to return to the old roots – to that
which is more real, direct, or more truly communal and involving.

The avant-garde is saying that we must use the new tools and
techniques which progress has provided to return to the old truths.
Thus, what seems to be a shattering of tradition is, in reality, a re-
affirmation of it. We see this for example in the new movements
towards ecumenism in our religious institutions. And in the arts it is
plainly apparent in the recording of 'Switched on Bach, ' produced by
the Moog Synthesizer. No instrument is "played" in the ordinary sense
and yet the interesting thing is that the Moog Synthesizer is no more

radical than the organ. I'm sure that if Bach were alive today he would be composing for the Synthesizer and not the organ. The really significant point is that the Synthesizer can create not only the more traditional sounds but wholly new sounds as well.

We are witnessing the emergence of new attitudes in all of the arts. There is a move away from protest and retreat which characterised much of artistic expression in the years following World War II. The theatre of the absurd, which portrayed man as totally isolated and victimised, along with abstract expressionism, which similarly depicted man as alienated and estranged from society, are fading from the scene.

TECHNOLOGY: NEW ALLY OF THE ARTS

In an almost unprecedented venture, America is taking the lead in every art form. This is the outgrowth, I believe, of a fundamentally new attitude toward technology. By and large, the artist has looked upon technology in the past as an enemy. Today, he is probing the possibilities of using technology to extend the limits of creative expression.

Technology, more than any other force, is giving us a new sense of choice – of almost unlimited choice. This sense of free choice seems to be taken for granted by many of our young people and to a degree that is often perplexing to their parents.

Technology has contributed to the artist's expanded perspective in another important dimension; it has made him aware of the possibilities of working not simply as an individual but as a member of a creative team. This realisation has served to intensify the hybridisation movement in the arts.

The result of these new attitudes has led the artist to be less concerned with creating lasting works of art than at any time in the past. More and more, he seeks personal reward in the process rather than in the product of his labour. It is symbolic perhaps that the Museum of Modern Art now maintains a permanent collection of disposable art.

In sum, what really has happened is that technology has made art a part of our environment and in so doing it has involved art in every aspect of our lives. **Art is no longer something that you go to, it is something that you live with.**

THE IMPULSE BEHIND CALIFORNIA INSTITUTE OF THE ARTS

These radical changes which the new movements in the arts are reflecting are also boldly manifest in our educational institutions – and especially in those institutions committed to the training of artists. Clearly, the turmoil in our schools, from the earliest grades to the universities, indicates that something fundamental has gone wrong with the educational process. The discontent of students is shared by their teachers; both are decrying the scene that has become depersonalised, fragmented and without relevance. Each time violence cuts short the dialogue, repression follows and the impasse is frozen. The problems remain and even amplify.

The arts have always made us more aware of the nature of reality as it actually is, and for this reason they provide those kinds of perceptions which point to the solutions of our fundamental problems. That is the impulse behind California Institute of the Arts.

We start from scratch, and from a commitment. If the arts are to play a role in the shaping of things, art for art's sake must be supplanted by art for the sake of the world. Education in the arts must be committed to this premise. From it should come insights and solutions to the struggles that beset education, and possibly the even larger problems which perplex society as a whole.

We are becoming more and more aware of how interrelated everything is in life, in the physical world as well as that of the psyche. It should not come as a surprise. The arts have been demonstrating this increasingly since World War I, and the confluence of science and social issues since World War II has developed the unified swell of a tidal wave. Traditional studies have been dispossessed from their isolation. Economic and social welfare programmes to alleviate poverty are colliding with politics.

Physics first merged with biology and has today become astrobiophysics. Architecture, as such, no longer exists detached from traffic patterns, air pollution, school systems, shopping centres and marketing processes. Everything is interconnected and present educational programmes do not reflect that our educators have adequately faced up to this fact. Schools have maintained the separateness of studies, producing the specialist, mono-faceted and polarised. The condition has forced even the artist into a new stereotype, the solitary man "doing his own thing".

California Institute of the Arts will be addressing itself to this situation with the concept of a community of the arts. Embracing six schools – art, design, music, theatre and dance, film/video, and general studies – it will neither establish an enclave of ivory towers nor eliminate the privacy of the artist. It will constitute a way of life and learning through which the artist will come to recognise that his creativity is part of his total existence, that only by mastery of his medium will he be able to express his individual identity and at the same time assume a responsible role in his society.

While the schools for each art form will be separate, their nexus will become inevitable once students, faculty and facilities begin life together with a sense of commitment to each other. Aiding the basic idea of an arts community will be the internal structure of the building, externally innocent of the unorthodox interplay within. All six schools will be housed under one roof. Time will not be reckoned in the usual calendar of semesters.

Work and projects will measure chronology. Even the corridors will contribute to the correlation of the arts. Instead of avenues of passage, they will be galleries, performance areas, and spaces for action. In this atmosphere students of the different disciplines will mingle, observe, interrelate, participate and learn.

COMMON PROCESS SHARED

No longer will the focus be just on "doing your own thing" which, as an idea, has degenerated into a rather spurious form of existentialism. No one really creates his own essence. We all share in a common process. At best, to do one's own thing has its limits which are reached more rapidly than we suspect. Moreover, to "do his own thing", each person must acknowledge not only his existence in relation to the community but also those demands imposed by the collective will of the community to do "our thing." If the artist is to participate in this joint process, he must come with three attributes: he must have something to give; what he has to give must be viable; and he must have the discipline to take responsibility for what he gives.

It is not possible for an artist to make a gift of his talent to "our thing" without the ability to control his medium. Training and discipline are essential in the community of the arts. They are not readily nurtured by the artist off by himself; nor are they begotten by magisterial dictum. They are not present simply because he's "always done it that way". The creative act requires design and arrangement as well as intuition and spontaneity. Even to plan a birthday party or a holiday celebration calls for organisation and discipline, and executing the plan is a source of excitement and joy.

There can be joy in the process of acquiring discipline, if it is conceived as making possible the act of giving. The reverse is to work hard "to be free", and that is obsolescent 19th century romanticism. The passion of discipline is that it frees us to participate. That's really what the whole kick of "encounter groups" is about, to eliminate gulfs and engender community. That's why this new school is really an institute, and more a community than an institute. Its rhythms, in so far as it is possible, will be those of the life cycle rather than of an educational system, parallel to the rhythms of the artist as we help him to define himself.

Parenthetically, it is our belief that these rhythms apply equally in other areas of human activity, in the social sciences, for example. It is impossible to solve the problems of the ghetto if they are approached as the task of freeing people from confinement instead of bringing different people together.

What California Institute of the Arts offers the artists who have joined its community — and both the faculty and the students are regarded as artists — is the opportunity to explore further the innovative paths which they have already trod both as artists and as educators. The Deans of each of the schools, for example, have not assumed their posts to become administrators. Herbert Blau, co-founder of the San Francisco Actor's Workshop and formerly co-director of the Lincoln Center Repertory, joined the Institute to create a new kind of theatre. Mel Powell, a distinguished composer and Dean of the Music School, regards the musician as an explorer in hitherto off-limit territory. The painter, Paul Brach, believes the teachable things in art are alternative systems of making things; techniques of reproduction; developing the young artist's awareness of what he is doing and what has been done before him; and above all, transmitting to him the systems by which man has been striving to explain himself to himself. This is hardly the perspective of an artist who does not see beyond his own palette and canvas.

PLACE TO "DO THEIR THING"

To each of these men, and scores like them — including Allan Kaprow, Robert Irwin, Nam June Paik, Victor Papanek, Richard Farson, Leonid Hambro, Morton Subotnick, Ravi Shankar, Nicholas England, Marni Nixon, Fernando Valenti, Sally Jacobs, Bella Lewitzky, Mark Harris, Ruby Cohn, Alexander MacKendrick, Don Levy, Terry Sanders, Clayton Eshelman, and Emmett Williams — California Institute of the Arts will afford the possibility to do what they know they must if they are to remain alive creatively. This will be the place, with its facilities and human resources, where they will be able to fulfill their particular arts, "do their own thing" by functioning in the broader context of the subcommunity of the Institute, and in turn, in the community of the larger environment.

The environment of our day is information, and the arts are part of the environment. People don't even have to go to museums. They live within the orbit of art without being aware of it.

The world itself is a theatre of endless creation and individually we all play roles. We affect different personalities at different hours of the day, according to whom we plan to see, in what light we wish to appear, and how best to make the desired impression. We constantly exercise disciplines to control these elements. We are constantly conscious of our need to express ourselves within our environment. We cannot, however, expect to be truly successful until we make our environment compatible by contributing to it, by making it our own. To say it another way, we have to create our community in order to be able to "do our own thing". The arts point the way.

Robert Corrigan

Clean and Dirty Words on the Drama Wall

4. Ideas
Projects
Materials

'Scar': Devon Drama Curriculum Project

One of the challenges of the seventies will be to make sure that drama really is in education and not, like all the other arts at present, merely tolerated as a fringe activity operating on the edge of the curriculum with inadequate resources, too few teachers and little or no money. 'The Arts and the Adolescent' (Schools Council Project) has documented the poverty and depression of the arts in secondary education with disturbing accuracy, and research surveys such as 'Enquiry I' leave us in no doubt as to pupil and parent attitudes to the arts on a national level.

The real challenge lies in the 11-16 school, the College of Further Education, the youth club. Very little drama is done once the youngster enters the fourth year; fifth and sixth year drama work is non-existent in most schools, little of value occurs in youth clubs and only recently have courses grown up in a few enlightened Colleges of Further Education. There is much to do. It is in this area that drama and the arts generally have yet to prove themselves relevant in the whole process of state education.

It was this problem of the relevance of the subject and the increasing awareness of the lack of drama as a regular and serious activity amongst the majority of older secondary pupils which led the drama specialists in Devon to devise what has come to be known as a Drama Curriculum Project, named 'Scar.'

Thanks to the work of an earlier Adviser, Derek Bowskill, the County was well endowed with Area Drama Organisers. There are now seven, all employed by the L.E.A. and all required to work as a team on every Friday of every week on projects and productions. Up to three years ago they worked almost exclusively in the adult field, touring productions and demonstrations in an attempt to raise the standard of amateur theatre in the County.

They are now touring 'Scar' after a nine month research and rehearsal period. The project takes a full day, concentrates on fourth

and fifth years in secondary schools with special emphasis on early
school-leavers. It is placed carefully within the context of preliminary
staff meetings involving teachers over a whole range of subjects, and
involves an intensive follow-up scheme using pupil-packs and teachers'
boxes which contain a considerable amount of resources and material.

The aims and description of the day itself which are quoted below
are taken directly from the teachers' booklet which is circularised before the drama team visits the school:

> "The solution which I am urging is to eradicate the fatal dis-
> connection of subjects which kills the vitality of our modern
> curriculum. There is only one subject matter for education,
> and that is Life in all its manifestations. You may not divide
> the seamless coat of learning." (A. N. Whitehead: 'The Aims
> of Education.')
> "Faced at the secondary stage with a sudden transition to a
> subject curriculum and a bell every 40 minutes, children
> seem to lose much of the interest and spirit of enquiry that
> characterises their approach in the primary school."
> (I.L.E.A. Report on Secondary Education still to be released,
> quoted in the 'Guardian.')

The Project — Aims

1. To demonstrate how, through educational drama methods
and theatre, young people in the 4th and 5th years of their
secondary education can be involved deeply in social, economic
and political history and to enable teachers to utilise that involvement in subsequent work.

2. To demonstrate how through personal and immediate experience in local environment and history young people can be drawn
from the particular concept into the general concepts outlined in
(1).

3. To show that first-hand experience and the emotional and
intellectual involvement of the whole person is essential in the
learning process, and that academic study by itself is a pointless exercise for many unless need and interest are aroused
initially by first-hand experience.

4. To illustrate ancillary curriculum possibilities of the theme
in terms of arousing interest in mineralogy and geology,
science, biology and ecology in relation to conservation,

191

English, geography, mathematics, religious knowledge, art and music.

5. To link schools and young people with the Dartington Amenities Research Trust and its Field Study Centre at Morwellham in the Tamar Valley, and to encourage residential study visits and the use of the Youth Hostel for that purpose.

The Theme
(Warning - please do not tell youngsters of these plans beforehand)

The day's activities are based on the life of the Devon Great Consolidated Copper Mine in the Tamar Valley between 1844 and 1900. Personalities and events are largely factual, departing only from strict accuracy when the need has arisen to condense diffused and lengthy events or to crystallise attitudes in certain personalities. We believe the spirit and atmosphere of the period to be more important at this stage than a strict attention to detail.

For the first 35 minutes the youngsters — up to 60 in number, a maximum teacher/pupil ratio of 7 to 1 — are asked to watch three short scenes dealing with the decision to begin mining on the Duke of Bedford's land and the effects of that decision in terms of the movement of the farm labourer from an agrarian to an industrial culture.

The youngsters are then split into eight groups for discussion and briefing. Gradually, over the following hour, they are asked to build cottages for themselves and to assume roles as members of farming families in the 1840's - Cobbett's "hungry forties." Once the groups have started work in earnest and with a real sense of involvement they are informed that unless they agree to become miners they will be evicted immediately. Three cottages are in any case to be demolished, because the land will be needed for mining. The alternative will be to go to the Workhouse in Tavistock. Stress is laid throughout the day on the youngsters' own decision-making within the choices open historically to their characters.

When the above has been resolved an announcement is made that Captain James Phillips, a Mines Manager, (one of the team in character) will give a talk illustrated with lantern-slides on mining in the Village Hall. The youngsters then

move, still in role as farmers, to a room in the school previously prepared for the talk. A considerable amount of factual
information is conveyed with the help of visuals, including an
explanation of the system of pitch-bidding at Auctions held by
Company representatives.

There is then a break for lunch after which the boys are
grouped into three "pitch-gangs" and the girls into two groups
of "bal-maidens". They are then told that there is a need for
a mine and they are invited to build one using rostra, drapes,
lighting if available, polystyrene sheets and chairs and tables.
This activity is a deliberate use of constructional and creative
play at adolescent level; essentially the learning process is
much the same as that in operation when a group of infants
build a Wendy-house for domestic play — although one would
not dream of telling them so.

Once the mine has been constructed there is an official
opening by Josiah Hitchens, who was the prime mover in
forming the D.G.C.C.M. A pitch auction is then held, with
the Mines Manager stating the offered Company price for a
pitch; and the pitch gangs, bidding against each other, endeavour to secure a number of shillings from the Company in
every £1 worth of ore brought up. The pitch gangs are then
issued with numbered discs and mining tools and the bal-
maidens are instructed in their task of sorting and breaking
ore.

There follows an intense period of work as the mine is
brought to life by the youngsters and the team, all working
"in role" or in character.

After the mining sequence there is a brief period allowed
for them to re-form in family groups to discuss the experience
followed by an explanation of a time-jump of roughly twenty
years in the life of the mine.

A meeting at Tavistock Town Hall then occurs, with
youngsters complaining at a public meeting to the Duke of
Bedford and Company representatives about their housing
conditions. This is based on an actual petition organised by
the Portreeve of Tavistock in the 1860's as a result of "the
revolting and overcrowded living conditions in and around
Tavistock."

At the end of this meeting the miners and their families
are informed of the Company's decision to cut the pitch-prices

by two shillings in every pound. They are given time to decide
on what action they are to take before a further auction is held.

This last session is open-ended and has always in the past
brought a sharp awareness of the need for and consequences of
industrial action and the withdrawal of labour. The youngsters
are bound by the labour and economic conditions of the time,
but the contemporary parallels are obvious and the need for subsequent discussion, research and teaching equally so.

Note

Often violence is near the surface — how can young people experience eviction from their homes and the exploitation of
their labour without this happening? The team have structured
the day so that if overt violence breaks out there are immediate
and effective ways of controlling it — unlike similar situations
the youngsters will be facing in adult life. We make no apolo-
gies for this, neither should any be necessary; if young people
are **really** going to understand social issues of this kind then
they must experience them and their emotions must be engaged
as well as their minds. Perhaps through this, understanding
and awareness will come — which is what education is about.

The scar is evident today on man's spirit as well as on
his environment — the conservation of the land and seas begins
with the nurture and conservation of inner values and aware-
nesses, which is at the root of this project.

It will be evident immediately that if this project is to
succeed in curriculum terms a number of specialist teachers
involved in teaching the 4th years should attend the full day
and observe.

The presence of the history, geography, English, drama and
art specialist teachers is essential and that of the science, maths,
music and RE teachers desirable for at least part of the day.

Obviously there will be timetabling difficulties, but it is
in the interest of both children and teachers if Headmasters
encourage staff to attend the full day.

The pupil packs and resource boxes are supplied free to the school
with enough packs for one to be shared by five pupils. They are professionally designed with graphics by lecturers and artists on the
Regional Resources Centre team based at Exeter University Institute
of Education.

Schools visited so far have responded well and evaluation of the project is being organised by the Exeter University Institute.

As the County's Drama Adviser, apart from the enjoyment gained from working for a complete day a week with so many Devon fourth-years, the most rewarding aspect for me has been the response from so many teachers who had never before been able to observe and in some cases participate in educational drama and role-play. This, more than anything else, has broken down barriers and removed suspicions and I think helped the drama teachers in the schools visited. Several Heads, who had hitherto not employed a drama specialist, are now advertising for one or considering it seriously.

It has not always been plain sailing; in a project which allows youngsters to make their own decisions things have a habit of departing from the plan. In some cases resentful and difficult youngsters, immediately identifying us as teachers (rightly) decided to use the role-playing game to disrupt the whole project; but the power and fascination of genuine role-playing is such that, if you are quick-witted enough, some sort of agreement can be reached, or at the very least a truce. But sometimes we were not quick-witted enough.

In one school, a group of youngsters barricaded themselves into their "house" and refused to attend the lecture on mining, asserting their right to remain farm-labourers. After protracted negotiations they set up a farm and farm they did, right through the mining sequences of the whole afternoon. They even came down the mine selling home-made pasties to the miners and set up an apple stall during the public meeting with the Duke of Bedford.

The conclusion has yet to be reached; many schools will have to be visited before a thorough evaluation can take place, but one thing is certain: the strength of the team lies in the fact that for four days of each week they are in close contact with children, students and teachers in their roles as Area Organisers. It is in this way that they maintain their knowledge and experience of the realities of the teaching situation.

The quality and thoroughness of the follow-up work is inevitably dependent on the degree of identification with the project on the part of the teachers; one of its weaknesses is that, however carefully discussed and prepared, it is still a structure imposed from outside and not an organic growth from the school itself. Secondary curriculum structures still lack the amoeba-like elasticity of a good primary school, where the nourishment of constantly changing events in the world outside is eagerly ingested and used as raw material for renewing the life of the learning process within the organism. Nevertheless it has been accepted as a serious excursion into interdisciplinary work, it relates very much to problem-solving, decision-making and language and speech registers; it works in a practical way to enable youngsters to absorb facts and events in terms of a historical context, and to drive home the limitations of environment and social evolution on human endeavour; it has contemporary political relevance and does not disregard the struggle between reason and emotion.

It certainly lacks the cohesion and focus of a theatre experience; the simplistic realism of the role-playing inhibits entry into symbolism; symbolism, that is, in the theatrical sense. As a genuine experience of learning, however, the involvement and passions aroused in the youngsters have left us in no doubt as to its validity.

John Butt
Devon County Drama Adviser

Four Plays for Less Able Pupils

In 1970 we first visited remedial departments in Secondary Modern and Comprehensive schools and talked to specialist teachers. The remedial pupil has a short concentration span, so that economy of style and variety are desirable. They need encouragement to stick at a concept long enough to master it, but above all one should not underestimate them. We therefore decided on a mixed bill, four short plays, each demanding different kinds of response, presented in the round at the Holyhead Drama Centre.

'NED CROFT'S COMEBACK'

Ned is a wrestler. He has given up the ring, tried to be a salesman and failed. He and his wife Beth are in debt. Lomax, a wrestling promoter, offers Ned a fixed fight for £50. A spotlight picks up Ned. He speaks to the audience. Should he be bought? Some pupils say no, others approve but tell him to ask for more money.

Ned and his opponent Kenny Peters wrestle. When he comes to the third round he should throw the fight, but he is too proud and fights to win. The excitement rises but his opponent Kenny smashes Ned. Lomax walks out on him. Kenny hears that Ned has no money and comes to offer him a loan. He holds out a handful of pound notes. Should Ned take it?

The concept we were exploring was pride. Some would tell him to take it for his wife. Others could see Ned's pride. We let them discuss Ned until they could begin to understand him. Ned then refuses the money. "I don't need charity." Some pupils called him stupid or a bighead. The strength of the situation lay in Kenny offering real banknotes in his outstretched hand. Money was a very strong temptation for them. For a man to refuse it prompted them to consider his motives.

'THE MARK OF THORG'

We changed the style completely to fantasy. Barney is on his way to a football match with a ten-bob piece, when ... he is transported to a strange kingdom of masked figures. The ten-bob piece leads them to hail him as the guardian of the seven-sided earth rock. He must lead them against their enemy Thorg.

The climax was a moment of high excitement with ultra-violet light and sound, before Barney returned to earth and we took an interval.

'BRONTOSAURUS'

Jim, a workman, digs a hole out of which comes a black polythene monster with a retractable neck so that he can curl up small or tower above everyone. Jim has to teach it how to adapt to civilisation.

'WHO WAS TO BLAME?'

The final play was the most demanding. By now we had built a strong relationship to the audience and we could revert to the character method of the first play and extend it.

Mick is a young man. We meet him on his milk round. He seems to be pretty unambitious. We see him at home. His father wants him to get on and find a better job. Mick is off-hand to his father who loses his temper. His mother wants him to settle down and marry. We see Mick with Monica, his girl friend. He is moody and can't explain what's wrong. They meet some friends in a pub, Spud and Sue. Spud is a mixer. He boasts about the big money he earns and his car. He pokes fun at Mick. Sue is a brainless girl who laughs at all Spud's jokes. Mick and his girl leave.

The following day Mick has a misunderstanding with his foreman. Alone, baffled and in a rage he takes it out by smashing milk crates to pieces. That night he and Monica bump into Spud and Sue again. Spud is very offensive and jeers at Mick. Mick hits him then loses control, hits him again and again and fractures his skull.

Coventry Magistrates' Court: Mick charged with Grievous Bodily Harm. Who was to blame?

One of the cast chairs an enquiry. The audience can ask any questions of any of the people in the situation. Spud is to blame! He defends himself. He was just joking. Individual pupils talk to him. You're bigheaded – "No you're just jealous of me." – You were needling Mick – "You've got to have someone to liven things up. Mick's such a drag." Spud sits down to boos.

His father is blamed for ... a pupil searches for the words ... not letting Mick choose for himself. His mother is asked what Mick

was like as a child. He was a lovely baby, but now he's very difficult
and moody. Why does she always take Dad's side?

Monica is questioned. This is more difficult. Why does she go
out with Mick. She likes him. Does he kiss her? Does she love him?
Why does she always seem to protect him? Some of the audience think
she should ditch Mick – will she? No, she'll stand by him.

Mick himself is inarticulate in the way some of the audience are.
They ask him who he thinks is to blame. He supposes he is. The
pupils begin to form a deeper concept of his character. You should
speak up for yourself. You shouldn't get moody. Why didn't you talk
things over with Monica? Some of the audience start to argue with
each other. Mick should have turned his back on Spud, should have
hit him once only, not repeatedly. No, Spud deserved all he got.

One pupil starts to put to Mick what he is beginning to understand.
He searches for the words ... you only hit him because you couldn't
think of what else to do. You didn't want to. The audience nod. They
have agreed on something.

The organiser takes a vote. Who was to blame? Hands go up
thoughtfully, weighing the evidence as they see it.

The scene took 15 minutes, the enquiry 20 - 25 minutes.

'WHO WAS TO BLAME?'

The Script

STUART: Have you ever felt fed up? Have you ever felt everyone was
getting at you? Have you ever felt so black that you could smash
someone?
I know someone who always gets bottled up inside himself.
This story starts early one morning.
(Enter Mick, whistling)

STUART: Do you like your job?

MICK: It's all right.

STUART: No, I mean are you really happy in your work?

MICK: I suppose so. I've been doing it for about three years.

STUART: What is there to like in it?

MICK: Well I mean, as soon as I leave the depot I'm my own boss.
I can take as long as I like on the round. My time's my own.

MRS BERRY: Oh, I'm glad I've caught you. I'm just off to the shop. It's two weeks I owe you for and a yoghurt. That's fifteen shillings.

MICK: I'll put it in the book, Mrs Berry.

STUART: How long does the round take you?

MICK: It depends. In the winter I go fast to keep warm but in the summer it's different. Sometimes in the summer when it's really hot I take an hour to do those houses back of the wood and there's only two.
What's it to you?

STUART: I'm interested in other people's jobs.

MICK: There's work down at the depot, if you want a job.

STUART: That's Michael. Lives in a council house with his mam and dad. His Dad's a scaffolder – that's me.
(Dinner time)
(Edie comes up with coat and cap)

EDIE: What time will you be in then Stan? So I know what time to do your tea?

STANLEY: I'll be in about eight o'clock love, I'm working over.

EDIE: That's the third time this week.

STANLEY: Well, I've got to get some money to pay off the caravan at Rhyl.

EDIE: But I never see you Stan.

STANLEY: But it'll be nice this summer when we've got our own little place at the seaside. We'll be able to get the whole family together again.

EDIE: You coming again this year Mick?

STANLEY: No, he'll be going off with that Monica, won't he (wink). How are you getting on then, son?

MICK: Keep the big fellow out.

STANLEY: Now just watch it, and while I'm on the subject, why don't

you get yourself a decent job, proper man's job. Bloody milkman,
ain't you?   (Exit)
(Leaves Mick smouldering)

EDIE: Now you know you shouldn't asnwer your dad back, Mick. When
are you going to settle down, Mick? You've been going out with that
Monica nearly two years now. Ever such a nice girl she is. I think
it's about time you made up your mind about it one way or the other.
Mick? I never get a word out of you these days. (He stands)
Where are you going now?

MICK: Out.
(Outside Owen Owen's store)

MONICA: Hello Mick. Sorry I wasn't here before. Mr Lucas gave
me some stuff to do five minutes before I left.

MICK: What's on?

MONICA: I thought you would have arranged something tonight Mick,
as it's a special night. Don't you remember Mick? Well we met
two years ago today. Do you like my dress? Got it specially (quick
cuddle) Tell you what, Mick, why don't we go out for a meal tonight?

MICK: I've had my tea.

MONICA: Where are we going then?

MICK: Down the pub.

MONICA: Do we have to?

MICK: (cuddle)   .

MONICA: All right. But don't let's stay too long.
(In the pub)

SPUD: Hello Sunshine. Right on time. Mine's a light ale. How are
you doing? We could do with a sparkle, this place is dead.

MONICA: Hello.

SPUD: Hello love – How are you? Eh, I like your dress. You know
what it takes eh?

MONICA: I'm glad someone noticed.

SUZY: Hello Monica. Oh it's lovely that.

SPUD: Hello, do I detect a touch of bitterness Monica? Now come on Mick, own up, didn't you notice her dress? Have you failed to do the social duties? You can do better than that, keep the lady happy, give her what she wants, ha ha.

SUZY: Oh, leave him alone Spud.

SPUD: You're right love, a man doesn't have to talk — he's got his powers, strong silent type eh, Mick, I'll do you a favour. Dandy Time 3 o'clock. Can't lose. Won me 50 quid at Newmarket the other day, flashed past the lot of them with weight on it's hooves. (to Monica) How's it going then love?

MONICA: What do you mean?

SPUD: Sunshine keeping you happy?

MONICA: Lay off him for a moment will you?

SPUD: What do you mean? I'm bolstering him.

MONICA: Look, if he doesn't want to talk he doesn't want to talk, O.K?

SPUD: Now look love, don't get shirty with me, O.K?

MONICA: I'm not getting shirty, but just lay off will you?

SPUD: O.K. O.K. peace, peace, all you need is love.
Tell us a joke then Mick.
(Long pause)

SUZY: I heard a funny one the other day.

SPUD: Oh spare us?

SUZY: What's white and has a black collar?

SPUD: What's — a dirty ice cream cornet.

SUZY: A vicar on a moped. Oh no that's not right.

SPUD: Where are you going? Mick?

MONICA: Well Mick and I have got something arranged. It's a special night for us.

Ideas, Projects, Materials

SUZY: Oh, has he popped the question Monica?

SPUD: What's this, a bit of the starshine, the whispered music, rubbing noses, Eskimo talk. And don't forget to tickle.
(Tension sound)

MONICA: Let's go to the Locarno.

SPUD: Locarno on a Tuesday night? You're bold. Give my love to Jill.

MONICA: Who's Jill?
(They go)

SUZY: He's a bit of a drip, that Mick.

SPUD: What Mick? No, he's all right, he's a good lad, he can take a joke.

STUART: Next morning. Mick's foreman is checking the books.

FOREMAN: Come on, get those floats emptied, we haven't all day.
(Mick unloads)
Where's your accounts book, Mick?
(Mick produces it)

FOREMAN: Mrs Berry rang up, said you overcharged her. Says it was 13/6 not fifteen shillings. What did you overcharge her for? Hey, wait a minute, it's not entered anyway. Get that money into the office. I'm saying nothing this time. But I'm watching you.
(leaves)
(Mick stacks his crates. The tension rises in him till suddenly he begins to throw the crates about. This releases the tension and he knocks over the pile of crates. He finishes the job whistling)

STUART: (to audience) Have you ever felt like that? Did knocking the crates over help him? That evening in the Rose & Crown.

MONICA: Can I have a Babycham?

MICK: Crisps?

MONICA: Is that Spud coming down tonight?

MICK: I don't know.

MONICA: He always manages to ruin every evening. I'm off if he comes in. (Pause) Oh for God's sake aren't you going to talk to me tonight? You in one of your moods?
(Enter Spud and Sue)

SPUD: Evening all. End of a perfect week. The weekend starts here. Get me a light, sunshine. Hello gorgeous.

MONICA: Oh – hello (to Sue) I though you two were going to Liz's party tonight.

SUE: Didn't know there was one. Fancy a party, Spud?

SPUD: No. We don't need a party. We got sunshine ... This new job of mine is a real cracker. It's got the lot you know. Got the lot. 40 quid. 40 quid a week basic. Cumfy chair to sit in and a couple of nice birds on the machine. Wouldn't you like that Mick? Yesterday this bloke came in – tipped me the wink. He leant over and he said "Spirella, Leopardstown, 4 o'clock." So I thought, why not? Give it a whirl. Came in! at 100 to 8, well that was a small monkey. Go towards a new car.

SUE: You what? Are you going to get a new car?

SPUD: Eh – did you go down the Locarno Thursday?

MONICA: Yes we did.

SPUD: Did the lover-boy behave? How was Jill then, how was Jill? Did he make you jealous, did he go off in the arms of another woman leaving you the blooming wallflower?

MONICA: Shut up. Are you going to ruin another evening? Does nothing get through to you!

SPUD: I've been hurt love. I've been hurt. All human life is here.

SUE: Which one's Jill? Is she the redhead?

SPUD: Shut up love.
(Pause)

SPUD: Well we are sparkling tonight. Is it the work? Met any good cows lately? Confucius he say "Too much yoghurt, not enough milk" (to Monica) Does he ever open his mouth?

Ideas, Projects, Materials

MONICA: Do you ever stop talking?

SPUD: Vicious, vicious. Somebody's got to do the work, he's hardly the life and soul is he? (Pause) Come on, let's not argue. Tell you what, I had a thought today. I was thinking of you Mick – trudging mile after mile with your little float and you know what – a horse could do your job. All you gotta do is train it to open garden gates with its ears or something and it could carry the bottles in its teeth. Do you fancy that, sunshine? Mick the Magnificent Milk Horse.

SUE: He could have a straw hat with holes in for his ears.

MONICA: Is that supposed to be funny? (squeak from Sue) I'm sick and tired of your babbling on. Can't you leave him alone for a moment.

SPUD: Now look love – don't get touchy. It's only a joke. (prodding her)

MONICA: Keep your hands off.

SPUD: You really got a nursemaid. Does she fight all your battles? A nursemaid for the milkmaid.

MONICA: You can talk to yourself. Come on Mick. Let's go.

SPUD: That's right love. Go along with your nursemaid. Have a bit of fun.
(The pressure is too much for Mick. He begins to crack. Spud prods him. There is a tense, powerless feeling among the bystanders. Mick lashes out. The more Spud struggles the more Mick hits him. Finally Spud is unconscious on the ground. Mick steps back, not able to believe what he has done)

STUART: Who was to blame for this? (to audience)
Mick?
Or Spud?
Or anyone else?
(The actors clear)
We are now going to hold an enquiry. Spud is in hospital with a fractured skull. Mick may be charged with Grievous Bodily Harm. Who was to blame?
(to audience)

Who would you like to question first?

The characters are called to the centre rostrum one by one.

The Audience ask them questions or criticise them:

- Mick should not have bottled everything up inside him.
- Spud should not have goaded him.
- Sue was a bystander but she contributed to the teasing of Mick.

What do you think of Monica? What about his mother and father?

(If points come up about which the audience disagree or if there is need for further investigation, parts of the scene can be re-run. This will give the slower children a greater chance to form attitudes to the people in the story and to evaluate those attitudes.)

STUART: Bulletin from the Infirmary. James Dunn (known as Spud) is recovering but will be in hospital for ten weeks. The Magistrate could have sentenced Mick to six months in prison. However, as he had not been in trouble before he asked for a probation report. What are you going to do?

MONICA: I'll stand by him. I hope he doesn't go to prison but I feel I was more to blame than anyone. I'll stand by him.

Stuart Bennett
and the Coventry Belgrade
Theatre in Education Team

Mirror Image

The County of Oxford Link Theatre has recently concocted a programme called 'Reflections' in which fourteen members explored, through a kind of Grotowski experience, and for four months, the following idea.

A universal community is established, showing the establishment of a camp or area; birth; fire and food; agriculture; hunting; initiation and death.

Two strangers appear bringing with them an object which they exchange mutually with the "residents". They exchange for the initiate who goes off with them.

They leave behind mirrors. We see every aspect of the mirrors. Ideas are explored and humour prevails until the property of power and dazzling emerges. One individual takes over the community and gradually collects its mirrors. He grows in power and corruption and eventually smashes the mirrors, leaving his former friends blind and masked. The initiate returns . . . . .

The group has just filmed this (in 16mm Ektachrome: the finished product should run for about twenty-five minutes). A sound track of non-verbal noise and percussion will be added once the editing is complete.

Tony Butterfield

Making a Play

There were a certain number of kids in the school who were very keen to do some drama apart from the regular work they did each week in class. They came mainly from the second and third year. Perhaps because the headmaster had made going on the stage taboo, they felt that they wanted to do a play at Christmas and perform it on the stage for the rest of the school. The Head agreed. "Something that would fill an hour" on the last morning of the term. I talked with various lads who said they were interested. "What do you want to do?" I asked them. They said "Anything". So I thought we'd cater for most tastes and do a traditional Christmas story, but with a different twist. The film 'Scrooge' was going the rounds of the local cinemas so I decided to take the Christmas Carol story. I re-read the book, but didn't ask the kids to. I just re-told the outline to them and from this they worked out their own story. The second year boys actually took the Scrooge story and worked upon it and included scenes that did not come from Dickens: scenes in the office where there wasn't just Bob Cratchit and Scrooge but four or five other people. Cratchit was the butt of fun and very much the underdog.

I had left five of the lads working. "What you need to get over," I said to them "is that it's very near Christmas and cold. You are terribly miserable and you don't like working for Scrooge. There is just one pleasant aspect about it all and that is it's near Christmas and you are going to have your day's holiday." They worked out the character of Scrooge in relationship not only to Cratchit but to the other three boys in the office. Cratchit became a very easy going type and always being blamed for the pranks that were carried on. (Obviously drawn from classroom situations!) They also worked on a scene where they took Bob Cratchit out in the evening, but this didn't work so well and they weren't too keen on it, so we cut it out.

Bob Cratchit's wife was a girl who came from the girls' school

next door. She really was a very good improviser, aware of others
and obviously capable of building on what she saw of her own mother
around the house. She led the boys in creating a scene in which she
was trying to hold together the family on very little money.   In this
kind of way the basic plot developed. But we wanted it to be a 'Scrooge'
with a difference. The Ghosts of Christmas Past and Future were our
opportunity. The Ghost of Christmas Past was to concern a Christmas
long ago that wasn't anything to do with Scrooge himself directly, but
very much to do with Christmas itself and the world today. So we put
in the story of the massacre of the innocents by Herod and worked
basically from the Wakefield Mystery Plays' version. This was an
opportunity to bring in youngsters from another year, since there was
a self contained element in this part of the overall play. It was the
third year boys who took this on. It developed in fact into a dream of
the past totally unrelated to any of the other characters in the play and
so enabled us to conduct rehearsals separately.

This group, too, made it their play and developed it very much on
their own lines, changing the story to some degree. There were
several mothers and after the killing of one child the soliders dragged
on another mother and her baby to Herod. A soldier told Herod that
this was the Christ child. One member of the guard said he couldn't
stand the killing any more; it made him sick and so they made Herod
kill this child himself. He was angry at the dissension of the guard
and the guard who had dissented was dragged off to be whipped. Herod,
in a rage, then took a sword and killed the baby. And that was where
that part of the story ended. Another rather able girl had taken the
part of that mother and she really made us all feel for her plight. She
threw herself about over the baby and distractedly caressed this strag-
gling mess. It was all very moving.

After that I felt we needed a future with some hope in it, but again
it seemed to need some kind of conflict and we found our answer in the
future of Christmas in the trenches, 1914. The famous story of the
men coming over and greeting one another in the first World War,
both sides celebrating Christmas together became friends. Everything
else in the plot we considered to have taken place in the mid nineteenth
century. Then came the Christmas Present.

The Ghost of Christmas Present asked Scrooge what he was going
to do about this moment now and a light came up on the Cratchit family
sitting there as in a family portrait. This ghost asked Scrooge what
he was going to do about the present. He said "You can work on them!"
This idea came from the children, and they said "We will just have the

Cratchit family there because that is what Scrooge does. " They didn't move much, just sat there as if a family photograph. No attempt to talk to Scrooge was made and Scrooge made no attempt to talk to them but they each knew what had to be done. Then Scrooge jumped out of bed, dashed around to various shops and in a grand Christmas shopping scene he bought presents. The presents were very much the traditional things, lots of toys, food and so forth. The only thing they added to the traditional story was that Tiny Tim was walking along the road singing carols with his brother and Scrooge came out and discovered them. He was just about to tell them to run off when suddenly he remembered the ghost. It was interesting to feel that they were aware that Scrooge's character wouldn't change particularly just like that, there would remain an element of his old personality under the surface. We found one lad who had perfect pitch and he sang a carol beautifully to round off the performance. So the cast enjoyed themselves, the school were appreciative, the Head didn't look too displeased and the holy of holies, the stage, had actually been trodden on by the second and third years.

Ian Bowater
Teacher, Birmingham

Language Workshop: Sponsored by the American Language Institute in New York

Together in one group were students who represented fourteen nationalities; spoke languages as different as Czechoslovak and Thai; bridged the age gap between eighteen and forty; and had occupations as dissimilar as civil engineer and fashion designer. Primarily we had three goals:

1. to stimulate spontaneous English dialogue;
2. to use English outside the classroom situation;
3. to increase socialisation, especially between students of different national and cultural backgrounds.

In addition the group was asked to provide entertainment for an end of the year party. The students elected to meet twice weekly. The combined constraints of posited goals and limited time created a need for exercises specifically designed to coordinate the educational and social objectives of the group. We used theatre games; those which follow proved the most successful.

'One Line/Retort' was an exercise virtually designed to stimulate "instant dialogue." One person began the game by addressing a simple phrase to the person on his right whose role it was to answer naturally and spontaneously. Samples of these questions and answers included "Your eyes are green, aren't they?" "No, my eyes are blue." The first person addressed his phrase to each member of the group, each time changing his stress so as to change the meaning of the sentence. The second person similarly addressed his own phrase to each group member, followed by the other students, each with his own phrase, changing the meaning each time. The result was a serpentine combination of mayhem and babble.

Aside from its muddled appearance, however, 'One Line/Retort' served an extremely important function for this group. Not only did it provide an unpressured situation for integrating simple one line responses into eventually enlarged dialogue, but it stressed rapidity of thought in English, and ability to convey emotion as well.

Another exercise, 'Can I Help You?' was designed to encourage cooperation in English, and to sensitise individuals to the needs of others. The students' were asked to submit four "who's" on separate pieces of paper, which were then mixed up in an old hat. Samples of submitted "who's" included: Lawyer; Mailman; Photographer; Bullfighter. Two people were asked to participate in the game, the first picking a "who" card. After he began an activity prompted by his occupation, the second person approached him asking: "Can I help you?" The objective of the first person was to find as many things as possible for the second person to do: and likewise, the goal of the second person was to make himself as helpful as possible.

'Can I Help You?' was of real value in breaking down barriers of communication and inhibition. By working together, students of different backgrounds created a real group feeling which fostered openness, and reinforced both trust and cooperation.

'I'm Sorry I only Speak English' was intended as an experiment to increase fluidity of communication. Following the pattern of other Gibberish games, 'I Only Speak English' involved one person who spoke English and one person who spoke Gibberish.* The Gibberish-speaker's objective was to make himself understood and his partner's job to translate what was said.

One final exercise will be mentioned here which was simply called 'Game.' In it, two people were told to make up a game in a confined period of time. After the time was up, they were asked to explain the rules and play the game for the rest of the group. 'Game' demanded both quick and pressured communication in English, and enormous creativity besides. Far from stimulating bad feeling and embarrassment, 'Game' stimulated both quick wits and competitive fun.

English teachers at The American Language Institute reported significant changes in many of the students which they attributed to the drama group. Two students will perhaps illustrate results.

Angela, from Ecuador. Her teachers reported that for almost two years — the normal course of study is one — Angela was not able to complete a sentence when called upon and did not participate in class discussion. After the first session, she reported to her teacher that she hadn't enjoyed herself. Nevertheless, she continued attending drama group activities, including Friday's which was her day off.

---

*Spolin, Viola, 'Improvisation for the Theatre' pp. 126, 226

Despite her initial inhibited and withdrawn behaviour, as a sense of group feeling was established, she began to interact more freely with her fellow students. In a similar fashion, her teachers noted a 100% improvement in her relaxation, freedom of speaking, and class participation which they attributed to her activities in improvisation.

And an even more poignant example of dramatic change was Ide, a student from Japan. He not only had trouble expressing himself, but had a stuttering problem in English as well. After participating in the drama activities, Ide mentioned his former problem to his English teacher, but added that he no longer stuttered in English, due to his experiences with improvisation.

There was a generally marked change, in social interaction between members of different groups. Once English conversation was established as a common social link, Spanish-speaking, Greek-speaking, etc. groups dissolved somewhat, and English became the common language. Naturally enough, it seemed particularly difficult for people of the same language group to speak English together, but this too eventually diminished.

The informal presentation at the end of the year was successful. Approximately one hundred guests were invited to the church-run coffee house which served as the group's meeting place. Most of the guests were participants in a weekly English conversation programme with the students. Basically, the performance used the games already described. Each game was performed two or three times by the students, then audience members were invited to participate. This yielded some interesting results, especially where English-speaking people were asked to switch roles and speak Gibberish.

The success of this year's brief programme has prompted The American Language Institute to include the drama group as a scheduled activity next year.

The Teaching Performance Center of New York University School of Education made a video-tape of a work session. This tape will serve as a pilot film to aid similar international groups in the future to explore developing English conversation skills through improvisation.

Michael E. Rosenberg
Student, New York University

Festival of Mime: Sponsored by the National Deaf Children's Society

The first N.D.C.S. Festival of Mime was held in July 1970, and the intention was to encourage the use of mime as a means of self-expression and creativity in schools for the deaf. Now, with the second Festival behind us, it is clear that the event has had the desired effect; more schools are taking part, and the general standard of work being presented is higher than it was in the first year. By "higher," I mean more original and less stilted. Even though some of the schools who do enter for the Festival show work which is still too formal and over-directed, too many schools still hold out, saying, "We should not encourage mime because it does not encourage the children to speak" — to which the Director of the N.D.C.S. replies, "Why do you allow swimming? That doesn't encourage the children to speak either."

Understandably the necessity to get deaf children to speak and the teaching of language through speech and lipreading have dominated this special education for several decades. This, however, keeps a child rooted to his desk, encased in wires and instruments, entirely receptive and dependent on his teacher for the greater part of his school life. Of course, labour is necessary. Deaf children must learn to speak and lipread if they are ever to take a place in a hearing world. But the method emphasises the need for some purely expressive outlets, and freedom to enable personality to develop.

The Festival of Mime sets out both to give an outlet for this and to encourage an interchange of ideas. The Festival of Mime develops, at its best, naturally in the classroom drama work. On a recent mime workshop for teachers of the deaf, we discussed whether speech should be incorporated into the Festival of Mime. There was general agreement, "No." They felt that mime was something the children could do with grace and perfect coherence, whereas their speech would immediately stamp them as being handicapped. The speech of the deaf, in most cases, is unintelligible to people who are not used to it. Even with a most successful pupil, the speech will remain "different" and

214

imperfect, and this is a fact that idealistic teachers must face.

Deaf children absorb a great deal through their eyes and often have far greater knowledge and understanding than they can ever express in language. Being given a certain situation, or a problem to solve in terms of action, will spark them off in a way that nothing else can do, and their natural inventiveness has a chance to grow. Freed from their struggle to express themselves through speech and writing, they often get right to the heart of the matter with incredible clarity and confidence. Their perception and observation is most acute. Some will even achieve a kind of wit and repartee in mime which is the equivalent of word play and puns which delight hearing children. Sometimes speech will come quite spontaneously out of the situation and it will be unusually clear and alive because it is in context and not merely imitative. This kind of experience in breaking through all the barriers and frustrations can lead to a renewed quest for language later on.

Perhaps the word "mime" is daunting. To some it suggests a specialised technique which is difficult to teach to children even when you have it yourself, but this is not necessary. I never try to teach technique to children and, in my experience, they often find a better way of doing things for themselves. So in this sense, mime, or "acting without words" is no different from other forms of creative drama.

The search for ideas which really interest the children, of any given age group, can lead to a much more contemporary approach to mime and avoid all the clichés of romance and sentiment and what I call "airy-fairy" mime. Good modern mime only works in terms of continuous action, and response to action. Children need a background of fable and fairy tale and bible stories, it's true, and this is where deaf children miss out because they don't have the bedtime story from an early age. Mime is a good way to help them understand these traditional stories, but creative drama should also be directly related to life as we live it, and they shouldn't miss out on that either. Deaf children can, and need to, make their own contribution, and my experience is they are more likely to do this with an original story about robots or football or the space race than they are if given the story of Joseph.

The gap between this kind of creative work and a Festival is not so great, I believe, as it might seem. Improvisations have to be polished for presentation, but if the children are consulted all through the polishing process ("That bit isn't very clear, what can we do to tidy it up?") then it remains a creative piece of work and they don't lose interest, as they will if they become mere chessmen being directed. I saw one

happy presentation in a recent Regional Festival, where the ending
was very confusing and when I remarked on this the teacher said,
"Well, they do it differently every time and that one wasn't quite so
good! "

Finally, schools for the deaf tend to be isolated and insular, a
little world on their own, especially in places like Aberdeen and Belfast,
where there is only one, and opportunities for getting together and seeing what everyone else is doing are rare, but very welcome. In this
way, the performance aspect can be played down, and the sharing of
ideas, and the "participation" aspect, can be played up.

If the Festival attracts the notice of the general public, this is all
to the good. The agreement these days is for the deaf to become more
and more integrated. Even a most severe handicap like deafness does
not exclude people from living full and happy lives nor, as we are beginning to realise does it exclude them from making a useful and valuable contribution to society as a whole. They are no longer purely on
the receiving end. There are many things they can show us, and the
art of mime is one of them.

Pat Keysell
Director, Theatre of the Deaf

Leeds International Children's Theatre Festival: July 1971

The Festival ran for two weeks, with a host of companies and activities accommodated in five theatres in the city, and with cooperation and coverage from the local press and television and radio. Leeds Playhouse's Director of Theatre in Education, Roger Chapman, organised the Festival and brought companies from all over Britain, the United States, Holland and Russia. The active, positive cooperation of the Leeds education authority meant that head teachers had been well informed in advance of the nature and scope of the Festival and had opportunities to book school parties into the presentations well in advance, and at fairly moderate charge. Most took advantage of this, though there were glaring examples of "progressive" schools who seemed unaware of the opportunities offered to them. With any festival of this nature, calling upon so many groups, there is bound to be an element of disaster as well as success. Certain companies seemed ill-chosen to work for children, arrogant and insensitive in their approach, and a small proportion of teachers and children had cause to complain at what they were offered. (And criticisms of bad performances may simply be because they were bad, not because the school is "square.") But many of the offerings were of a high standard and brought interesting ideas and methods to view. One national paper reviewer remarked that the Festival rather knocked one's traditional idea of what children's theatre was all about and emphasised that far from dealing with Goldilocks and the Three Bears it was often concerned with immediate issues that children could grasp. But it would take a hard-hearted critic to knock a festival that brought huge double-decker bus-loads of children streaming into five theatres five days a week for two weeks and sent the great majority of them away happy and stimulated. Reservations about the Festival, however, did exist, and we record them here not to carp but for information.

Is it a good idea to bring such a wide variety of groups together?

Inevitably to do so is to have a proportion of dross amongst the gold
and that's a bit rough on the kids who only see that. Did enough pre-
selection go into the planning of which groups to invite? If so, on what
basis? Shouldn't there be a clear philosophy behind the invitations?
Is a fortnight's concentrated children's theatre, with the effort and expense it implies, less worthwhile than a steady concentrated year-
through project? Answers to these reservations are available. Variety
of choice may be healthier than pre-selection, for the basis of pre-
selection may be arguable. The effort is worthwhile because the impact
of the concentrated fortnight is memorable and reinforces continuing
work that is already established or planned. Yes, it is expensive, but
only by the miserly relative standards of the kind of money we are prepared to spend on children's theatre.

Was it all worthwhile? Surely, warts and all.

Lowestoft Theatre Centre: An Education Authority Project

The idea of creating a Theatre Centre in Lowestoft, arising from the
work of the East Suffolk Drama Advisory Body in the mid-sixties, was
given weight by a group of young people in Lowestoft itself. For some
years, groups of young people had been attending week long drama
courses taken by local drama teachers, and it was they who asked why
they couldn't carry on the sort of creative drama work that occupied
them on the course. At the same time (the spring of 1967) the General
Studies Department was looking for someone to teach drama to full and
part-time students. The Drama Advisor, the local authority and the
College came together, the top part of an old school building was made
available as a base for the creation of a youth theatre group, and I was
appointed to the staff of the College. Part of my work was to be done
in the General Studies Department, the remainder creating the youth
group, working closely with the County Drama Advisor.

In the old school building, three huge classrooms were knocked
into one large hall, and an overhead grid (made out of aluminium scaffold bars) was rigged. The local electricity board wired some sockets
across the grid, the cheapest Strand Electric control board was bought,
and the Centre (or rather its one room) was opened in January, 1968.
In spite of a bitterly cold winter, barely any heating and absolutely no
comfort, forty or so young people came to see what was going on,
formed a group and put on a production. The original members of that
group still remember the tables they disguised as rostra and the mirrors
collected for the dressing room with a nostalgia usually reserved for
those three times their age. By the spring we had also accomplished
a production for the General Studies Department. Using other members
of staff we ran Pinter's 'The Dumb Waiter' twice a day for a week,
bringing coach-loads of students to see the play. For many of them it
was the first time that they had seen live theatre, and the controversy
that raged through the College — much of it centring around "wasted
time" and "lousy play" — was quite amazing.

Encouraged by the initial success of these two projects, several hundred posters were printed proclaiming the merits of a Theatre Centre with almost evangelist zeal. The response was leaden; the youth group continued, but no-one else seemed to know that the Centre existed. Our work was known about inside the education service, but we were quite obviously not reaching the most important group – those who had left school without being interested in theatre or drama work and who would never set foot inside a Theatre Centre on principle.

It was not in fact a success until it was realised that like the butcher who sells the best meat or the best pub in the town, a Centre must become known by people talking to each other, and coming because they've heard that something is going on. There was, and to a certain extent still is, some suspicion that a Centre administered by a local education authority would at best be a dull and institutional place and at worst show a smug and patronising face to the town.

By the Autumn of 1968, work had begun on transforming the old cloakroom areas into a very basic coffee bar, and this small investment gave the building a new air of confidence. The Centre's creative work was linked to an active social life.

Eighteen months after the opening of the Centre, my teaching work at the College was reduced and the activities at the Centre began to expand.

The foundation of a beach theatre company whose members attended local secondary schools, and who performed during their summer holiday to children on local beaches; the transferring of the local film group's programme of modern films to the Centre and the creation of an adult theatre company helped to give the place a busier atmosphere, and therefore to spread its name. Throughout the Centre's development the impetus for new things has been given by those who come to the Centre, and we have tried not to begin new activities until there really is a demand for them.

The clearest idea of the way the Centre has developed can be given by summarising the events of the past year.

Two children's theatre companies have been set up to tour local schools. The first, consisting of local teachers who meet to rehearse after school, has just finished taking around a semi-documentary programme based on two smuggling stories set in Lowestoft. The production involves the children in the action and encourages them to do research and follow-up work in and around Lowestoft. The second company is touring the infant schools with a play/drama session. The members of this company are young housewives whose children attend school and who are more than willing to give up part of each week to create and perform plays for children.

Two youth groups, an adult company and film making continue, groups from local secondary schools are now timetabled into the Centre for drama work, film making and studies of all kinds.

Last Autumn, the Centre's youth group put on a production which was created for them (and indeed partly by them) based on three of Chaucer's 'Canterbury Tales.' The show used a great deal of contemporary music written by the composer Gordon Crosse who lives near, and a full orchestra of young people from the surrounding area, together with a children's choir, was recruited. After the performances were over, a number of the cast who had taken part in the movement and dance sequences asked if they could start a dance workshop. We eagerly took up their offer, and began Saturday afternoon sessions. Through these, we met a very good local professional rock band. They said that they wanted to do something with the dance group, and we have brought together the band, the dancers and one of our companies to do a production this summer.

In the Spring, working with the Students' Union at the College of Further Education, we were able to organise a month-long festival of entertainments and events in the arts which ranged from a mixed media evening devised by a group of students to an attempt to create a 19th century fishermen's "Smoker" — a late night session of songs and stories, and which included visits by underground theatre groups, films and plays. All the events were very well attended.

Early in the planning for the festival, I met a local artist who had a huge collection of very good paintings which he had never been able properly to exhibit. He came into the festival, and in return for hanging space created huge murals across the Centre's vast and ugly wall spaces as a background for his paintings. During his exhibition, someone else asked if they too could display their paintings, and it looks as though exhibitions will become a regular part of our programme.

If one adds to this the Women's Institute groups, the occasional courses, and work in local schools, it seems more than ample justification for the setting up of a centre which deals in an informal and straightforward way with the performing and associated arts, a place where the main emphasis is placed upon individuals enjoying themselves through the arts, where the only limit on the amount of activities that can be undertaken is shortage of time — a true people's theatre.

Patrick Redsell
Director, Lowestoft Theatre Centre

The Lincolnshire Youth Theatre: Establishing a Workshop and a Name

Four years ago the University of Nottingham Extra-Mural Department first sponsored a Youth Theatre Workshop to run for a week in July at Pilgrim College, Boston. Each July, young people in their final year at school have met to work on an improvised drama project. But this year's workshop had two rather special features: it was both a premiere and an anniversary. It was the first workshop course of the newly-formed Lincolnshire Youth Theatre. After the previous year's venture a group of those who had attended from the outset declared that they wanted to inaugurate the L.Y.T. They also recognised that this year was special for Boston in that it is the 350th anniversary of the sailing of the Mayflower. So on Tuesday, 14th July, at Blackfriars Theatre in Boston, thirty young people met, most of them for the first time. They had come from a variety of town and country areas throughout the county of Lincolnshire. About half the company were resident and were accommodated not far from the Theatre in Fydell House, run as Pilgrim College by Nottingham University Extra-Mural Department. From the outset, these young people showed a sense of occasion and leapt into work immediately.

The first evening was a "getting-to-know-you" session, with a series of improvisations designed to help the young players in gaining confidence, a group spirit and some sensitivity towards each other. The overall project, of course, was to research, sift, improvise and shape a production about the Pilgrim Fathers and their aspirations. In this first evening, then, the topic was introduced and the players began to express their own ideas and share their knowledge of the involvement of Boston in the saga. The first evening culminated in a series of improvisations centred around a T.V. programme called 'Topic for Tonight'. In one scene there was a group of American visitors who came to talk to the Mayor about their connections with this part of old England; another depicted something of the background history of the Pilgrim

Fathers' arrival in America; a third scene contrasted the idea of it being illegal to enter this country without permission, while 350 years ago, it was illegal to leave it without sanction. Work continued to about 9 p.m. but discussion went on over coffee and refreshments.

The next day was devoted to further research and investigation. Activities were under way straight after breakfast. At 9.15 in the movement class, 17th century crowds were listening to preachers; there was gossip, rumour and dissent. After coffee the company was divided into groups and worked on different scenes from the early history of the Pilgrim Fathers. These all came together at the end of the morning and effectively presented some of the main features of the attempt of the early Separatists to escape from Boston by boat for Holland. There was a scene, too, showing how the Catchpole had prevented their sailing; another dramatised how they had been brought back to the Guildhall in Boston where several of them were imprisoned for weeks and eventually brought to trial and fined.

It was fortunate that next to Fydell House, and not far from Blackfriars Theatre, there stood Boston's 15th century Guildhall. This year, anticipating the visitors, the town has spent some money in restoring its interior. How ideal then, after lunch, to make arrangements for the whole company to spend some time looking over this building. In fact they were able to take their knowledge of events and bring them to life within this stimulating environment. Every one of the actors spent some time in the very cells where William Bradford, William Brewster, Richard Clifton and the others had been imprisoned! After this experience the young players all assembled upstairs in the Court Room and conducted a mock trial.

From here, groups undertook a series of further investigations in and around Boston, scrutinising documents, perusing maps, looking up photographs and examining places which had any light to throw upon the Pilgrims in their time. In the evening, work continued in Blackfriars Theatre and further scenes were developed and performed. These covered particularly the period the early Brownists spent in Holland.

On the day following, the company again assembled prompt at 9.15 a.m. On this occasion their movement activities were concerned with voyage, storms and the sea. From these explorations emerged a most effective ship scene and "voyage" to America. Simply using a rope to represent the side of the ship and a ship's wheel standing on a table, they conveyed through movement and sound the setting sail, the storm-tossed seas and the hazards of the long and wearisome journey. Though young and for the most part inexperienced in drama the company showed a remarkable discipline and a keen sense of timing. In succeeding rehearsals many other movement scenes were developed. There grew up one scene in which the players showed the clearing of areas in the New World and the building of the first settlement; another, using Fulke Clifton's list of "Provisions needful for such as intend to plant themselves in New England", developed a packing and embarkation scene.

One of the most effective of all the scenes was one in which there was hardly a spoken word. The players had learnt of the early settlers' discovery of an Indian who spoke a little English learnt from previous traders. Working on this idea led them to evolve a scene in which an Indian came upon some sleeping Pilgrims. Wakened by his intrusion they frightened him into submission with the firing of a musket. Then, once he had submitted, the Pilgrims sought to win his confidence. In actions, they showed the Indian how the musket worked, instructed him in loading the powder and shot, and even taught him to fire it. They used signals to instruct him in the ways they employed in the hunting of rabbits. Encouraged by this show of trust the Indian returned their kindness and shared with the Pilgrims his knowledge of trapping animals. He mimed the scooping out of the earth and laying of a trap. So off they went together on a hunting expedition: the Indian keen to explore hunting with the musket and the Pilgrims eager to experiment in the trapping of animals.

A range of material tackled in a variety of ways began to be assembled. The scenes in which dialogue were employed were helped by a study of Arthur Miller's play 'The Crucible'. The sense of dignified speech and archaic phrasing were soon appreciated from improvised work developed from acquaintance with this text and several scenes were reshaped in the light of this study. Much of the Saturday and Sunday was spent in scripting some of the more complicated scenes using the improvised ideas as a basis. Not surprisingly, the trial scene in 'The Crucible' impressed everyone. All were particularly struck by the fact that just seventy years after the Pilgrim Fathers left England to build their new society on more ideal lines, a new generation were, in fact, trying people even more severely than their forefathers had been tried. The sought-after freedom did not seem to have been realised to the extent everyone had wished. In Miller's trial scene there were many of the elements which could be discerned in the earlier struggles of Nonconformists who sought to leave England.

A scene which linked the two periods of time through letters written by relatives to England was used. This led neatly into the trial scene, played much as Arthur Miller had written it. It stood in clear parallel to the scene which had taken place early in the produc- tion — the Guildhall trial. At the end of the Miller scene, just as Mr. Hale leaves the court room having denounced the proceedings, Danforth calls after him. It was at this point that the company decided to pick up the idea of names and to call others, as it were, for trial and judge- ment. Their final scene recalled many of the names which had appeared throughout the story of the Pilgrim Fathers and Proctor embodied their resistance in refusing to conform. After his final agonised refusal to sign his submission "because it is my name", voices echoed other names down the corridor of history from that time to this: names of those who had tried to force conformity alongside names of those who had sought to resist it. The final moment was a speech spoken from the darkness, "Leave me my name".

In just about one week these thirty people had established some- thing of an ensemble in their playing and had developed and shaped all kinds of ideas into dramatic form. In the days which followed, their self-discipline and control were further called upon when they took Lincolnshire Youth Theatre on tour to other parts of the county. Each day they had a run-through in which they were prepared to be critical of their skills in acting and communication. Everyone was keen to go on building the effectiveness of their work throughout this period and much confidence and growth was achieved. They too, they realised, were pioneers aiming to build and establish a worthwhile name.

The Birmingham Youth Theatre

Proposals for the formation of an amateur theatre company for young people attending secondary schools in Birmingham, to be under the auspices of the Birmingham City Council

The construction of the new Educational Drama Centre, at the Paradise Complex in Birmingham, places at the disposal of Birmingham people a spacious and well-equipped building for activities in drama. This scheme proposes to use the facilities of the centre annually at the end of the academic year and in the summer holidays for the presentation by selected Birmingham secondary school children of an original play. At present there is no organisation offering solely to those Birmingham schoolchildren who are talented at and keen on dramatic art the opportunity of taking part in a theatrical activity of some prestige closely identified with the City; thus such a scheme would complement on a regional level the work done nationally by the National Youth Theatre. The theatre would be directed by two part-time leaders, and there may be two or three additional technical assistants; costs would be low, covering only payment of leaders, small production costs (which could be recovered in part by sale of tickets) and publicity.

The foremost aim of such a theatre would be to provide for Birmingham an annual young people's production of a standard comparable to that achieved by the National Youth Theatre. Secondly, the play would always be original, and linked in some way with Birmingham, as an expression of the environment which produced it; the cooperation of professional writers may well be sought in the making of some plays. Thirdly, this scheme would aim to allow young people to develop their interests in conditions and facilities which are at once easily accessible, and near to professional standard. Experience of working with young actors in schools indicates that there exists a considerable amount of talent which at present is untapped, and which could be channelled very fruitfully in this way.

D. F. Nicholls and
R. A. Speakman

A Children's Film Theatre

At the Paris-Pullman Cinema we began in July 1971 the first Children's Film Theatre.

The idea is, first, to provide at the moment one, but in time, we hope, many cinemas with special matinees for children and parents of films that have been selected on the grounds that they have an aesthetic quality which nobody need be ashamed of and at the same time can be enjoyed by both the young people and their parents. Secondly, we are at the moment planning with the I. L. E. A. a series of themed programmes to run on weekdays through the school term. Themes we have chosen include conflict, growing up and a history of man. We are probably also going to do a series on biographies and a series on the film of the book — this could turn out to be the dullest of the lot, but nevertheless it seems important. The aim is to programme films which are not necessarily the most obvious in posh film terms. We want to treat subjects filmically, which is often very different from a literary treatment. We shall, I think, be using a lot of fairly standard, very glossy Hollywood movies simply because they so often treat their subjects filmically. Hitchcock's work, for instance, treats all sorts of subjects, particularly themes of man against society and questions of guilt, in extremely effective and gripping ways. It would be difficult to write a literary version of a Hitchcock movie.

We want to relate the work to schools in several ways. We may have a short introduction to each film and a brief discussion at the end of each film. In both of these we aim to stimulate further argument. later on. We also hope for a feedback from teachers as to the kind of material they need and want and a discussion about the ways in which we are programming the films. We shall also be using the I. L. E. A. closed circuit television system (probably not immediately because of their scheduling problems) to link our work to a series of programmes on the television screen, so taking it further. In this way film, television and classroom can be used in a much more integrated fashion. Eventually we are hoping to have our own cinema, one we can convert to our own needs because we need to do more than just run films and have short discussions and so on. Most people watching films in schools do so under the worst possible conditions with enormous noisy rackety 16mm projectors. Prints are often bad and there is usually not much space to see things.

I think there is a very good reason for getting out into a proper cinema. There is no reason at all to stop building cinemas in schools but it is a question of priorities and resources. One of the things I would like to do is to build a cinema with retractable seating. Then if we wanted to use it as an improvisational theatre it could be done and also, rather more important as far as film is concerned, to be able to get a great many disabled kids in to see the films. To be able to wheel them in their wheel chairs, so they could get an opportunity of seeing films regularly at a place that is purpose-built for them. There are also specially captioned films for deaf children which could be shown. Another project would be to show something like, say, five Hamlets. I would like to project them all because then kids realise that there are different ways of approaching a play like this and film is a very simple way of showing this kind of variety. We could show extracts to indicate how different people have treated the same subject in different ways. Another programme I would seriously like to do is one on propaganda. Not so much straightforward propaganda as the ways in which a film carries a message and the subtlety with which it does it. Then when we have the time and the facilities for doing it we need to encourage children to make films on 8 mm. It would be interesting to work with teachers using the themes that we have been using and developing films around them.

So the place could become a kind of cultural centre for children rather than just a cinema with other kinds of art work and we could interrelate the work that was being done in drama, painting, sculpture, pottery. So lectures, discussions, movements, would move into a sort of workshop situation with the facilities for kids to learn how to edit and put together a film and have their own attempt at shooting a film. Eventually perhaps we could produce our own films for our own circuit and when our one children's film theatre has grown to one hundred we could do that. Meanwhile there is still plenty of opportunity with the single children's film theatre. There is no need for a film to run through the whole week. There could be a set of films each week or different programmes every day. As it is, the schools

programme each day will have something different. And there is opportunity for programmes for kids just coming out of school at 4 o'clock.
There is really no limit to the number of things which could develop
but we need permanent premises, sufficient money and adequate support.

Michael Segal

Radio Link-Up

'Stage' is the name of a weekly programme, transmitted by Radio Oxford, one of the country's twenty local radio stations.

Radio Oxford takes some pride in the amount of involvement it creates among its potential listening public and this regular thirty minute programme is certainly one of few if not the only one both dedicated to drama and theatre work and also run by those in the local drama scene.

It began originally as a fifteen-minute programme but by last Christmas it had been lengthened to thirty minutes. A repeat is transmitted at 1.45 on Saturdays and the original transmission, live, is at 6.30 each Wednesday. The extra fifteen minutes has included a substantial part of 'Workshop,' a series devoted to work-in-progress by local groups and this has ranged from pantomime by a local amateur group to a new radio play presented by the City of Oxford Theatre Guild; there were also two sequences from schools in Banbury and Oxford City. The Workshop session from this autumn will become the responsibility of Theatre in Education, the circle of teachers, lecturers and advisers which meets regularly in Oxford.

The programme's format is constantly being watched and revised. The two theatres – the New and the Playhouse – have their work regularly reviewed and often clips from a performance are included, as well as interviews with key directors and actors. Outstanding local amateur and educational work is featured. There is the usual 'What's On' column; frequent studio interviews; correspondence is invited; occasional features occupy the whole thirty minutes and these have included ones on Stratford at the beginning of the season and the Oxford Playhouse Company on tour in Glasgow. Future plans for features include one on a local girl about to leave the Central School to enter the profession and an audience-orientated programme.

Tony Butterfield

Developmental Drama as a University Discipline

From 1968, Canadian universities offered undergraduate and graduate degrees in Developmental Drama – a wider concept than the British "Drama" (universities) or "Dramatic Education" (colleges), or the American "Creative Dramatics & Children's Theatre". It is the study of dramatic enactment within human development – personal, cultural, and artistic. Philosophically, it accepts the existential consciousness and, thus, work is based on ipso facto empiricism, phenomenology, and a "whole" view of man. All enactments have their own specific elements of process and form, which are not seen within classifications but as aspects of a whole consciousness.

Use is made of the concept of Developmental Stages (from Piaget and others): there are certain steps through which man evolves, each being a constituent element within the subsequent step. We can study development individually (psychologically and/or artistically) or socially (through anthropology and/or sociology). The fundamental step, however, occurs at about 10 months old when the baby first externalises his identification through an act of impersonation; he acts his Mother – symbolises her in action – discovers he can control the external world. Dramatic action is seen as "the substitute" for mental imaginative activity and it is through this mechanism that we develop. Art, for example: we first express imagination by acting (with the elements of sound and movement) which becomes the art form of theatre; we displace the sound of our acting-self (to music and litera- ture) and the movement of our acting-self (to dance, three-dimensional and two-dimensional art). Other substitutions lead to abstraction, natural methods of learning, and the way we live with our fellows through "the mask and the face".

Thus has evolved a Theory of Imagination and Learning which can be applied at all steps where process (drama) and form (theatre) are practised. There are practical fields tending towards process (play, creative drama, creative movement and speech, improvisation) or towards form (theatre, cultural dramatic enactment, theatre for young audiences, youth theatre, role-playing), which have their own physical requirements. In addition, there are a number of applied fields: education; human relations, inter-action, and communication; recreation and leisure; social work and medicine; business and industry. Methodology is in a three-fold sequence: experiential; descriptive, particularly phenomenological; and only then theoretical. Theoretical fields that relate include: theatre, philosophy, psychology, sociology, and anthropology – all within a gestalt that is specifically non-disciplinary.

Richard Courtney
Professor of Drama
University of Calgary

The Oxford and Cambridge Shakespeare Company: A Touring Theatre Venture

The Oxford and Cambridge Shakespeare Company was the brainchild of two Cambridge undergraduates. During the Christmas vacation of '65/66 Stephen Wright and Jonathan James Moore met on the Cambridge University Experimental Theatre Group's European tour production of 'Cymbeline'. The following year they were elected President and Secretary of the E.T.G., and 'Comedy of Errors' was chosen as the production. The tour was a great success (the total proceeds of £8 were the first profits ever realised by a tour), and during the following Cambridge run they were shown rare marks of favour by the University. Peter Avery, the Senior Proctor at the time, not only gave permission for a midnight matinee to be held, but even ventured to come and see it. Lord Butler, the new Master of Trinity, was also sent tickets for the production; his wife came – and appeared to enjoy it ...

In the following year, Wright was tour-escort for a touring American Chapel Choir. The Conductor's wife and tour-director was at the time Chairman of the Artists Series at Penn. State, and when Wright told her about the E.T.G. tour she suggested, "Why not tour the USA?" She explained the Artists Series system, whereby touring groups were booked to play on the campuses for worthwhile fees. Then, at a small and anonymous Parisian restaurant, Wright and Bruce Kerr – a fellow courier and Oxford "homme de theatre" – conceived the idea of a joint Oxford and Cambridge Shakespeare production which would tour the United States.

In the meantime Moore, as the new President of Footlights, had been organising a revue using the joint talents of Oxford and Cambridge. Thus when the other two asked him to join them he suggested that a joint undergraduate revue should accompany the main production. They felt that after 'Beyond the Fringe' the potential was enormous. Plans were made, and a preliminary budget was drawn up. It was decided that the '66/67 production of 'Midsummer Night's Dream' would be a sort of pilot production for the American tour the following year.

During September and October Wright and Moore attempted to

obtain Senior Members and Patrons for the company.   Lord Butler
consented to become Senior Member on the strength of the E. T. G.
'Comedy of Errors'; Peter Avery became Senior Treasurer, and Ralph
Richardson, Yehudi Menuhin and Paul Scofield became Patrons. After
Wright had compiled a list of American universities from 'The World
of Learning', 500 letters were sent out. A miscalculation on postage
necessitated his grandfather lending £37, the first of many loans to the
company.

Through December and January replies trickled back; by February
there were enough guarantees from the States to make a tour possible.
Now that the tour was a feasible project theoretically, the problems of
sponsoring and financing it had to be faced. Various foundations were
approached – with little success – until the Cambridge Societies Syndi-
cate granted £250 against loss.

Support finally came in the form of a film contract. The Oxford
and Cambridge Shakespeare Company Ltd., which was incorporated on
May 8th, signed a contract with a film company for the film rights of
the production 'Midsummer Night's Dream', and the revue 'Strictly for
Kicks', for £12, 500. Richard Cottrell was contracted to direct both
shows, and Paul Scofield and Ralph Richardson both agreed to dub
soundtrack commentaries for the film.

During the Summer term the revue and play were cast from Oxford
and Cambridge, and the company had every reason to be optimistic,
with guarantees from the States now totalling about £10, 000.

In late August, in view of Peter Hall's imminent film of the Royal
Shakespeare Company's 'Midsummer Night's Dream', it was agreed
that an extended revue should be filmed instead of the two productions.

At the end of September, 'Midsummer Night's Dream', after a
month's rehearsing, was performed at the ADC Theatre, Cambridge,
before an invited audience. The success was clearly an inspiration to
the company.

The following week, the revue was scheduled for filming in the
Arts Theatre, Cambridge, but disaster struck: it was understood that
the unions had blacked the film because of lack of funds. They managed
to keep the film crew unaware of the film being blacklisted, and after
a week the film was completed. Moore took the film personally to the
Denham Laboratories for processing to avoid seizure. Sorrows,
coming in battalions, appeared now in the form of a deep artistic rift
in the revue between Richard Cottrell and Clive James, who had been
commissioned by Moore to help. The cast split into factions and the
Oxford participants backed out. It was agreed, accordingly, that

an all-Cambridge revue should go to the States.

The failure of the film company to meet the contracted date for payment of £12,000 plunged the company into a dire financial predicament. The payment schedule had been built on the expectation of this £12,000. At first it was thought that it might yet come through, but this notion gradually evaporated as deadline after deadline expired. Attempts were made to finish and market the film, but to no avail: prospects of it realising any money became dimmer and finally faded altogether. The possibility of legal action was all that remained, and still remains.

After the completion of the filming Wright flew to the States with a colleague to search for new bookings and, if possible, to increase payments on standing ones. They managed to raise the total to $20,000, a figure which included a 12-night run at the Ferris Booth Hall in Columbia University, New York.

During the pre-tour period, Moore was fighting off the creditors and facing the immediate cash problems. With the help of Lord Butler he arranged for an overdraft facility of £2,500 on guarantee, and simply did not pay bills.

Then the crucial week in Oxford arrived. 'Midsummer Night's Dream' played to capacity audiences for 6 nights at the Playhouse, and drew unanimous press approval. On the Tuesday, the company was made aware of the enormity of the financial situation and the final decision was made to take the tour. The company obtained 50% credit on the air fares, and various loans from friends and institutions totalling £2,200 – £1,000 of this presented by cheque to Wright and Moore over tea at the Randolph Hotel in Oxford; when Moore emptied his bank balance and added £700, the money had been raised.

The first tour was lived in a tense pioneering spirit, with problems being faced and solved and/or totally ignored. As was to be expected, there were a chapter of them: visas which were only valid for three days; the set and costumes somehow travelling via Rome. A good review from the New York Times boosted morale, and it stayed high until the beginning of the 12-night run at Columbia. Influenza had hit the cast, and the New York fuel strike was producing minimal audiences. Some of the principals were literally carried to the stage. Moore received a telegram that his mother had died – the show went on.

Clive Barnes, who was subsequently to show little mercy to the company, recommended that a booking agent be found, and himself contacted the enormous Sol Hurok agency. Harold Shaw of Hurok came to see the show and after breakfast the following morning he agreed to consider acting as agent. At the end of the tour, with half an hour to spare, Wright and Moore secured from Shaw a letter promising to book the next tour, which was to be 'Twelfth Night, ' and expressing confidence that $50, 000 could be raised. And so the first tour was completed with the "little piece of paper" providing for the future.

On their return, Wright and Moore still had to face the £12, 000 deficit. The creditors were faced and asked to wait until guarantees for the following year's bookings came through. With the help, again, of contracts, an advance of $26, 000 was obtained from the Bank of America on the strength of guarantees totalling $40, 000 from Hurok.

Meanwhile Jonathan Miller had consented to direct 'Twelfth Night' for the company, his first Shakespeare production, and Wright had received an invitation for the play to be performed at the Middle Temple Hall before the Queen Mother, as part of the Quatercentenary celebrations.

By the beginning of rehearsals for the 'Twelfth Night' tour, the company had suddenly established itself as an institution. The administrative facilities of Moore and Wright became broadened and refined, and the whole project, by virtue of its history of disasters, had assumed an unassailable conviction. For the first time, a feeling of security pervaded the company's members.

It was in this spirit that rehearsals began with Jonathan Miller in the Italia Conti Stage School in Clapham. Miller, in a characteristically in-theatrical way, led the company through a series of improvisational pastiches on the play: the same scene was presented in the style of Oscar Wilde, Pinter, a Western, Chekhov; the last exercise proving the most fruitful. Each time the success or failure was discussed, and new insights were thrown upon the characters involved. The final exercise, to create a Chekhovian atmosphere, was approached more methodically, and as the improvisation continued, more and more came out of it. The actors involved established fully developed relationships in minutes, and slowly strange and subtle nuances appeared. This improvisation certainly coloured Miller's conception of the play considerably, and to some extent his subsequent conception of Shakespeare in the later productions; 'Lear', 'The Tempest', and 'The Merchant of Venice'.

'Twelfth Night' opened at the Arts Theatre, Cambridge, to full houses and, again, much critical approval. Even by the end of the run in Cambridge, the cast of the play had gelled in a curious way. The success was repeated in Oxford, and two weeks later, the company of 30 arrived, after a considerable journey, for its first booking in New

York to find Miller awaiting them.

The 'Twelfth Night' tour was different from its predecessor for several fundamental reasons. Firstly, Miller's influence was strong. He provided an enormous intellectual stimulus which arose from a combination of commonsense and eccentricity. He was at all times a member of the company, and his presence on the first half of the tour fused its members in a way that had not been possible on the 'Midsummer Night's Dream' tour. Secondly, Moore and Wright had, with the help of the notorious Cambridge impresario David Frost, and a considerable amount of experience from courier work in the summer, planned the tour impeccably. The cast were provided for at every turn, from breakfast to the habitual party after the performance. Where on the 'Midsummer Night's Dream' tour differences over meal allowances widened into rifts between the administration and the cast, on 'Twelfth Night' they disintegrated into intellectual exercises, and sometimes into improvisations. The only significant administrative blunder was to book the company into the notorious Y.M.C.A. in New York, where the long-haired group of actors were welcomed with warm anticipation. The company moved the following day "en masse" to the seedy, but secure, Paris Hotel in uptown New York.

By various meetings and arrangements, and for the first time by reputation, the company was honoured with a reception at the British Embassy, Washington, given by Mr. and Mrs. John Freeman, then Ambassador. In return for their hospitality, the cast performed a never-to-be-forgotten extract from the play for the assembled guests – the play was not being performed in full there – in cold blood and ordinary clothes, and the social graces of the Embassy entourage were strained to the full as straggled laughs were desperately produced to fill the silences.

The critical response in the States was variegated, ranging from almost speechless wonder at Miller's approach – it must be understood that the American view of Shakespeare is largely a rigidly conventional one – to Clive Barnes' outpouring of vitriol in the New York Times. Shaw undertook to book Jonathan Miller's 'Hamlet' notwithstanding the influence of this edict.

The company parted at London airport to return to their respective "alma maters", mostly convinced they had experienced something extraordinary, even if it had been fleeting and intangible. Reunion followed with a performance of selected scenes on the late James Mossman's 'Review' programme, and at the Middle Temple before the Queen Mother.

During the year of 'Twelfth Night', the company had started a series of fund-raising events including a benefit recital by Vladimir Ashkenazy and a poetry and music recital at the Arts Theatre, Cambridge, devised by George Rylands, and performed by Alan Bennett, Judi Dench and others. Gradually, with the small but important profit from the 'Twelfth Night' tour, the company eroded its deficit of £12,000. All looked well for the 'Hamlet' tour until Shaw wrote that the recession in America was affecting bookings badly, and Moore hurriedly departed for the States between the runs in Cambridge and Oxford to do as much patching as he could. By means of cutting back on accommodation expenses, and arranging some last minute bookings, the tour was financed and was again triumphant, although this time critical response in the press carried long chastisements against Miller's sacrilegious treatment of "the Bard".

The possibility of presenting 'Hamlet' in the West End had been explored tentatively before departure for the States, and Michael White had shown considerable interest and promised to put the show on, dependent on theatre availability. In March, the Fortune Theatre went dark and 'Hamlet' was booked for a 3-week run in April.

At the time of writing, the Company is about to embark upon the fourth production, 'Julius Caesar', and is within reach of erasing the deficit altogether. When and if it does this, and when it begins to earn money on a scale unprecedented in University drama, the company will take upon its shoulders a considerable responsibility, and its character will change abruptly, from that of the worthy cause struggling for security, to the well-endowed institution bulldozing the smaller societies from which it sprang into obscurity.

The company has certain facilities at its disposal, which are not available to the older university societies, and which are a direct consequence of the revenue it earns in the States. The most important of these is that it can afford to employ a permanent full-time administration, unique in university drama in so far as it is not beset by tripos or other distractions, and firmly committed because it is dependent financially on the Company. At the moment, the successors of Moore and Wright, two graduates from Cambridge, John Madden and Jon Amiel, must devote their energies to benefit evenings (the last spate, hopefully) and fund-raising activities. When the company is on a financially even keel, their time may be spent devising enterprises for the company itself and for Cambridge and Oxford drama generally. Eventually, a university version of the Old and the Young Vic might be envisaged, the "parent" Shakespeare production and the American tour perhaps providing backing for a second or third annual non-Shakespeare production to tour elsewhere. The company also hopes to establish a permanent base for centralised administration of larger Oxford and Cambridge schemes. But the primary aim of the company is that it should be able to assist, foster, and develop dramatic projects on a university level from its position of financial strength. In order to maintain this position, it is necessary to set up a residual fund to compensate for a financial crisis, such as might ensue from an artistically disastrous tour.

The dangers of this sort of policy are obvious – that artistic ends will be subordinated in commercial ones. To this the only defence is statement of intent: that making a profit is not, and will not, be the primary aim of the company and, even if it were to make no profit, then it justifies itself simply in that it offers an opportunity for undergraduates in England and America to compare their attitudes to drama and to Shakespeare.

John Maddon and
Jon Amiel

Books

CHILD DRAMA. Peter Slade. University of London Press (1954)

Originally published in 1954, Peter Slade's book is central to the understanding of the development of much work concerning drama in education, and has acted as guide and inspiration to many teachers and students. The influence and success of CHILD DRAMA has, paradoxically, made much of the book sound rather old-fashioned now — one has heard it all before! But mainly because Slade said it. The book remains essential reading.

DEVELOPMENT THROUGH DRAMA. Brian Way. Longmans (1967)

An influential book in which Brian Way has crystallised much of his thinking and practice. There is much useful example and helpful discussion of both the how and the why of classroom drama and free improvisation in larger spaces.

THE PLAYWAY. Henry Caldwell Cook. Portway

It is good to see this early book in print again. Those who think they have discovered English into Drama and Drama into English in recent years will find it was all happening a good 50 years ago. Caldwell Cook sees improvised drama in the full educational context. It is both exhilarating and humbling to read him again.

AN INTRODUCTION TO CHILD DRAMA. Peter Slade.
University of London Press (1958)

An introduction to Mr. Slade's major work, CHILD DRAMA. A useful reference but no substitute for the full book.

IMPROVISED DRAMA. Peter Chilver. Batsford (1967)

This book has a large number of interesting ideas from which improvisation may start, and this is quite useful, but there is a disappointing lack of any real discussion of improvisation techniques or basic guidance to using improvisation positively and variably.

TEACHING DRAMA. R. N. Pemberton-Billing and J. D. Clegg.
University of London Press (1965)

This is a very useful and practical guide to drama work in secondary schools, bringing together ideas from a variety of sources and being very sensible about the realities of the school situation.

CREATIVE PLAYMAKING IN THE PRIMARY SCHOOL. Paul Cornwell.
Chatto & Windus (1970)

Based on his experience in Primary School play making, the author has set out in some detail his approach to particular projects and themes. This is a modest book, perhaps rather too much of a record and too restricted in its ideas, but nevertheless a useful book for the primary teacher whether experienced or not in playmaking. Mr. Cornwell has clearly produced excellent results with his own pupils and his painstaking methods have much to commend them.

MOVEMENT AND DRAMA IN THE PRIMARY SCHOOL. Betty Lowndes.
Batsford (1970)

This is a very interesting book, full of ideas and examples for the use of the primary teacher, rich in experience and creativity. Pleasant illustrations do much to illuminate the text, and in addition to general discussion and critical theory, six "work" chapters (on Sensory awareness activities, Body awareness, Locomotion, Creative movement, Mime, and Verbal Drama improvisations) provide detailed information of one teacher's obviously successful approach.

(Lack of space forces us to restrict our book coverage in 'Drama in Education I'. A fuller survey will appear in 'Drama in Education II')

Index